INNATE IDEAS

edited by
Stephen P. Stich

INNATE IDEAS

University of California Press
Berkeley   Los Angeles   London

University of California Press
Berkeley and Los Angeles, California

University of California Press, Ltd.
London, England

ISBN: 0-520-02822-8
Library of Congress Catalog Card Number: 74-81441
Copyright © 1975 by The Regents of the University of California

Printed in the United States of America

TO JUDE

Contents

Preface

The idea of a volume on the controversy over innate ideas and innate knowledge emerged from conversations between Arnold Kaufman and myself in 1969. The format that evolved divides the volume into three parts—the first containing classical statements on both sides of the debate, the second devoted to modern commentary on the classical statements, and the third to the work of contemporary philosophers and linguists among whom the controversy has flared anew.

As work progressed, a number of friends and colleagues pitched in with advice and assistance. Nicholas White prepared a new translation of parts of Plato's *Meno*. Robert Adams arranged and edited the debate between Locke and Leibniz. Martha Hinman and Frithjof Bergmann helped render into English some of the difficult German quoted in the selection from Professor Chomsky's *Cartesian Linguistics*. Three colleagues, Adams, W. D. Hart, and Alvin Goldman went so far as to prepare original essays which appear in this volume for the first time. To all of them I am most grateful, as I am to the authors who allowed their work to be reprinted here. I owe a debt of another sort to those of my colleagues who failed to warn me of the efforts involved in preparing an anthology such as this. But for their silence the work would never have begun.

When work on the manuscript was largely complete, we learned that Arnold Kaufman, in the very prime of this years, had lost his life in a plane crash. Kaufman's death along with other events resulted in a three year delay during which the volume expanded somewhat and found a new publisher. Without the continuing cooperation and support of the contributors during these years, the volume might never have seen the light of day.

Ann Arbor   S. P. S.

June 1974

Introduction:
The Idea of Innateness

Philosophical controversies are notoriously long-lived. And in point of venerability the controversy around innate ideas and innate knowlegdge is equal to any. It differs, however, from many of its cousins of comparable ancestry. For in the last decade it has emerged anew as a lively debate whose participants include some of the most important philosophers in the English-speaking world. The debate is unique, too, in having been rekindled not by philosophers but by linguists who based their arguments on the findings of modern generative grammar.

It is not surprising that in a controversy extending over two millennia the strands of the argument have become knotted and intertwined. My aim in this introductory essay is to untangle a few of the strands of the argument, with the hope of making it a little easier for the reader new to the debate to find his bearings.

The controversy is easy enough to summarize: Some philosophers, as well as linguists, psychologists, and others, allege that human beings have innate knowledge or innate ideas. Others deny it. But what is it to have innate knowledge or an innate idea? There is a pattern running through much of the debate in this area. Advocates of the doctrines of innate ideas and innate knowlege commonly take the notion of *innateness* itself to be unproblematic. They explain it with a few near synonyms, "inborn" or "unlearned," or with a metaphor or an allegory, and leave it at that. The doctrine's opponents often begin by puzzling over just what the doctrine could possibly *mean*. They go on to construct a variety of accounts, arguing against each in turn. The advocate's rejoinder, as often as not, is that he has been misunderstood. Thus, in approaching the debate over the innateness doctrine, we would do well to ponder what we are saying of someone when we say that he knows something or has an idea innately.

In working toward an analysis of innateness there are two

pitfalls we must avoid. First, we should unpack the concepts
in such a way that there *might* be innate ideas or innate knowledge. An account of these notions, which makes the claim
that a person has innate ideas or knowledge either straight-
forwardly logically impossible or patently empirically false,
holds little promise as an explication of what those who advance
the claim have in mind. Their view may be false but, if we
are to interpret them sympathetically, it will not be trivially
false. Second, our account should portray the innateness
doctrine as an interesting view about human cognitive mechanisms. An analysis would be suspect in this quarter if it entailed
that all knowledge or ideas are innate. Advocates of innateness
usually took themselves to be advancing an exciting thesis
about a special sort of knowledge or idea. But if, on a given
analysis, all knowledge or ideas are innate, there is reason to
be suspicious that this exciting thesis has been exchanged for
the humdrum claim that, on a special sense of "innate," all
knowledge or ideas count as innate.

   While counting all knowledge as innate is a symptom that
an account is philosophically uninteresting, it is not a sufficient
condition. In particular, we should note two historical caveats.
In some of his writings Plato seems to endorse the view that
all knowledge is innate. But on Plato's view, only part of what
we commonly think we know is known innately. The rest
isn't worthy of being called knowledge at all. Plato's move is
not to bloat the concept of innateness to encompass all
knowledge, but rather to shrink the concept of knowledge
until it coincides with what we know innately. Descartes, too,
sometimes maintains that all ideas are innate. However, as
Prof. Adams' essay in this volume points out, there is both a
narrow and a broad sense in which an idea might be innate for
Descartes. When Descartes claims that all ideas are innate he
is using the broad sense. But the interesting hypothesis about
our cognitive mechanisms is the claim that we have innate
ideas in the narrow sense. While Descartes advocates this
latter hypothesis, he abjures the stronger one that *all* ideas are
innate in the narrow sense.

Innate Diseases

> I observed . . . that there were in myself certain thoughts that did not
> proceed from external objects, nor from a determination of my will, but
> only from the thinking faculty that is in me; and therefore, in order to
> distinguish the ideas or notions that are the content of these thoughts
> from other ideas which are *adventitious* or *manufactured,* I called them
> *innate.* It is in the same sense of the word that we say generosity is innate
> in certain families; or again that in others certain diseases, e.g. gout and
> the stone, are innate; not that infants of these families suffer from these
> diseases in their mother's womb, but because they are born with a cer-
> tain disposition or liability to contract them. (Descartes, *Notes on a
> Certain Programme)*

In calling ideas *innate,* Descartes tells us, he is using the
same sense of the word we use when we say certain diseases are
innate. So let us launch our analysis of innateness by pursuing
Descartes' hint and asking what it is to be afflicted with an
innate disease. Our strategy then will be to seek an analysis
of the notion of an innate disease. Armed with our analysis we
will return to tackle the thornier problem of innate knowledge.

To begin let us imagine a disease that at a certain stage,
is always characterized by a unique and easily observable set
of symptoms. (The lurid details are left to the reader.) In
imagining a disease *always* characterized by a unique set of
symptoms, we are making a simplifying assumption about the
relation between a disease and its symptoms. But the prey we
are stalking is *innateness,* not *disease.* A more realistic assumption would complicate the discussion while shedding no further
light on the concept that interests us.

Now, under what conditions would we be willing to say
that someone having such a disease has it innately? A natural
first move is suggested by the parsing of "innate" as "congeni-
tal" or "inborn." Perhaps to have the disease innately is just to
have the symptoms of the disease from birth. But, as Descartes
notes, this will not do. For a person may well have an innate disease though none of its symptoms are evident at birth.
It may be that the symptoms appear only at some specific
stage later in life—during a certain age span, say, or accom-
panying some normal bodily change like puberty or menopause.
In such a case we are prepared to say that the person has the

disease even before the appearance of the symptoms. Of course, unless there is some way to predict the future occurrence of the symptoms, we may not know the person has the disease until he begins to exhibit the symptoms. Still, there is nothing unusual about the claim that he had the disease all along, though we didn't know it until the symptoms appeared. The parallel to the notion of innate knowledge is clear. Those who advocate the doctrine of innate knowledge are often willing to attribute such knowledge to a person even though he has not yet come to believe the proposition he is alleged to know. But here we are getting ahead of ourselves.

We have, then, what appear to be two sorts of innate infirmities, those whose symptoms are present at birth and those whose symptoms appear only later. Let us focus for a while on the second sort. Under what conditions can we properly say that a person is afflicted with such an innate malady? We have seen that the symptoms themselves need not yet have appeared. So perhaps what is called for is an analysis in the form of a conditional: To say that a person has a disease of this second sort innately is to say that if he is of the appropriate age (or at the appropriate stage of life) then he has the symptoms.

To be at all plausible, this proposal demands at least one modification. If the "if . . . then" locution it uses is understood as a material conditional, true if the consequent is true or the antecedent false, then the account as it stands has the consequence that everyone who has yet to attain the appropriate age has the disease innately. What is wanted, rather, is a subjunctive locution forming not a material conditional but a *counterfactual conditional.* With this modification, our analysis becomes: To say that a person has a disease of the second sort innately is to say that if he were of the appropriate age (or at the appropriate stage of life) then he would have the symptoms.

I think it could be argued that similar moves will be needed in the analysis of the first sort of innate disease, the cases where the symptoms are present at birth. This would, for example, enable us to make sense of talk of a fetus having an innate disease before showing any detectable abnormalities.

But rather than pursue this line, let us keep our attention restricted to the second type of case. For ultimately the subjunctive analysis will prove inadequate.

Returning, then, to cases of the second sort, let us attend to a pair of further problems with the analysis as it stands. First, consider the case of an infectious disease caused, say, by a bacterial infection. Let us suppose that, while the disease can be acquired at any age, the symptoms appear during or after puberty. So a child may contract the infection while still an infant. This, it would seem, is a clear case of a person having a disease that is not innate. Yet our analysis, as it stands, implies that the child has the disease innately. From the time he contracts the infection onward, it is true of him that if he were at puberty then he would have the symptoms. Second, our analysis focuses on the period of latency when the symptoms have yet to appear. Thus it does not enable us to segregate innate from noninnate diseases once the symptoms are present. Both these difficulties can be patched if we swap a counterfactual locution for an "independent-of-factual" conditional which is true of the victim from the beginning of his life. We have, then: A person has a disease innately if and only if, from the beginning of his life it is true of him that if he is or were of the appropriate age (or at the appropriate stage of life) then he has or would have the disease's symptoms.

This leaves us with the nice problem of saying just when a life begins. On the answer turns the distinction between innate diseases and diseases caused by abnormal pregnancy. Here I have no solutions to suggest. My suspicion is that the distinction is a fuzzy one, and that on this score the notion of innate disease is fuzzy. My only proposal is that for purposes of our investigation we take life to begin sometime before birth. This will collapse the distinction between the two sorts of innateness, leaving our analysis applicable equally to each.

Unhappily, our analysis is still not adequate. Its fault is excessive pessimism. In defining the notion of innate disease we have left no room for possible cures. Imagine an innate disease whose symptoms, in the normal course of events,

appear at age ten. Imagine further that a cure has been
developed and administered to one of the disease's victims at
age five. Intuitively, we want to say the young patient had
the disease until he was five. But this is blocked by our
account. For it is not true of him during his first five years
that if he were ten years old then he would have the symptoms.
Rather what is true of him during these years is a watered-
down subjunctive that we might render: If he were ten years
old, then, in the normal course of events, he would have the
symptoms. So our account, full-blown at last, becomes:

A person has a disease innately at time t if, and only if, from the
beginning of his life to t it has been true of him that if he is or were of
the appropriate age (or at the appropriate stage of life) then he has or
in the normal course of events would have the disease's symptoms.

Timid conditionals, hedged with "in the normal course
of events" and the like, are familiar to philosophers who have
reflected on the relation between counterfactual and dispositional locutions. Dispositionals, like "x is soluble" or "x
is flexible," are commonly weaker than unhedged counter-
factuals.[1] For to attribute a dispositional property to an
object is not to say what the object would do under certain
conditions, but rather to say what it would do under these
conditions if surrounding circumstances were normal or natural.
So we can, with some justice, dub our final analysis the
"dispositional account" of innateness. Descartes it seems had
much the same idea. Those who suffer innate diseases, on
his account, "are born with a certain disposition or liability
to acquire them."

The notion of innate disease, if our dispositional account is
correct, is tied essentially to concepts of naturalness or normalcy.
The job of unpacking these concepts, of saying what is natural or
normal (or when "other things are equal") is notoriously difficult.
While clear cases of normal situations and of abnormal ones
can be found, there is substantial vagueness in the middle. Our
analysis would lead us to expect that this vagueness is reflected in
the concept of innateness. The reflection is not hard to find.

Consider the distinction between an innate disease and
a susceptibility. To suffer from an innate disease is to be
disposed to acquire its symptoms at the characteristic time

in the normal course of events. To be susceptible to a (non-innate) disease is to be disposed to acquire its symptoms under certain *special* circumstances. Certain toxic diseases, for example, can be acquired only by certain people. A susceptible person, when exposed to the toxic substance, will come down with the symptoms. At the extremes, the distinction seems clear enough. But notice how the two shade into each other. Suppose a person becomes ill after ingesting a certain amount of a particular chemical. (We can imagine the effects to be cumulative.) Suppose also that the chemical occurs naturally in the drinking water of the person's community. Is this a case of an illness caused by the substance, or of an innate disease whose onset can be prevented by avoiding the substance? Vary the example, now, so that the substance is nitrogen in the air, and ask the same question.

These examples illustrate a central feature of the notion of an innate disease. There are commonly a host of necessary environmental conditions for the appearance of the symptoms of a disease. If these conditions all occur naturally or in the normal course of events, the symptoms will be counted as those of an innate disease. But it is often unclear whether the occurrence of a certain necessary condition *is* in the normal course of events. So it will often be unclear whether a person is afflicted with an innate disease or is, rather, susceptible to a (noninnate) disease.

There is much more that might be said on the topic of innate infirmities. But it is time to take such conclusions as we have reached and see if they can be applied in our study of innate knowledge.

INNATE DISEASES, INNATE KNOWLEDGE, AND INNATE BELIEF

Let us begin by trading one problem for another. Questions about the nature and varieties of knowledge are as controversial as any philosophers are wont to consider. But on one point, at least, there is fair agreement: At least one sort of knowledge is a species of belief. This is so-called propositional knowledge or knowledge that, commonly attributed by locutions like "Christopher knows that the earth is round."

Not every belief, of course, is an instance of knowledge. False beliefs are counted out; and even among true beliefs further discrimination is needed. Specifying the principles of discrimination is a problem of celebrated difficulty. Happily, it is a problem we can conveniently avoid. For innate knowledge, on the view of most of those who hold there is any, is innate propositional knowledge. And if there is innate propositional knowledge, there are innate beliefs. Let us see what sense we can make of the doctrine that people have innate beliefs. This will prove problem enough so that we need not feel guilty about leaving to others the question of whether innate beliefs are instances of innate knowledge. [2]

By taking innate belief in exchange for innate knowledge we have traded up to a more manageable problem. The notion of belief is not without its puzzles, of course. Still, every analysis must take something as clear. So let us presume that our workaday grasp of the concept of belief is sufficient for the task at hand. Before attending to innate belief, it is worth reminding ourselves that beliefs need not be objects of current reflection. We all now believe many propositions we are not presently thinking about, and some we have never consciously entertained. Thus, in all likelihood, you have long believed that your left thumb is smaller than the pyramid of Cheops, though you have never reflected on the belief until now. Following familiar terminology, we will call those of our beliefs that are currently being entertained "occurrent beliefs" and those we are not currently entertaining "dispositional beliefs."

Enough said on the topic of belief. Let us ponder, now, what might be meant by "innate belief." According to Descartes "innate" in "innate idea" has the same sense it has in "innate disease." Pursuing our strategy of following up this hint, let us see how well our analysis of "innate disease" can be adapted to "innate belief." Making appropriate changes, our account energes as follows:

A person has a belief innately at time t if, and only if, from the beginning of his life to t it has been true of him that if he is or were of the appropriate age (or at the appropriate stage of life) then he has, or in the normal course of events would have, the belief occurrently or dispositionally.

This account is not without its virtues. As our introductory quote from Descartes suggests, we can use it to wind our way through some of the more obvious moves in the debate over the doctrine of innate knowledge. Infants, the doctrine's detractors argue, believe nothing; or if they have some beliefs they surely do not include the sophisticated propositions proposed by the doctrine's advocates. But what sense is there to the claim that one of a man's beliefs is innate if he did not have the belief at birth? Here our account has a ready answer. One can have a belief innately without believing it (occurrently or dispositionally) at birth much as one can have a disease innately without showing its symptoms at birth.

There are, however, other problems that our Cartesian (or dispositional) account dodges less successfully. Most critical are problems with the interpretation of the qualification "in the normal course of events." While on the topic of innate diseases we took note that the phrase was uncomfortably vague. Still, we had a passable intuitive feel for cases that were to be clearly counted in or clearly counted out. The trouble with the dispositional account when warped into an analysis of innate belief is that the *same* intuitions seem to swell the ranks of innate beliefs beyond all tolerable limits. For they seem to count in just about all banal truths about commonplace objects. In the normal course of events children are disposed to develop the belief that night follows day and day follows night, that things fall when dropped and that drinking water quenches thirst. Yet surely a notion of innateness distended enough to count these beliefs as innate is bereft of philosophical interest.

In the face of this difficulty we might consider a more liberal construal of "the normal course of events," allowing in those intuitively abnormal cases of children raised in a world of total darkness, without gravity or water.[3] Following this strategy we would read "the normal course of events" as "any physically possible course of events." But this tack is in danger of running aground on the opposite shore. If we allow as "normal" circumstances that are sufficiently bizarre, it seems likely that our account will count no beliefs as innate. Although the issue is an empirical one, it would be surprising if it were shown that there are some beliefs people acquire no matter how bizarre their experiences may be. Beliefs, after all, involve concepts. One cannot believe that armadillos are animals without having the concept of armadillo. Nor can one believe that everything is identical with itself if one is without the concept of identity. And, I suspect, for any concept there is *some* course of (physically possible) experience which would leave a child without the concept.

Is there, perhaps, some middle course, some way to construe "the normal course of events" which will leave the dispositional concept of innate belief neither empty nor cluttered with unwelcome occupants? One possibility is suggested by our recent observation on the interdependence of beliefs and concepts. Let us allow that having sufficiently exotic experiences a person may find himself lacking any given concept. Still, there may be beliefs that innately accompany concepts; given that a person has had experience sufficient to acquire the concept, he will be disposed to develop the beliefs in the natural course of events. The beliefs, then, are conditionally innate. Here, of course, we must interpret the residual reference to the natural course of events liberally, allowing in any experience compatible with the person having the concept. A more restricted construal would have us again class many banal beliefs as innate.

There is also a new danger. Having a particular concept may *entail* having certain beliefs involving the concept. To take an extreme case, it would be absurd to say a person had the concept of an armadillo but held no true beliefs about armadillos.[4] If it is the case that having a certain concept entails having certain specific beliefs, then the claim that these beliefs are conditionally innate is vacuous. A belief is conditionally innate if a person is disposed to acquire the belief on acquiring a given concept. But if acquiring a concept consists, in part, in acquiring the belief, then the claim that the belief is conditionally innate amounts to the tautology that if someone has a belief then he has it.

Despite this danger, the concept of conditional innateness remains a plausible candidate in our quest for a philosophically interesting unpacking of the dispositional notion of innate belief. While some beliefs may be conditionally innate only in the vacuous way lately considered, others may be conditionally innate for nontrivial reasons. These will be those conditionally innate beliefs the holding of which is not entailed by having the concept they embody. Whether there be such beliefs is open to dispute. But I see no straightforward argument that there are none.

Still, it would be nice to have some examples. Perhaps one of Kant's examples of synthetic a priori knowledge can be bent into an illustration. Kant held that the truths of elementary arithmetic, like $7 + 5 = 12$, were known a priori. He also contended that the judgments these truths express are nowhere contained within the concepts they employ. They are synthetic not analytic truths. Now if we construe a priority as conditional innateness and if we take the claim that "$7 + 5 = 12$" is synthetic to entail that having each of the concepts involved does not entail having the belief that $7 + 5 = 12$, then the belief that $7 + 5 = 12$ is a nonvacuous example of conditional innateness. But the example is not entirely a happy one. Quite apart from its dubious Kant scholarship, the claim that "$7 + 5 = 12$" is synthetic is at best a matter of controversy. Frege and the logicists who followed him undertook to show that it was analytic. While in more recent times Quine and others have denied that there is any distinction to draw between analytic and synthetic truths. Here the course of our investigation into the dispositional notion of innate belief merges with the dispute over the nature and existence of the analytic-synthetic distinction. To pursue Descartes' suggestion any further along the path we have come would take us too far from the central concerns of this essay.

Our interest in conditional innateness was provoked by the quest for some plausible way to construe "the normal course of events" which would be more liberal than the construal invoked in our concept of innate disease but more restrictive than mere physical possibility. The proposal was that we relativize innate beliefs to specific concepts, and allow as normal any course of events sufficient for the person to have the concept. This move suggests a still more permissive

account of normalcy within the boundaries we have staked
out. Rather than demand normal experiences be sufficient
for the acquisition of some specific concept, we can relax
our requirement and demand of normal experience only that
it be sufficient for the acquisition of some concept or other.
Or better, we can drop the reference to concepts altogether
and take as normal any course of experience that is sufficient
for the acquisition of some belief or other. A belief is innate
for a person, then, if he is disposed to acquire it under any
circumstances sufficient for the acquisition of any belief. Here
we have a second proposal on how the notion of dispositional
innateness might be employed in an account of innate belief.
As in the case of conditional innateness, it is not obvious
that there are beliefs innate in this sense. Nor, so far as I can
see, are there straightforward arguments that there could be
none.

    Before leaving the topic of dispositional innateness, let
us pause to explore one proposal of considerable interest
which is not directly in the line of our current reflections. We
have lately observed that having a concept, in one plausible
sense of this nebulous notion, may involve having certain
beliefs. But there is another sense to this notion which is
quite independent of belief. To illustrate, suppose an animal
or an infant can discriminate red from nonred things; it can
be conditioned to respond to red stimuli and can be taught
simple tasks that presuppose the ability to discriminate between
red and nonred things. We might, under these circumstances,
say that the animal or the child has the concept of red even
though it has *no* beliefs about red things. Concepts in this
sense are prime candidates for *innate* concepts in the sense of
innateness modeled after innate diseases. For if simple conditioned learning is to take place, the organism that does the
learning must be able to discriminate stimuli that are being
reinforced from those not reinforced. And since most organisms
can, in fact, be conditioned to some stimuli from birth, some
concepts must be innate.[5] This is the theme elaborated by
W. V. Quine in his contribution to this volume.

It is time to take stock of our progress so far. Our strategy
was to follow up Descartes' suggestion by seeking an account
of innate belief on the analogy of our analysis of innate disease.
We discovered that the analogy is not so straightforward as
Descartes may have thought. For buried in the notion of
innate disease is an appeal to the normal or natural course
of events. And while our intuitions about what is normal or
natural serve passably well when we attend to innate disease,
the same intuitions yield an intolerably broad notion of innate
belief. In casting about for a more restrictive account of what
is to be allowed as "normal," we have come upon two possi-
bilities. The first led to the concept of conditional innateness;
the second counted a course of experience as "normal" if it
led to the acquisition of any belief at all. These alternatives
are at best tentative proposals. There is much work yet to be
done on the dispositional account of innateness. But in this
essay we must abandon the topic here and turn our attention
to a quite different attempt at explicating the notion of
innate belief.

THE INPUT-OUTPUT MODEL:
ANOTHER APPROACH TO INNATE BELIEF

The dispositional account of innateness was suggested by
Descartes' analogy between innate ideas and innate diseases.
The alternative account that is our current topic can be coaxed
from the exchange between Socrates and the slave boy in
Plato's *Meno*. Though Socrates succeeds in eliciting from the
boy the solution to the problem he has posed, Socrates nonetheless insists that he has not *taught* the boy anything. Rather,
he tells Meno, he has uncovered something that was in the boy
all along. Thus Socrates claims that the boy has some sort of
innate belief. But it is clear that it is not a dispositionally
innate belief. For at the beginning of the interrogation the
boy does not believe what he later "recollects," nor need he
ever have come to believe it. The questioning played a crucial
role. There is no suggestion that the belief would have arisen
without the questioning as part of the normal course of
events. Moreover, the questioning did not serve to supply the
boy with new concepts. He seems to have all the requisite

conceptual apparatus before the questioning begins. So the beliefs he comes to hold are not conditionally innate. How are we to understand this nondispositional sense of innateness Plato seems to be using?

One idea that takes its cue from Plato's remarks is to view the role of the Socratic interrogation as akin to the role of a trigger or a catalyst. It sets off a process that results in the acquisition of the belief. But, as a catalyst is not part of the end product of a chemical reaction, so the questioning process does not supply the content of the belief. The content of the belief was contained within the boy much as the content of a tape recorded message was contained upon the tape. The questioning experience, like the throwing of the tape recorder's switch, serves only to set off the appropriate mechanism. On this model we can begin to make sense of the claim that the beliefs contained within the boy are innate even though they require certain sorts of experiences to bring them out.

There is at best scant textual evidence for the hypothesis that Plato would have expanded his doctrine along the lines that we have taken. With later authors, however, it is quite clear that they flirted with the model we are considering. Leibniz, for example, contends "the mind has a disposition (as much active as passive) to draw [necessary truths] from its depths; although the senses are necessary to give it the occasion and attention for this and to carry it to some rather than others."[6] He makes much the same point with his favorite metaphor. "It is a disposition, an aptitude, a preformation which determines our soul, and which brings it about that [necessary truths] may be derived from it. Just as there is a difference between the figures which are given to the stone or marble indifferently, and those which its veins already mark out, or are disposed to mark out, if the workman profits by them."[7] A natural reading of the metaphor is that in acquiring knowledge of necessary truths the mind uses experience only as a catalyst providing the occasion or cause for the knowledge being uncovered, but providing little or none of the content of the knowledge, just as when an appropriately grained block of marble is transformed into a statue the workman need only tap and chip a bit to uncover the figure. In the selection from

Cartesian Linguistics included in this volume, Noam Chomsky finds evidence of this view of experience as a trigger for innate cognitive mechanisms in thinkers as diverse as Schlegel and Herbert of Cherbury.

In several of his discussions of the catalyst or trigger metaphor, Chomsky suggests a variant on the figure. He proposes that we look on belief acquisition as an input-output process, with sensory experience as input and belief as output. If the beliefs that result from a particular pattern of sensory experience are richer or contain more information than the experience, then this added information must be the mind's contribution. If the total sensory input up to a given moment in time is poorer in information than the beliefs acquired to that moment, the excess information is innate. Where the disparity is particularly great, the sensory input contributes little or nothing to the belief acquired. It acts merely as a trigger, setting off the innate cognitive mechanisms.

It is important to see that though Chomsky's suggestion is couched in terms rather more modern than those used by Leibniz, it is nonetheless little more than a metaphor. Chomsky is proposing that belief acquisition be viewed as an input-output process and that the mind is interestingly similar to an input-output device. If we are to pursue this proposal seriously, trying to turn it into more than a suggestive metaphor, we should have to give some account of how we measure the comparative richness—or information content—of experiences and beliefs. Existing accounts of information content will not do. They treat of the information in a proposition or sentence, not the information in a belief or stretch of experience. Also, familiar accounts of information content count logical truths as containing minimal information. So adopting such an account for our present purposes would lead us to exclude belief in logical truths as innate beliefs, though such beliefs have often been taken as paradigms of what is known innately.

Even without any developed account of the appropriate notion of information content, we may note one quite fundamental difference between the input-output model of innateness and the pair of dispositional concepts developed previously. On either dispositional account the hypothesis that there are

innate beliefs is moot. On the input-output model, however,
there can hardly be any doubt that many beliefs are in part
innate. Most any empirical belief, for example, will be richer
in information content than the experience that led to its
acquisition—and this on any plausible account of the appropriate information measures. This is a consequence of the
philosophical commonplace that the evidence a person has for
an empirical belief rarely entails the belief. While we may
come to believe that all armadillos are omnivorous by observing the eating habits of a fair sample of armadillos, the generalization is not implied by any number of propositions attributing
varied tastes to particular armadillos.[8]   In the case of mathematical or logical beliefs it is rather harder to specify the
relevant experiental input. But again it seems that on any
appropriate measure of information content the information
contained within our mathematical and logical beliefs outruns
that contained in our total sensory history.

The upshot of these observations is that when pursuing
the input-output model of innate belief, the interesting question
is no longer whether there are beliefs that are (in part) innate.
Rather what is interesting is *to what degree* our various beliefs
are innate. Also of interest is the detailed story about the
cognitive mechanisms that lead from sensory input to belief.
In developing his theory of the acquisition of language, Chomsky
is making a tentative effort at sketching in some of these
details.

A PRIORI KNOWLEDGE AND INNATE IDEAS: TWO MORE THREADS TO UNTANGLE

The project with which we began this essay was to untangle some of the strands that run through the long history
of the argument over innate ideas and innate knowledge. So
far we have succeeded in separating out two basic concepts
which historically have often been run together. The several
related notions of innateness which flow from Descartes' analogy
between innate ideas and innate diseases contrast sharply
with innateness conceived on the input-output model. It
would be tempting to see much of the historical debate over

the innateness doctrine as a consequence of the failure to
distinguish these two sorts of innateness. But, though tempting, it would be inaccurate. For, though some of the historical
(and modern!) debates can no doubt be traced to the failure
to distinguish these two concepts, problems were multiplied
by still other confusions. In particular there is a pair of
notions whose history is wound together with the history of
the idea of innateness. One of them is the concept of a
priori knowledge.

In the preceding two sections we retreated from tackling
the notion of innate *knowledge,* and focused instead on innate
belief. In so doing we avoided need to talk of *warrant* or
justification—a property a true belief must have to be an instance of knowledge. We thus avoided confronting the issue
of a priori knowledge, which is tied to the concept of justification.

For some of the propositions we know our justification
is (at least in part) to be traced to sensory experience. But,
on the view of many philosophers, we know some propositions
whose justification is entirely independent of experience. These
are the propositions we know a priori. Our belief in these
propositions may have been (in part) *caused* by experience.
But the *justification* we have that makes instances of a priori
knowledge more than mere belief is not to be found in the
experience that caused the beliefs, nor in any other experience.
To say that a bit of knowledge is a priori, then, is to say
something about its justification, while to say that a belief is
innate is to say something about its cause or genesis.[9]

Though the distinction between innateness and a priority
seems passably clear, the two have not always been distinguished.
Thus Leibniz writes: ". . . very often the consideration of the
nature of things is nothing else than the knowledge of the
nature of our mind and of those innate ideas which we do not
need to seek outside. Thus I call innate those truths which
need only this consideration *in order to be verified.*"[10] And
elsewhere: ". . . it is always clear in all the states of the soul
that necessary truths are innate and are proved by *what is
internal.*"[11] Here there is maddening tangle. If the truths
are verified from within, proved by what is internal, then it

is their justification that is independent of experience. So it
is a priority not innateness that is at issue. Perhaps Leibniz
thought that all and only innate knowledge was known a
priori. But once the two have been distinguished the claim
that they coincide in extension is itself in need of justification.

   The second of the pair of concepts whose history is
bound up with the history of the doctrine of innate knowledge
is the notion of an innate *idea*. Talk of belief or knowledge
slips easily into talk about ideas. Indeed, in previous pages I
have occasionally slid back and forth from one to the other
with a studied equivocation. But though sometimes talk about
ideas is but a colloquial variant on talk about knowledge, it
is not always so. For the Classical Rationalists, who have
loomed large in our discussion of innateness, had quite a
unique use for the term "innate idea." Their doctrine of
innate ideas is to be understood against the background of the
Aristotelian scholasticism that flourished in the late Middle
Ages, and it admits of no tidy summary. Happily we need not
here attempt an explication of their views, since the job is
done with great clarity in Robert Adams' contribution to
this volume.[12]
   While the controversy between Classical Rationalists and
Classical Empiricists on the topic of innateness was focused
as often on innate ideas as on innate knowledge, the modern
"rationalists," who would argue their innateness doctrine
from the theories of modern grammar, talk mostly of innate
knowledge. So in the remaining section of this essay, I will
attempt a brief sketch of the nature of modern grammar. I
can then indicate where questions of knowledge—innate or
otherwise—are likely to arise.

GRAMMAR AND KNOWLEDGE[13]

   A grammar is a theory. The grammarian's principal data
are the judgments speakers make about expressions—judgments,
for example, that expressions are or are not grammatical
sentences, that sentences are ambiguous, that pairs of sentences are related as active and passive or as simple declarative

and yes-no (or wh-) questions, [14] and a host of others. Roughly
speaking, the grammarian tries to build a theory which will
entail that expressions have the properties speakers judge them
to have. If a grammar is to be an adequate theory of the
language of a speaker, it must entail that an expression has
a given grammatical property if the speaker would judge the
expression to have the property.

This brief account must be modified in several directions.
First, speakers' judgments are not the only data a grammarian
may use. Data about what a speaker does and does not say
in unreflective speech, data about pronunciation peculiarities
and a host of other phenomena may also be taken into account. Also, a grammar is an *idealized* theory. The grammarian
will systematically ignore certain discrepancies between what
his theory says of some expressions and what the speaker says
of the same expressions much as, in the theory of ideal gases,
we systematically ignore deviations between predicted correlations of temperature, pressure and volume and observed
correlations. In both cases the motive is much the same—the
expectation that construction of a complete theory that
accurately describes all the phenomena is best approached by
breaking the job into several parts, first giving the idealized
theory, then explaining the deviations.

Commonly a grammar will consist of a set of *rules* (phrase
structure rules, transformational rules, and perhaps some others)
and a set of *definitions.* [15]   The definitions and rules entail a
variety of statements. They entail many of the form:

S is a grammatical sentence

where 'S' is replaced by the name of an expression; many of
the form:

e is the subject of sentence S;

many of the form:

Sentences S and S' are related as active and passive, etc.

It is these consequences of the rules and definitions which
must agree with speakers' judgments. The rules and definitions

form an integrated empirical theory, and both rules and
definitions may be modified in the face of recalcitrant
data.

The grammarian's theory construction does not stop with
a grammar. Having made some progress at grammars for several
languages, he turns his attention to *linguistic theory* or the
theory of grammars. Here the goal is to discover linguistic
universals, general features of the grammars of human languages.
These universals may be general constraints on the form of
grammars—that all are divided into phrase structure and transformational components, say, or that all use rules only of a
specified sort. The universals may also include particular
rules or definitions which are the same in the grammar of
every natural language. If any rules or definitions are universal,
they need no longer be specified along with the more idio-
syncratic details of individual grammars.

The linguistic theory is also concerned with the acquisition
of grammar—how a person comes to have the grammar he does.
Here the strategy is to find a function ranking humanly possible grammars. The goal is to find a function that ranks
highest among humanly possible grammars that grammar which
the child actually acquires, when we first exclude from the
class of humanly possible grammars all those that are incompatible with the observed utterances and other data available to
the child. Specification of linguistic universals and a measure
function of the sort described would provide a (low level)
explanation of how the speakers of a language come to have
the grammar they do.

These are the two sorts of theories the grammarian constructs. If the theories are correct, they will describe certain
facts about speakers' linguistic intuitions (for grammars) and
certain facts about all human grammars (for linguistic theory).
About what aspects of these theories might speakers be thought
to have knowledge? In the essays that follow there are, I
think, three distinct proposals.

First, it might be thought that speakers know the linguistic universals, that they know (perhaps innately) that all human
languages have phrase structure and transformational rules,
or that the grammar of every language contains some specific

rule or that in every natural language an expression is a noun phrase if and only if ———. In short, this first suggestion is that speakers know that p where 'p' may be replaced by any statement belonging to linguistic theory.

Next it might be held speakers know that the particular rules of the grammar of their language are rules of the grammar of their language, or that they know the definitions that, along with the rules, constitute the grammar of their language.

Third, and most plausibly, it might be thought that speakers have knowledge of the consequence of the rules and definitions of their grammar. If this suggestion is correct then speakers of English will know that "Mary had a little lamb" is grammatical, that "Mary" is its subject, and that it is several ways ambiguous. Each of these views is considered in the debates that follow among Chomsky, Putnam, Katz, and Harman.

NOTES

1. Cf. Nelson Goodman, *Fact, Fiction and Forecast* (2d ed.), chap. II, sect. 2 (Indianapolis: Bobbs-Merrill, 1965).

2. Some argument on this topic can be found in the debate between Professors Hart and Goldman included in this volume. Cf. also R. Edgely, "Innate Ideas," in *Knowledge and Necessity,* Royal Institute of Philosophy Lectures, vol. 3 (London: Macmillan, 1970).

3. Note that each of these circumstances must be counted as abnormal by the account of normalcy required for innate diseases. Symptoms that appear in the absence of gravity are not symptoms of an innate disease.

4. This is, of course, not sufficient to establish the stronger claim that there is some specific belief the holding of which is necessary for the possession of the concept.

5. Though this argument seems straightforward enough, there is a problem buried here. Let me indicate it briefly. We have contended that conditionability requires a preexisting concept or, as Quine would have it, a "quality space" or "qualitative spacing of stimulations." Now in the case of colors, tones, and other relatively elementary sensory qualities, our contention seems to have some rudimentary explanatory value. We would like to know much more about quality spaces. But still, to say an organism prior to conditioning must have a qualitative spacing of stimulations seems to add something to the bare observation that the organism is conditionable. Now contrast these cases with other

instances of conditionability. Some organisms (some people, for example) can be conditioned to respond differently to paintings in the style of Rubens, as contrasted with paintings in the style of Monet. Other organisms (I presume) cannot be so conditioned. The case seems, for all we have said, quite analogous to the case of colors and tones. But here it seems perverse to postulate that the conditionable organisms have a preexisting quality space. Such a move appears explanatorily vacuous. It adds nothing to the bare observation that the organisms *are* conditionable. All this is impressionistic. But if my impressions are correct we are left with a problem: Why is the postulation of a preexisting quality space plausible in one sort of case and perverse in the other?

6. Leibniz, *New Essays* (1703-1705), I, i, 5.

7. Ibid., 11.

8. As this observation indicates, the notion of innateness built on the input-output model is not inimical to empiricism. Hume's doctrine of "natural belief" required an inborn faculty or mental mechanism by which we acquire our beliefs about matters of fact. The beliefs acquired are not entailed by the sensory evidence we have for them. Thus, in the sense of innateness under consideration, they are in part innate. This theme is taken up briefly in Professor Harman's essay included in this volume.

9. There is some precedent for a rather narrower notion of a priority. Kant, for example, made it a "criterion" for a "judgment" being a priori that it be "thought as necessary." Following Kant's lead we might say that a person has a priori knowledge of a proposition (in this narrower sense) when he knows the proposition and his justification is independent of experience and the proposition is necessarily true.

10. Leibniz, *New Essays*, I, i, 21; emphasis added.

11. *Ibid.*, p. 5; emphasis added.

12. The reader should be warned that not each occurrence of "innate idea" and kindred expressions in Descartes or Leibniz is intended in the sense Professor Adams explains. Sometimes their use of the term is better taken as meaning "innate knowledge" or "a priori knowledge."

13. This section is adapted from my essay, "What Every Speaker Knows," *Philosophical Review*, Vol. LXXX, no. 4 (October, 1971).

14. E.g., "Max went to the store" and "Did Max go to the store?" are related as simple declarative and yes-no question; "Max went to the store" and "Who went to the store?" are related as simple declarative and wh-question, as are "Max went to the store" and "Where did Max go?"

15. The literature on modern or generative grammars is vast and growing. A good starting place for the reader new to the subject would be N. Chomsky, *Aspects of the Theory of Syntax* (Cambridge, Mass.: MIT Press, 1965).

PART I

1

Plato, Meno

Translated by NICHOLAS P. WHITE

Socrates: . . . concerning virtue: what it is I do not know; but you, while perhaps you knew before you came in contact with me, are as good as ignorant now. Still, I am willing to investigate with you and to inquire what it is.

Meno: But in what way, Socrates, will you inquire after something when you do not know what it is at all? What sort of thing, among those things which you do not know, will you set up beforehand as the object of your inquiry? Or to put it otherwise, even if you happen to come right upon it, how will you know that it is that which you did not know?

Socrates: Meno, I understand what you mean. Do you see how contentious the argument is which you are introducing, that it is not possible for a man to inquire after that which he knows or that which he does not know? He would not inquire after that which he knows, since he knows it and there is no need of inquiry for such a thing, nor after what he does not know, since he does not know what he is inquiring after.

Meno: Well, does it seem to you a good argument?

Socrates: No.

Meno: Can you tell me why?

Socrates: I can; for I have heard men and women of wisdom in divine matters. . . .

Meno: Heard them saying what?

Socrates: Something true, I thought, and splendid.

Meno: What is it, and who are they?

Socrates: They are among those priests and priestesses who

make it their business to be able to give an account of the matters with which they deal; and in addition there are also Pindar and many other poets with divine inspiration. What they say is as follows—see if they seem to you to be telling the truth. They say that the soul of a man is deathless, that it at one time comes to its end—this is what people call death—and at another time is born again, but never perishes, and that accordingly one must live life as piously as possible, since those

from whom Persephone the penalty of ancient grief receives, their souls she restores again to the sun above in the ninth year; from them splendid kings arise, and men swift in strength and great in wisdom, and for the rest of time they are called holy heroes by men. [Pindar, fragment 133]

Inasmuch, then, as the soul is deathless and has been born many times, and has seen what is in this world and in the underworld and indeed all things, there is nothing which it has not learned. So there is nothing to wonder at in its being capable of recalling the things which it knew before about virtue and other things. For since all nature is akin, and since the soul has learned everything, there is nothing to prevent a man, having recalled just one thing (this recalling is what men call "learning") from finding everything else if he has courage and does not give up inquiring. For inquiring and learning are nothing but recollection. We should not, accordingly, be persuaded by this contentious argument, since it would make us lazy and is pleasant to those who are soft, while the other makes us energetic and inquiring. I am persuaded of the truth of this view, and am willing to inquire with you what virtue is.

    Meno: Yes, Socrates; but how do you mean the claim that we do not learn, but that what we *call* learning is recollection? Can you teach me that it is so?

    Socrates: Just now, Meno, I said that you would stop at nothing and now you ask me if I can teach you, me who say that there is no teaching but only recollection. Your purpose is to make me contradict myself right away.

    Meno: No, Socrates, really. I did not say it with that in view, but out of habit. But if you can somehow make it clear that things are as you say, do so.

    Socrates: It is not easy, but I am willing to make the effort for your sake. Call over one of these attendants of yours, whichever you like, for me to use to make it clear to you.

Meno: By all means. Come here.

Socrates: Is he a Greek, and does he speak Greek?

Meno: Certainly—he was born and brought up in my house.

Socrates: Observe carefully whether he strikes you as recollecting or as learning from me.

Meno: I will.

Socrates: Tell me, boy: do you know that a square is a figure of this sort? [A, B, C, D]

Slave: Yes.

Socrates: So a square is a figure having all of these lines equal, the four of them?

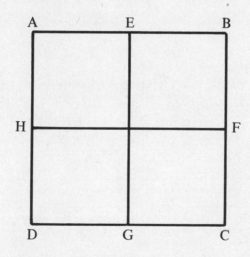

Slave: Yes.

Socrates: And having these lines through the middle equal too? [EG, HF] Correct?

Slave: Yes.

Socrates: And mightn't there be a larger or smaller figure of this sort?

Slave: Yes.

Socrates: Then if this side is two feet and this is two feet, how many feet would the whole be? Think of it this way: if it were two feet this way and only one this way, of course wouldn't the space be two feet taken once?

Slave: Yes.

Socrates: But since it is two feet this way also, doesn't it become two taken twice?

Slave: It does.

Socrates: So it becomes two times two feet?

Slave: Yes.

Socrates: How many, then, are the two times two feet? Figure it out and tell me.

Slave: Four.

Socrates: Mightn't there be another figure double this one but of the same sort, having all of the lines equal, like this one?

Slave: Yes.

Socrates: How many feet will it be?

Slave: Eight.

Socrates: Now, try and tell me how big each of its sides will be. Each side of this one is two feet. What of the side of the one which is double?

Slave: Obviously, Socrates, it will be double.

Socrates: Do you see, Meno, that I am teaching him nothing, but only asking? Even now he thinks that he knows what sort of side the eight-foot figure comes from—or do you not think so?

Meno: I do.

Socrates: Does he then know?

Meno: By no means.

Socrates: But he thinks it is double the side of the other?

Meno: Yes.

Socrates: Now watch him recollecting things in series—as one must recollect. Tell me, boy: do you say that the double figure is constructed on a side of double length? I mean this sort of figure, not long this way and short this way, but rather let it be equal in all directions like this one here, but double it—that is, eight feet. See if you still think it is constructed on a side which is double.

Slave: I do.

Socrates: Won't this line [DN] be double this one [DC] if we add here another [CN] like the latter?

Slave: Of course.

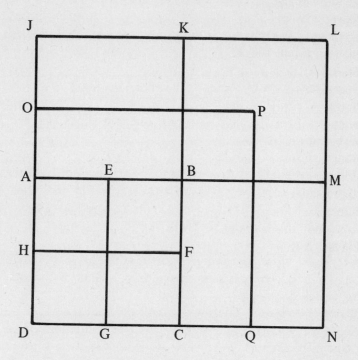

Socrates: On this, you say, the eight-foot figure will be constructed, if there are four such lines?

Slave: Yes.

Socrates: Let us draw in four equal lines from it [i.e., JL, LN, JD, DN, using DN as a base]. Would this be what you say is the eight-foot figure?

Slave: Certainly.

Socrates: Aren't there four figures in it, each equal to this four-foot one [ABCD]?

Slave: Yes.

Socrates: How big, then, is it? Is it not four times this one [ABCD];

Slave: Of course.

Socrates: So a figure which is as big as this one taken four times is double it?

Slave: No!

Socrates: What, then?

Slave: Quadruple.

Socrates: So on the line of double length, boy, there is constructed a figure which is quadruple, not double.

Slave: True.

Socrates: For four times four are sixteen, aren't they?

Slave: Yes.

Socrates: But on what sort of line is the eight-foot figure constructed? Isn't the one on this line [DN] quadruple?

Slave: It is.

Socrates: And this one on the line of half its length [DC] is four feet, isn't it?

Slave: Yes.

Socrates: Fine. But isn't the eight-foot figure double the latter and half the former?

Slave: Yes.

Socrates: Won't it have a side greater than that of the latter, but less than that of the former?

Slave: It seems so to me.

Socrates: Good—always answer as it seems to you. Tell me me, then: wasn't this line [DC] two feet, and this one [DN] four feet;

Slave: Yes.

Socrates: Therefore the side of the eight-foot figure must be larger than the two-foot line and smaller than the four-foot line.

Slave: It must.

Socrates: Try and say how big you think it is.

Slave: Three feet.

Socrates: If it is to be three feet, then we shall add half of this [CN] and it [DQ] will be three feet? These [DC] are two feet, and this [CQ] is one; and this way likewise these [DA] are two feet and this [AO] is one; and this [OPQD] is the figure you speak of.

Slave: Yes.

Socrates: If it is three feet this way and this way, isn't the whole figure three times three feet?

Slave: It seems so.

Socrates: How many feet are three taken three times?

Slave: Nine.

Socrates: But the double figure was supposed to be how many feet?

Slave: Eight.

Socrates: Therefore the eight-foot figure is not constructed on the three-foot line.

Slave: No.

Socrates: But from what sort of line? Try to tell us exactly; and if you do not want to count it up, show by pointing what sort of line it is.

Slave: But, Socrates, I don't know.

Socrates: Do you realize, Meno, how far he has reached in recollecting? He did not know at first, just as he now does not yet know, what the side of the eight-foot figure is; but at any rate he then thought he knew the line, and answered confidently as though he knew, and did not consider himself in any difficulty. But now he does think that he is in difficulty, and just as he does not know, he does not even think that he knows.

Meno: True.

Socrates: Isn't he now in a better position with respect to the matter which he did not know?

Meno: That seems so too.

Socrates: So we have not harmed him, have we, by putting him in perplexity and numbing him like the sting ray?

Meno: It doesn't seem to me that we have.

Socrates: And we have given him some help toward finding out what is the case. For now he might inquire gladly, as one who does not know, whereas before he might readily think that he could speak well any number of times to any number of people about the double figure, to the effect that it has a side of double length.

Meno: Apparently.

Socrates: *Before* he fell into difficulty, considered himself not to know, and desired to know, would he have tried to inquire after, or learn, that which he then thought he knew but did not know?

Meno: I don't think so at all.

Socrates: Then being numbed was beneficial to him?

Meno: I think so.

Socrates: Now consider what, starting from this perplexity, he will discover inquiring with me, while I refrain from
teaching and do nothing but ask questions. Be on guard to
catch me teaching or explaining to him, rather than asking him
about his own opinions.

Tell me, boy: is this not our four-foot figure [ABCD]?
Do you understand?

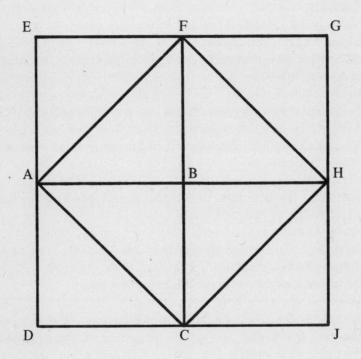

Slave: Yes, I do.

Socrates: Might we add to it this other one [BHJC], equal
to it?

Slave: Yes.

Socrates: And this third one [EFBA], equal to each of
them?

Slave: Yes.

Socrates: And we could fill out this one in the corner
[FGHB]?

Slave: Yes.

Socrates: So wouldn't we have four equal figures?

Slave: Yes.

Socrates: Now: this whole figure [EGJD] is how many times as big as the first [ABCD]?

Slave: Four times.

Socrates: But it was supposed to be twice as big, don't you remember?

Slave: Certainly.

Socrates: Doesn't this line from corner to corner cut each of these squares in half?

Slave: Yes.

Socrates: Don't we have these four equal lines, enclosing this figure [AFHC]?

Slave: We do.

Socrates: Now consider: how big is this figure [AFHC]?

Slave: I don't understand.

Socrates: Didn't each line cut off the inner half of each of these four figures?

Slave: Yes.

Socrates: How many figures of this size are there in this figure [AFHC]?

Slave: Four.

Socrates: And how many in this one [ABCD]?

Slave: Two.

Socrates: And how many times two is four?

Slave: Two.

Socrates: So how many feet is this figure [AFHC]?

Slave: Eight feet.

Socrates: Constructed on what sort of line?

Slave: This one [AC].

Socrates: The one going from one corner to the other of the four-foot figure?

Slave: Yes.

Socrates: The experts call this the "diagonal": so if we use the word thus, the figure of double area would, as you claim, be constructed on the diagonal.

Slave: That's right.

Socrates: What do you think, Meno? Did he answer according to any opinion not his own?

Meno: No.

Socrates: Yet he did not know, as we agreed just before.

Meno: That is true.

Socrates: But these opinions were in him, were they not?

Meno: Yes.

Socrates: So there are, in a man who does not know, true opinions concerning that which he does not know?

Aeno: Apparently.

Socrates: At this moment these opinions are stirred up in him as in a dream, but if someone asked him the same things often and in many different ways, you know that in the end he will have knowledge as exact as anybody's concerning them.

Meno: So it appears.

Socrates: Won't he then know—with no one teaching him, but only asking questions—but he himself having recovered the knowledge from within himself?

Meno: Yes.

Socrates: And is it not the case that to recover knowledge within oneself is to recollect?

Meno: Yes.

Socrates: Didn't he then either acquire at some time the knowledge which he now has, or else he always had it?

Meno: Yes.

Socrates: Then if he always had it, then he always knew, but if he acquired it at some time, he would not have acquired it in his present life. Or has someone taught him to do geometry? For he will behave in the same way concerning all geometry, and all branches of learning. So is there someone who has taught him everything? You ought to know, especially since he was born and raised in your house.

Meno: I know that no one ever taught him.

Socrates: But he has these opinions, doesn't he?

Meno: He obviously must have them.

Socrates: And if he did not acquire them in this life, is it not already evident that in some other time he had possession of them and had learned them?

Meno: Apparently.

Socrates: Isn't that a time when he was not a man?

Meno: Yes.

Socrates: So if there are going to be in him, both for the time when he is and the time when he is not a man, true opinions which become knowledge when they are aroused by questioning, won't his soul then always be in a state of having learned them? For clearly he always either is or is not a man.

Meno: Apparently.

Socrates: Isn't it the case that if the truth concerning things is always in the soul, the soul would be deathless; so that one should take heart and try to inquire after (i.e., recollect) what one happens now not to know (i.e., not to remember)?

Meno: Somehow or other it seems to me that you are right, Socrates.

Socrates: It seems so to me too, Meno. As for other things, I would not wholeheartedly endorse the arguments; but concerning this I would fight as well as I can in word and deed, that if we think we must inquire after what we do not know, we shall be better and braver and less lazy than if we think either that it is impossible to find, or that it is not necessary to inquire after, what we do not know.

Meno: In this too I think you are right. (80d-86c).

Socrates: . . . true opinions are a fine thing, as long as they remain; but they are not willing to remain a long time and they escape from the soul of a man, so that they are not worth much until one binds them by the calculation of reasons. This, Meno, is recollection, as we previously agreed. But when they are bound, first they become knowledge, and then permanent; and it is on this account that knowledge is more valuable than true belief, and knowledge differs from true belief in being so bound.

Meno: That certainly seems plausible.

Socrates: Certainly I do not speak as one who knows, but on the basis of likelihood. However I do not think it merely likely that true opinion and knowledge are different sorts of things, but if there is anything else which I would say I know—and there are very few—I would count this as one of them. (97e-98b).

Translator's note: This translation does not aim at elegance. It aims at accuracy, particularly on certain key points which should be remarked on here. I have uniformly translated Plato's '*zetein*' (which ordinarily takes a direct grammatical object) by 'inquire (after)' ('search for' might have been used instead). I have used 'know' to render both 'eidenai' and 'epistasthai.' These words occur in various constructions (e.g., 'to know X,' 'to know concerning *(peri)* X. . . .,' 'to know what X is,' 'to know X, what it is,' 'to know X, that it . . .'—these last two being fairly common in Greek), and except for the last two just now mentioned in parenthesis, I have tried to mirror these constructions faithfully. I have also tried to reproduce the informality of the vocabulary used by Plato in the geometrical parts of the passage (Plato's one departure from this practice is his use of the word 'diagonal' (see page 33); my only further departure is my use of the technical locution 'construct on,' and variants thereof, to render various phrases containing the nontechnical *'gignesthai'*). For Plato's *'peri'* I use 'concerning' and 'about' indiscriminately.

2

The Locke-Leibniz Debate

Edited and Arranged by ROBERT MERRIHEW ADAMS

[Leibniz's *New Essays* (mostly written 1703-1705) is a commentary on Locke's *Essay* (published 1690). Leibniz wrote it in the form of a dialogue, though that is not apparent from the selections presented here. In this anthology portions of Locke's work are printed (in ordinary Roman type, except for emphasized passages) with Leibniz's commentary inserted (in italics, except for emphasized passages) at the appropriate points, so that the relation of the two works may be more readily grasped. The passages of Locke form fairly continuous portions of three chapters, all omissions being indicated by punctuation (. . .). The passages of Leibniz do not form a continuous text, and not all omissions are indicated.]

LOCKE [Introduction, section 8] – . . . I must here in the entrance beg pardon of my reader for the frequent use of the word *idea,* which he will find in the following treatise. It being that term which, I think, serves best to stand for whatsoever is the *object* of the understanding when a man thinks, I have used it to express whatever is meant by *phantasm, notion, species,* or *whatever it is which the mind can be employed about in thinking;* and I could not avoid frequently using it. . . .

LEIBNIZ [*commenting on this passage, but in Book II, chapter i, section 1 of the* New Essays] *—I agree, provided you add that it is an immediate internal object, and that this object is an expression of the nature or the qualities of things. If the idea were* the form *of thought, it would spring up and cease* *with the actual thoughts which correspond to it; but being their object it can exist previous to and after the thoughts. External sensible objects are only* mediate *because they cannot act immediately upon the soul. God alone is the* external immediate *object. We might say that the soul itself is its own immediate* internal *object; but it is this in so far as it contains ideas, or what corresponds to things. For the soul is a little world, in which distinct ideas are a representation of God, and in which confused ideas are a representation of the universe.*

LOCKE [Book I, chapter i: "No Innate Speculative Principles"] —

1. It is an established opinion amongst some men, that there are in the understanding certain *innate principles;* some primary notions, κοιναὶ ἔννοιαι, characters, as it were stamped upon the mind of man; which the soul receives in its very first being, and brings into the world with it. It would be sufficient to convince unprejudiced readers of the falseness of this supposition, if I should only show (as I hope I shall in the following parts of this Discourse) how men, barely by the use of their natural faculties, may attain to all the knowledge they have, without the help of any innate impressions; and may arrive at certainty, without any such original notions or principles. For I imagine any one will easily grant that it would be impertinent to suppose the ideas of colours innate in a creature to whom God hath given sight, and a power to receive them by the eyes from external objects: and no less unreasonable would it be to attribute several truths to the impressions of nature, and innate characters, when we may observe in ourselves faculties fit to attain as easy and certain knowledge of them as if they were originally imprinted on the mind. . . .

LEIBNIZ— . . . *I have been for a long time of another opinion; . . . I have always held, as I still do, to the innate idea of God, which Descartes maintained, and therefore to other innate ideas, which cannot come to us from the senses. Now I go still farther in conformity to the new system,* and I believe even that all the thoughts and acts of our soul come from its*

---

* Leibniz referred to his own philosophy as a "new system."—Ed.

own resources, with no possibility of their being given to it by the senses, as you shall see in the sequel. But at present I will put this investigation aside, and, accommodating myself to the received expressions, since in fact they are good and tenable, and one can say in a certain sense that the external senses are in part causes of our thoughts, I shall consider how in my opinion one must say even in the common system (speaking of the action of bodies upon the soul, as the Copernicans speak with other men of the movement of the sun, and with cause), that there are some ideas and some principles which do not come to us from the senses, and which we find in ourselves without forming them, although the senses give us occasion to become conscious of them.

LOCKE—2. There is nothing more commonly taken for granted than that there are certain *principles*, both *speculative* and *practical*, (for they speak of both), universally agreed upon by all mankind: which therefore, they argue, must needs be the constant impressions, which the souls of men receive in their first beings, and which they bring into the world with them, as necessarily and really as they do any of their inherent faculties.

3. This argument, drawn from universal consent, has this misfortune in it, that if it were true in matter of fact, that there were certain truths wherein all mankind agreed, it would not prove them innate, if there can be any other way shown how men may come to that universal agreement, in the things they do consent in, which I presume may be done.

4. But, which is worse, this argument of universal consent, which is made use of to prove innate principles, seems to me a demonstration that there are none such: because there are none to which all mankind give an universal assent. I shall begin with the speculative, and instance in those magnified principles of demonstration, "Whatsoever is, is," and "It is impossible for the same thing to be and not to be"; which, of all others, I think have the most allowed title to innate. These have so settled a reputation of maxims universally received, that it will no doubt be thought strange if any one should seem to question it. But yet I take liberty to say, that these propositions are so far from having an universal assent, that there are a great part of mankind to whom they are not so much as known.

LEIBNIZ—*I do not ground the certainty of innate principles upon universal consent. . . . A consent sufficiently general among men is an indication, and not a demonstration, of an innate principle; but . . . the exact and decisive proof of these principles consists in showing that their certitude comes only from what is in us. To reply further to what you say against the general approbation which is given to the two great speculative principles, which are, nevertheless, among the best established, I may say to you that even if they were not known they would not cease to be innate, because they are recognized as soon as heard;* but I will add further that at bottom everybody knows them, and makes use at every moment of the principle of contradiction (for example) without considering it distinctly; and there is no barbarian who, in a matter which he takes seriously, is not offended by the conduct of a liar who contradicts himself. Thus, these maxims are employed without being explicitly envisaged. And in nearly the same way we have virtually in the mind the propositions suppressed in enthymemes, which are set aside, not only externally, but further in our thought.*

LOCKE—5. For, first, it is evident, that all children and idiots have not the least apprehension or thought of them. And the want of that is enough to destroy that universal assent which must needs be the necessary concomitant of all innate truths: it seeming to me near a contradiction to say, that there are truths imprinted on the soul, which it perceives or understands not: imprinting, if it signify anything, being nothing else but the making certain truths to be perceived. For to imprint anything on the mind without the mind's perceiving it, seems to me hardly intelligible. If therefore children and idiots have souls, have minds, with those impressions upon them, *they* must unavoidably perceive them, and necessarily know and assent to these truths; which since they do not, it is evident that there are no such impressions. For if they are not notions naturally imprinted, how can they be innate? and if they are notions imprinted, how can they be unknown?

LEIBNIZ—*If you have this prejudice, I am not surprised that you reject innate knowledge. But I am surprised that the*

* Or: as soon as they are understood.—Ed.

thought has not occurred to you that we have an infinity of knowledge, of which we are not always conscious, not even when we need it. It is for the memory to preserve this, and for reminiscence to represent it to us, as it often, but not always, does at need. . . . And it must certainly be that in this multiplicity of our knowledge we are determined by something to renew one part rather than another, since it is impossible to think distinctly and at once of everything we know.

LOCKE—To say a notion is imprinted on the mind, and yet at the same time to say, that the mind is ignorant of it, and never yet took notice of it, is to make this impression nothing. No proposition can be said to be in the mind which it never yet knew, which it was never yet conscious of. For if any one may, then, by the same reason, all propositions that are true, and the mind is capable ever of assenting to, may be said to be in the mind, and to be imprinted: [a] since if any one can be said to be in the mind, which it never yet knew, it must be only because it is capable of knowing it; [b] and so the mind is of all truths it ever shall know.

LEIBNIZ *[Two separate comments directed, respectively, to the statements ending at [a] and at [b] in the text of Locke above]—[a] I agree with you in regard to pure ideas, which I oppose to the phantoms of the senses, and in regard to necessary truths, or truths of reason, which I oppose to truths of fact. In this sense it must be said that all arithmetic and all geometry are innate, and are in us virtually, so that we can find them there if we consider attentively and set in order what we already have in the mind, without making use of any truth learned through experience or communicated to us by another, as Plato has shown in a dialogue* in which he introduces Socrates leading a child to abstruse truths by questions alone without giving him any instruction. We can therefore construct for ourselves these sciences in our private room, and even with closed eyes, without learning through sight or even through touch the truths which we need; although it is true that we would not envisage the ideas in question if we had never seen or touched anything. For it is by an admirable economy of nature that we*

---

*The *Meno;* see the selection printed in this anthology.—Ed.

cannot have abstract thoughts which have no need whatever of anything sensible, even if that would only be characters, such as the shapes of letters, and sounds, although there is no neces- sary connection between such arbitrary characters and such thoughts. And if the sensible signs were not required, the pre- established harmony between the soul and the body . . . would have no place. But that does not prevent the mind from taking the necessary truths from itself. You see also sometimes how far it can go without any aid, by a logic and arithmetic purely natural, as that Swedish youth does who, cultivating his own [soul], goes so far as to make large calculations instantly in his head without having learned the ordinary method of com- putation, nor even to read and write, if I remember correctly what has been told me of him. It is true that he cannot solve problems that involve working backwards, such as those which require the extraction of roots. But that does not show that he would not still have been able to draw them from his resources by some new turn of mind. Thus that proves only that there are degrees in the difficulty of becoming conscious of what is in us. There are innate principles which are common and very easy to all; there are theorems which are also discovered at once, and which compose natural sciences of which one person under- stands more than another. Finally, in a wider sense, which it is well to employ in order to have notions more comprehensive and more determinate, all truths which can be drawn from primi- tive innate knowledge can still be called innate, because the mind can draw them from its own resources, although often it is not an easy thing to do. But if someone gives another mean- ing to the terms, I do not wish to dispute about words.

[b] Why could not this have still another cause, such as the soul's being able to have this thing within it without one's being conscious of it? for since an acquired knowledge can be concealed therein by the memory, as you admit, why could not nature have also concealed therein some original knowledge? Must everything that is natural to a substance which knows it- self be known by it actually from the outset? Cannot and must not this substance (such as our soul) have many properties and affections such that it is impossible to envisage all of them from the very first and all at the same time? It was the opinion of the

*Platonists that all our knowledge was reminiscence, and that
thus the truths which the soul has brought with the birth of the
man, and which are called innate, must be remains of a previous
explicit knowledge. But this opinion has no foundation; and it
is easy to believe that the soul must already have had innate
knowledge in the preceding state (if there were any preexistence), however remote it might be, just as it must here; it would
then have to come also from another preceding state, or* it
would be finally innate, or at least created together [with the
soul], or else it would be necessary to go to infinity and make
souls eternal, in which case this knowledge would in effect be
innate, because it would never have any beginning in the soul;
and if anyone should claim that each earlier state has had something from another still earlier, which it has not left to the
succeeding, the reply will be made that it is manifest that certain evident truths must have belonged to all of these states;
and in whatever manner it may be taken, it is always clear in
all states of the soul that necessary truths are innate, and are
proved by what is internal, it not being possible to establish
them through experience, as we establish truths of fact. Why
should it be necessary also that we could possess nothing in the
soul of which we had never made use? And is it the same thing
to have a thing without using it as to have only the faculty of
acquiring it? If that were so, we should never possess anything
but the things which we enjoy; instead of which we know that
besides the faculty and the object, some disposition in the faculty or in the object, or in both, is often necessary, in order
that the faculty may exercise itself upon the object.*

LOCKE—Nay, thus truths may be imprinted on the mind
which it never did, nor ever shall know; for a man may live long
and die at last in ignorance of many truths which his mind was
capable of knowing, and that with certainty.

LEIBNIZ—*I see no absurdity in that, even though one cannot assert with certainty that there are such truths. For things
more exalted than we can know in this present course of life
may be developed some time in our souls, when they shall be
in another state.*

*It is possible that "where" should be read here instead of "or."—Ed.

LOCKE—So that if the capacity of knowing be the natural impression contended for, all the truths a man ever comes to know will, by this account, be every one of them innate; and this great point will amount to no more, but only to a very improper way of speaking; which, whilst it pretends to assert the contrary, says nothing different from those who deny innate principles. For nobody, I think, ever denied that the mind was capable of knowing several truths. The capacity, they say, is innate; the knowledge acquired. But then to what end such contest for certain innate maxims? If truths can be imprinted on the understanding without being perceived, I can see no difference there can be between any truths the mind is *capable* of knowing in respect of their original: they must all be innate or all adventitious: in vain shall a man go about to distinguish them. He therefore that talks of innate notions in the understanding, cannot (if he intend thereby any distinct sort of truths) mean such truths to be in the understanding as it never perceived, and is yet wholly ignorant of.

LEIBNIZ—*The mind is not only capable of knowing them, but further of finding them in itself; and, if it had only the simple capacity of receiving knowledge, or the passive power for it, as indeterminate as that which the wax has for receiving figures and the blank tablet for receiving letters, it would not be the source of necessary truths, as I have just shown that it is; for it is incontestable that the senses do not suffice to show their necessity, and that thus the mind has a disposition (active as well as passive) to draw them itself from its own resources; although the senses are necessary to give it the occasion and attention for this, and to direct it to some rather than to others. You see, then, . . . that these people, very able in other respects, who are of another opinion appear not to have thought enough upon the consequences of the difference which there is between necessary or eternal truths and the truths of experience, as I have already observed, and as all our discussion shows. The original proof of the necessary truths comes from the understanding alone, and the other truths come from experience or from the observations of the senses. Our mind is capable of knowing both; but it is the source of the former, and, whatever number of particular experiences we may have of a universal truth, we could not be assured of it for always by induction without knowing its necessity through the reason.*

The senses,* although necessary for all our actual knowledge, are not sufficient to give it all to us, since the senses never give us anything but examples, that is to say particular or individual truths. Now all the examples which confirm a general truth, whatever their number, do not suffice to establish the universal necessity of that same truth, for it does not follow that what has happened will always happen in the same way. For example, the Greeks and the Romans, and all the other peoples of the world which was known to the ancients, have always observed that before the lapse of twenty-four hours day changes into night, and night into day. But we would be mistaken if we believed that the same rule holds good everywhere else; for since then, the contrary has been experienced in the region of Nova Zembla. And he would still be in error who believed that, in our climates at least, this is a necessary and eternal truth, which will always endure, since we must think that the earth, and even the sun, do not exist necessarily, and that there will perhaps be a time when this beautiful star, together with its whole system, will no longer exist, at least in its present form. Whence it appears that necessary truths such as are found in pure mathematics, and particularly in arithmetic and in geometry, must have principles whose proof does not depend upon examples, nor consequently upon the testimony of the senses, although without the senses it would never have occurred to us to think of them. This distinction must be carefully made, and was so well understood by Euclid, that he often proved by the reason what is sufficiently seen through experience and sensible images. Logic also, together with metaphysics and ethics, one of which shapes natural theology and the other natural jurisprudence, are full of such truths, and consequently their proof can come only from internal principles which are called innate. It is true that we must not imagine that these eternal laws of reason can be read in the soul as in an open book, as the praetor's edict is read in his album without difficulty and

---

*This paragraph is part of the Preface to the *New Essays,* but I have introduced it here because it sheds light on what Leibniz is saying at this point.—Ed.

research; but it is sufficient that they can be discovered in us by dint of attention, for which the senses furnish the occasions, and successful experience serves to confirm reason, in much the same way as checking procedures in arithmetic serve for the better avoidance of error in calculating when the reasoning is long. Herein, also, human knowledge differs from that of the brutes: the brutes are purely empirics and only guide themselves by examples; for, so far as we can judge of them, they never attain to the formation of necessary propositions; while men are capable of demonstrative sciences. It is also for this reason that the faculty the brutes have for making inferences is something inferior to the reason of man. The inferences of the brutes are merely like those of simple empirics, who claim that what has sometimes happened will happen again in a case where that which strikes them is similar, without being able to judge whether the same reasons hold good. This is why it is so easy for men to entrap the brutes, and so easy for simple empirics to make mistakes. This is why persons who have become skilful through age and experience are not exempt [from error] when they rely too much upon their past experience, as has happened to many in civil and military affairs; because they do not consider sufficiently that the world changes, and that men become more skilful by finding a thousand new stratagems, while the deer and the hares of the present do not become more cunning than those of the past. The inferences of the brutes are only a shadow of reasoning—that is to say, they are only connections of the imagination and passages from one image to another—because in a new juncture which appears similar to the preceding they expect anew that which they formerly found connected with it, as if things were bound together in fact because their images are bound together in the memory. It is true that reason also counsels us to expect ordinarily to see that happen in the future which is conformed to a long experinece of the past, but it is not on this account a necessary and infallible truth, and success may cease when it is least expected to, when the reasons change which have sustained it. Therefore the wisest do not trust it so much as not to try to discover, if possible, something of the reason of this fact in order to judge when it is necessary to make exceptions. For reason alone is capable of establishing rules that are sure, and of supplying what is lacking to those which were not sure by inserting their exceptions; and of finding at last connections which are certain in the force of necessary implications—which often furnishes the means of foreseeing the result without the need of experiencing the sensible connections of images, so that that which justifies the internal principles of necessary truths also distinguishes man from the brutes.

LOCKE—For if these words "to be in the understanding" have any propriety, they signify to be understood.

LEIBNIZ—*They signify to us something else entirely. It is enough that what is in the understanding can be found there, and that the sources or original proofs of the truths which are in question are only in the understanding; the senses can suggest, justify, and confirm these truths, but cannot demonstrate their infallible and perpetual certainty.*

LOCKE—So that to be in the understanding, and not to be understood; to be in the mind and never to be perceived, is all one as to say anything is and is not in the mind or understanding. If therefore these two propositions, "Whatsoever is, is," and "It is impossible for the same thing to be and not to be," are by nature imprinted, children cannot be ignorant of them: infants, and all that have souls, must necessarily have them in their understandings, know the truth of them, and assent to it.

6. To avoid this, it is usually answered, that all men know and assent to them, *when they come to the use of reason;* and this is enough to prove them innate. I answer:

7. Doubtful expressions, that have scarce any signification, go for clear reasons to those who, being prepossessed, take not the pains to examine even what they themselves say. For, to apply this answer with any tolerable sense to our present purpose, it must signify one of these two things: either that as soon as men come to the use of reason these supposed native inscriptions come to be known and observed by them; or else, that the use and exercise of men's reason, assists them in the discovery of these principles, and certainly makes them known to them.

8. If they mean, that by the use of reason men may discover these principles, and that this is sufficient to prove them

innate; their way of arguing will stand thus, viz. that whatever
truths reason can certainly discover to us, and make us firmly
assent to, those are all naturally imprinted on the mind; since
that universal assent, which is made the mark of them, amounts
to no more but this—that by the use of reason we are capable
to come to a certain knowledge of and assent to them; and, by
this means, there will be no difference between the maxims of
the mathematicians, and theorems they deduce from them: all
must be equally allowed innate; they being all discoveries made
by the use of reason, and truths that a rational creature may
certainly come to know, if he apply his thoughts rightly that
way.

9. But how can these men think the use of reason necessary to discover principles that are supposed innate, when reason
(if we may believe them) is nothing else but the faculty of de-
ducing unknown truths from principles or propositions that are
already known? That certainly can never be thought innate
which we have need of reason to discover; unless, as I have said,
we will have all the certain truths that reason ever teaches us,
to be innate. We may as well think the use of reason necessary
to make our eyes discover visible objects, as that there should
be need of reason, or the exercise thereof, to make the understanding see what is originally engraven on it, and cannot be in
the understanding before it be perceived by it. So that to make
reason discover those truths thus imprinted, is to say, that the
use of reason discovers to a man what he knew before: and if
men have those innate impressed truths originally, and before
the use of reason, and yet are always ignorant of them till they
come to the use of reason, it is in effect to say, that men knew
and know them not at the same time.

10. It will here perhaps be said that mathematical demonstrations, and other truths that are not innate, are not assented
to as soon as proposed, wherein they are distinguished from
these maxims and other innate truths. I shall have occasion to
speak of assent upon the first proposing, more particularly by
and by. I shall here only, and that very readily, allow, that
these maxims and mathematical demonstrations are in this different: that the one have need of reason, using of proofs, to
make them out and to gain our assent; but the other, as soon as

understood, are, without any the least reasoning, embraced and assented to. But I withal beg leave to observe, that it lays open the weakness of this subterfuge, which requires the use of reason for the discovery of these general truths: since it must be confessed that in their discovery there is no use made of reasoning at all. And I think those who give this answer will not be forward to affirm that the knowledge of this maxim, "That it is impossible for the same thing to be and not to be," is a deduction of our reason. For this would be to destroy that bounty of of nature they seem so fond of, whilst they make the knowledge of those principles to depend on the labour of our thoughts. For all reasoning is search, and casting about, and requires pains and application. And how can it with any tolerable sense be supposed, that what was imprinted by nature, as the foundation and guide of our reason, should need the use of reason to discover it?

11. Those who will take the pains to reflect with a little attention on the operations of the understanding, will find that this ready assent of the mind to some truths, depends not, either on native inscription, or the use of reason, but on a faculty of the mind quite distinct from both of them, as we shall see hereafter.

LEIBNIZ—*Very well. But it is this particular relation of the human mind to these truths which renders the exercise of the faculty easy and natural with respect to them, and which causes them to be called innate. It is not, then, a bare faculty which consists in the mere possibility of understanding them; it is a disposition, an aptitude, a preformation, which determines our soul and which makes it possible for them to be derived from it. Just as there is a difference between the figures which one gives indifferently to stone or marble, and those which its veins already indicate, or are disposed to indicate if the workman profits by them.*

I have * *made use . . . of the comparison of a block of marble which has veins, rather than of a block of marble completely uniform, or of blank tablets—that is to say, of what is called among philosophers a* tabula rasa. *For if the soul were*

---

* This paragraph is part of the Preface of the *New Essays*, but expands on what Leibniz has said here.—Ed.

*like these blank tablets, truths would be in us as the figure of
Hercules is in a piece of marble when the marble is completely
indifferent as to whether it receives this figure or some other.
But if there were veins in the block which indicated the figure
of Hercules rather than other figures, this block would be more
determined thereto, and Hercules would be, as it were, in a
fashion innate in it, although it would be necessary to labor to
discover these veins, to clear them by polishing and by cutting
away what prevents them from appearing. Thus it is that ideas
and truths are innate in us, as inclinations, dispositions, conditions, or natural potentialities, and not as actions; although
these potentialities are always accompanied by some actions,
often insensible, which correspond to them.*

LOCKE—Reason, therefore, having nothing to do in pro-
curing our assent to these maxims, if by saying, that "men know
and assent to them, when they come to the use of reason," be
meant, that the use of reason assists us in the knowledge of
these maxims, it is utterly false; and were it true, would prove
them not to be innate.

12. If by knowing and assenting to them "when we come to
the use of reason," be meant, that this is the time when they
come to be taken notice of by the mind; and that as soon as
children come to the use of reason, they come also to know and
assent to these maxims; this also is false and frivolous. First,
it is false; because it is evident these maxims are not in the mind
so early as the use of reason; and therefore the coming to the
use of reason is falsely assigned as the time of their discovery.
How many instances of the use of reason may we observe in
children, a long time before they have any knowledge of this
maxim, "that it is impossible for the same thing to be and not
to be?" And a great part of illiterate people and savages pass
many years, even of their rational age, without ever thinking
on this and the like general propositions. I grant, men come
not to the knowledge of these general and more abstract truths,
which are thought innate, till they come to the use of reason;
and I add, nor then neither. Which is so, because, till after they
come to the use of reason, those general abstract ideas are not
framed in the mind, about which those general maxims are,
which are mistaken for innate principles, but are indeed dis-

coveries made and verities introduced and brought into the mind by the same way, and discovered by the same steps, as several other propositions, which nobody was ever so extravagant as to suppose innate. This I hope to make plain in the sequel of this Discourse. I allow therefore, a necessity that men should come to the use of reason before they get the knowledge of those general truths; but deny that men's coming to the use of reason is the time of their discovery.

13. In the mean time it is observable, that this saying, that men know and assent to these maxims "when they come to the use of reason," amounts in reality of fact to no more but this— that they are never known nor taken notice of before the use of reason, but may possibly be assented to some time after, during a man's life; but when is uncertain. And so may all other knowable truths, as well as these; which therefore have no advantage nor distinction from others by this note of being known when we come to the use of reason; nor are thereby proved to be innate, but quite the contrary.

14. But, secondly, were it true that the precise time of their being known and assented to were, when men come to the use of reason; neither would that prove them innate. This way of arguing is as frivolous as the supposition itself is false. For, by what kind of logic will it appear that any notion is originally by nature imprinted in the mind in its first constitution, because it comes first to be observed and assented to when a faculty of the mind, which has quite a distinct province, begins to exert itself? And therefore the coming to the use of speech, if it were supposed the time that these maxims are first assented to (which it may be with as much truth as the time when men come to the use of reason), would be as good a proof that they were innate, as to say they are innate because men assent to them when they come to the use of reason. I agree then with these men of innate principles, that there is no knowledge of these general and self-evident maxims in the mind, till it comes to the exercise of reason: but I deny that the coming to the use of reason is the precise time when they are first taken notice of; and if that were the precise time, I deny that it would prove them innate. All that can with any truth be meant by this proposition, that men "assent to them when they come to

the use of reason," is no more but this—that the making of general abstract ideas, and the understanding of general names, being a concomitant of the rational faculty, and growing up with it, children commonly get not those general ideas, nor learn the names that stand for them, till, having for a good while exercised their reason about familiar and more particular ideas, they are, by their ordinary discourse and actions with others, acknowledged to be capable of rational conversation. If assenting to these maxims, when men come to the use of reason, can be true in any other sense, I desire it may be shown; or at least, how in this, or any other sense, it proves them innate.

15. The senses at first let in *particular* ideas, and furnish the yet empty cabinet, and the mind by degrees growing familiar with some of them, they are lodged in the memory, and names got to them. Afterwards, the mind proceeding further, abstracts them, and by degrees learns the use of general names. In this manner the mind comes to be furnished with ideas and language, the *materials* about which to exercise its discursive faculty. And the use of reason becomes daily more visible, as these materials that give it employment increase. But though the having of general ideas and the use of general words and reason usually grow together, yet I see not how this any way proves them innate. The knowledge of some truths, I confess, is very early in the mind; but in a way that shows them not to be innate. For, if we will observe, we shall find it still to be about ideas, not innate, but acquired; it being about those first which are imprinted by external things, with which infants have earliest to do, which make the most frequent impressions on their senses. In ideas thus got, the mind discovers that some agree and others differ, probably as soon as it has any use of memory; as soon as it is able to retain and perceive distinct ideas. But whether it be then or no, this is certain, it does so long before it has the use of words; or comes to that which we commonly call "the use of reason." For a child knows as certainly before it can speak the difference between the ideas of sweet and bitter (i.e., that sweet is not bitter), as it knows afterwards (when it comes to speak) that wormwood and sugarplums are not the same thing.

16. A child knows not that three and four are equal to seven,

till he comes to be able to count seven, and has got the name
and idea of equality; and then, upon explaining those words, he
presently assents to, or rather perceives the truth of that proposition. But neither does he then readily assent because it is an
innate truth, nor was his assent wanting till then because he
wanted the use of reason; but the truth of it appears to him as
soon as he has settled in his mind the clear and distinct ideas
that these names stand for. And then he knows the truth of
that proposition upon the same grounds and by the same means,
that he knew before that a rod and a cherry are not the same
thing; and upon the same grounds also that he may come to
know afterwards "That it is impossible for the same thing to be
and not to be," as shall be more fully shown hereafter. So that
the later it is before any one comes to have those general ideas
about which those maxims are; or to know the signification of
those general terms that stand for them; or to put together in
his mind the ideas they stand for; the later also will it be before
he comes to assent to those maxims—whose terms, with the
ideas they stand for, being no more innate than those of a cat
or a weasel, he must stay till time and observation have acquainted him with them; and then he will be in capacity to know
the truth of these maxims, upon the first occasion that shall
make him put together those ideas in his mind, and observe
whether they agree or disagree, according as is expressed in those
propositions.

LEIBNIZ—*The intellectual ideas, which are the source of
necessary truths, do not come from the senses; and you admit
that there are some ideas which are due to the reflection of the
mind upon itself. For the rest, it is true that the explicit knowledge of truths is subsequent (in time or nature)* to the explicit
knowledge of ideas; as the nature of truths depends upon the
nature of ideas, before we explicitly form one or the other, and
the truths into which enter ideas that come from the senses
depend upon the senses, at least in part. But the ideas which
come from the senses are confused, at least in part; while the
intellectual ideas, and the truths dependent upon them, are distinct, and neither the one nor the other have their origin in the*

---

*This phrase in parentheses is in Latin, rather than French, in the
original.—Ed.

senses, although it may be true that we would never think of them without the senses.

LOCKE—And therefore it is that a man knows that eighteen teen and nineteen are equal to thirty-seven, by the same self-evidence that he knows one and two to be equal to three: yet a child knows this not so soon as the other; not for want of the use of reason, but because the ideas the words eighteen, nineteen, and thirty-seven stand for, are not so soon got, as those which are signified by one, two, and three.

LEIBNIZ—*I can agree with you that often the difficulty in the explicit formation of truths depends upon that in the explicit formation of ideas. Yet I believe that in your example the question concerns the use of ideas already formed. For those who have learned to count to ten, and the method of passing farther on by a certain repetition of tens, understand without difficulty what are 18, 19, 37—namely, one, two, or three times ten, with eight or nine or seven—but in order to draw from it that 18 plus 19 make 37, much more attention is necessary than to know that two plus one are three, which at bottom is only the definition of* three.

LOCKE—17. This evasion therefore of general assent when men come to the use of reason, failing as it does, and leaving no difference between those supposed innate and other truths that are afterwards acquired and learnt, men have endeavoured to secure an universal assent to those they call maxims, by saying, they are generally assented to as soon as proposed, and the terms they are proposed in understood: seeing all men, even children, as soon as they hear and understand the terms, assent to these propositions, they think it is sufficient to prove them innate. For, since men never fail after they have once understood the words, to acknowledge them for undoubted truths, they would infer, that certainly these propositions were first lodged in the understanding, which, without any teaching, the mind, at the very first proposal, immediately closes with and assents to, and after that never doubts again.

18. In answer to this, I demand whether ready assent given to a proposition, upon first hearing and understanding the terms, be a certain mark of an innate principle? If it be not, such a general assent is in vain urged as a proof of them: if it be said

that it is a mark of innate, they must then allow all such propositions to be innate which are generally assented to as soon as heard, whereby they will find themselves plentifully stored with innate principles. For upon the same ground, viz. of assent at first hearing and understanding the terms, that men would have those maxims pass for innate, they must also admit several propositions about numbers to be innate; and thus, that one and two are equal to three, that two and two are equal to four, and a multitude of other the like propositions in numbers, that everybody assents to at first hearing and understanding the terms, must have a place amongst these innate axioms. Nor is this the prerogative of numbers alone, and propositions made about several of them; but even natural philosophy, and all the other sciences, afford propositions which are sure to meet with assent as soon as they are understood. That "two bodies cannot be in the same place" is a truth that nobody any more sticks at than at these maxims, that "it is impossible for the same thing to be and not to be," that "white is not black," that "a square is not a circle," that "bitterness is not sweetness."

LEIBNIZ—*There is a difference among these propositions. The first, which declares the impenetrability of bodies, needs proof. Everybody who believes in genuine condensation and rarefaction, in the strict sense, as the Peripatetics and the late Chevalier Digby did, reject it in effect; not to mention the Christians, who believe, for the most part, that the contrary— namely, the penetration of dimensions—is possible to God. But the other propositions are* identical, *or very nearly so, and identical or immediate propositions do not admit of proof. Those which are about that which the senses furnish, such as the proposition which says that the color yellow is not sweetness, do nothing but apply the general identical maxim to particular cases.*

LOCKE—These and a million of such other propositions, as many at least as we have distinct ideas of, every man in his wits, at first hearing, and knowing what the names stand for, must necessarily assent to. If these men will be true to their own rule, and have assent at first hearing and understanding the terms to be a mark of innate, they must allow not only as many innate propositions as men have distinct ideas, but as many as

men can make propositions wherein different ideas are denied
one of another. Since every proposition wherein one different
idea is denied of another, will as certainly find assent at first
hearing and understanding the terms as this general one, "It is
impossible for the same thing to be and not to be," or that
which is the foundation of it and is the easier understood of
the two, "The same is not different"; by which account they
will have legions of innate propositions of this one sort, without mentioning any other.

LEIBNIZ—*The one (namely, the general maxim) is the
principle, and the other (that is to say, the proposition in which
one idea is negated of another opposed idea) is its application.*

LOCKE—But, since no proposition can be innate unless the
ideas about which it is be innate, this will be to suppose all our
ideas of colours, sounds, tastes, figure, etc., innate, than which
there cannot be anything more opposite to reason and experience. Universal and ready assent upon hearing and understanding the terms is, I grant, a mark of self-evidence; but self-
evidence, depending not on innate impressions, but on something else (as we shall show hereafter), belongs to several propositions which nobody was yet so extravagant as to pretend to
be innate.

LEIBNIZ— . . . *This proposition:* the sweet is not the bitter, *is not innate, according to the sense which we have given to
the term innate truth. For the sensations of sweet and bitter
come from the external senses. Thus it is a mixed conclusion*
(hybrida conclusio), *where the axiom is applied to a sensible
truth. But as regards this proposition:* the square is not a circle, *you can affirm that it is innate, for, in considering it, you
make a subsumption or application of the principle of contradiction to what the understanding itself furnishes as soon as you
are conscious that these ideas which are innate include incompatible notions.*

LOCKE—19. Nor let it be said, that those more particular
self-evident propositions, which are assented to at first hearing,
as that "one and two are equal to three," that "green is not
red," etc., are received as the consequences of those more universal propositions which are looked on as innate principles;
since any one, who will but take the pains to observe what

passes in the understanding, will certainly find that these, and the like less general propositions, are certainly known, and firmly assented to by those who are utterly ignorant of those more general maxims; and so, being earlier in the mind than those (as they are called) first principles, cannot owe to them the assent wherewith they are received at first hearing. . . .

LEIBNIZ—*I have already replied to that above. We build on these general maxims as we build upon the major premises, which are suppressed when we reason by enthymemes; for although very often we do not think distinctly of what we do in reasoning any more than of what we do in walking and leaping, it is always true that the force of the conclusion consists in part in that which is suppressed, and could not come from anywhere else, as one will find when one wants to justify it.*

LOCKE—21. But we have not yet done with "assenting to propositions at first hearing and understanding their terms." It is fit we first take notice that this, instead of being a mark that they are innate, is a proof of the contrary; since it supposes that several, who understand and know other things, are ignorant of these principles till they are proposed to them; and that one may be unacquainted with these truths till he hears them from others. For, if they were innate, what need they be proposed in order to gaining assent, when, by being in the understanding, by a natural and original impression (if there were any such), they could not but be known before? Or doth the proposing them print them clearer in the mind than nature did? If so, then the consequence will be, that a man knows them better after he has been thus taught them than he did before. Whence it will follow that these principles may be made more evident to us by others' teaching than nature has made them by impression: which will ill agree with the opinion of innate principles, and give but little authority to them; but, on the contrary, makes them unfit to be the foundations of all our other knowledge; as they are pretended to be. This cannot be denied, that men grow first acquainted with many of these self-evident truths upon their being proposed: but it is clear that whosoever does so, finds in himself that he then begins to know a proposition, which he knew not before, and which from thenceforth he never questions; not because it was innate, but because the consideration of the nature of the things contained in those words would not suffer him to think otherwise, how, or whensoever he is brought to reflect on them.

LEIBNIZ—*Both are true. The nature of things and the nature of the mind cooperate to produce this result. And since you oppose the consideration of the thing to the consciousness of that which is engraved in the mind, this objection itself shows . . . that those whose side you take understand by* innate truths *only those which would be approved naturally as* by instinct, *and even without knowing it, unless confusedly. There are some of this nature. . . . But what is called* natural light *supposes a distinct knowledge, and very often the consideration of the nature of things is nothing else than the knowledge of the nature of our mind, and of these innate ideas, which we have no need to seek outside. Thus I call innate the truths which need only this consideration in order to be verified.*

LOCKE—And if whatever is assented to at first hearing and understanding the terms must pass for an innate principle, every well-grounded observation, drawn from particulars into a general rule, must be innate. When yet it is certain that not all, but only sagacious heads, light at first on these observations, and reduce them into general propositions: not innate, but collected from a preceding acquaintance and reflection on particular instances. These, when observing men have made them, unobserving men, when they are proposed to them, cannot refuse their assent to. . . .

23. There is, I fear, this further weakness in the foregoing argument, which would persuade us that therefore those maxims are to be thought innate, which men admit at first hearing; because they assent to propositions which they are not taught, nor do receive from the force of any argument or demonstration, but a bare explication or understanding of the terms. Under which there seems to me to lie this fallacy, that men are supposed not to be taught nor to learn anything *de novo;* when, in truth, they are taught, and do learn something they were ignorant of before.

LEIBNIZ—*The question here is not of names, which are in some way arbitrary, whereas ideas and truths are natural. But with respect to these ideas and truths, you attribute to us . . . a doctrine from which we are far removed; for I agree that we learn innate ideas and truths either in paying attention to their source, or in verifying them through experience. Thus I do not make the supposition which you say, as if in the case of which you speak we learned nothing new. And I cannot admit this proposition:* all that one learns is not innate. *The truths of numbers are in us, and we do not cease to learn them—either by drawing them from their source, when we learn them by demonstrative proof (which shows that they are innate); or by becoming acquainted with them in examples, as do ordinary mathematicians, who, for lack of a knowledge of the proofs, learn their rules only by tradition, and, at most, before teaching them, justify them by experience, which they continue as far as they think expedient. And sometimes even a very able mathematician, not knowing the source of another's discovery, is obliged to content himself with this method of induction in examining it—as did a celebrated writer at Paris, when I was there, who continued rather far the testing of my arithmetical tetragonism, by comparing it with the numbers of Ludolphe, believing that he found there some error; and he had reason to doubt until someone communicated to him the demonstration of it, which excuses us from these tests, which could always be continued without ever being perfectly certain. And it is this very thing, namely the imperfection of inductions, which can also be verified by instances of experience. For there are progressions in which one can go very far before noticing the changes and the laws that are found there.*

LOCKE—For, first, it is evident that they have learned the terms, and their signification; neither of which was born with them. But this is not all the acquired knowledge in the case: the ideas themselves, about which the proposition is, are not born with them, no more than their names, but got afterwards.

LEIBNIZ— . . . *The intellectual ideas or ideas of reflection are derived from our mind; and I should much like to know how we could have the idea of being if we were not beings ourselves, and did not thus find being in ourselves.*

LOCKE—So that in all propositions that are assented to at first hearing, the terms of the proposition, their standing for such ideas, and the ideas themselves that they stand for, being neither of them innate, I would fain know what there is remaining in such propositions that is innate. For I would gladly have any one name that proposition whose terms or ideas were either of them innate.

LEIBNIZ—*I would name the propositions of arithmetic and geometry, which are all of this nature; and as regards necessary truths, no others could be found.*

LOCKE—We *by degrees* get ideas and names, and *learn* their appropriated connection one with another; and then to propositions made in such terms, whose signification we have learnt, and wherein the agreement or disagreement we can perceive in our ideas when put together is expressed, we at first hearing assent; though to other propositions, in themselves as certain and evident, but which are concerning ideas not so soon or so easily got, we are at the same time no way capable of assenting. For, though a child quickly assents to this proposition, "That an apple is not fire," when by familiar acquaintance he has got the ideas of those two different things distinctly imprinted on his mind, and has learnt that the names apple and fire stand for them; yet it will be some years after, perhaps, before the same child will assent to this proposition, "That it is impossible for the same thing to be and not to be"; because that, though perhaps the words are as easy to be learnt, yet the signification of them being more large, comprehensive, and abstract than of the names annexed to those sensible things the child hath to do with, it is longer before he learns their precise meaning, and it requires more time plainly to form in his mind those general ideas they stand for. Till that be done, you will in vain endeavour to make any child assent to a proposition made up of such general terms; but as soon as ever he has got those ideas, and learned their names, he forwardly closes with the one as well as the other of the forementioned propositions: and with both for the same reason; viz., because he finds the ideas he has in his mind to agree or disagree, according as the words standing for them are affirmed or denied one of another in the proposition. But if propositions be brought to him in words which stand for ideas he has not yet in his mind, to such propositions, however evidently true or false in themselves, he affords neither assent nor dissent, but is ignorant. For words being but empty sounds, any further than they are signs of our ideas, we cannot but assent to them as they correspond to those ideas we have, but no further than that. . . .

LOCKE [Book I, chapter iii: "Other Considerations Concerning Innate Principles Both Speculative and Practical"] —
1. Had those who would persuade us that there are innate principles not taken them together in gross, but considered separately the parts out of which those propositions are made, they would not, perhaps, have been so forward to believe they were innate. Since, if the *ideas* which made up those truths were not, it was impossible that the *propositions* made up of them should be innate, or our knowledge of them be born with us. For, if the ideas be not innate, there was a time when the mind was without those principles; and then they will not be innate, but be derived from some other original. For, where the ideas themselves are not, there can be no knowledge, no assent, no mental or verbal propositions about them.
2. If we will attentively consider newborn children, we shall have little reason to think that they bring many ideas into the world with them. For, bating perhaps some faint ideas of hunger, and thirst, and warmth, and some pains, which they may have felt in the womb, there is not the least appearance of any settled ideas at all in them; especially of *ideas answering the terms which make up those universal propositions that are esteemed innate principles.* One may perceive how, by degrees, afterwards, ideas come into their minds; and that they get no more, nor other, than what experience, and the observation of things that come in their way, furnish them with; which might be enough to satisfy us that they are not original characters stamped on the mind.
3. "It is impossible for the same thing to be, and not to be," is certainly (if there be any such) an innate *principle.* But can any one think, or will any one say, that "impossibility" and "identity" are two innate *ideas*?
LEIBNIZ—*It is quite necessary that those who favor innate truths maintain and be convinced that these ideas are also innate, and I confess that I am of their opinion. The ideas of* being, *of the* possible, *and of the* same *are so completely innate that they*

*enter into all our thoughts and reasonings, and I regard them as
essential to our mind; but I have already said that we do not always pay them particular attention and that we pick them out
only with time. I have already said that we are, so to speak, innate in ourselves, and since we are beings, beings is innate in us;
and the knowledge of being is wrapped up in that which we have
of ourselves. There is something similar in the case of other general notions.*

LOCKE—Are they such as all mankind have, and bring into
the world with them? And are they those which are the first in
children, and antecedent to all acquired ones? If they are innate,
they must needs be so. Hath a child an idea of impossibility and
identity, before it has of white or black, sweet or bitter? And is
it from the knowledge of this principle that it concludes, that
wormwood rubbed on the nipple hath not the same taste that it
used to receive from thence? Is it the actual knowledge of *im-
possibile est idem esse, et non esse,* that makes a child distinguish
between its mother and a stranger; or that makes it fond of the
one and flee the other? Or does the mind regulate itself and its
assent by ideas that it never yet had? Or the understanding draw
conclusions from principles which it never yet knew or understood? The names *impossibility* and *identity* stand for two ideas,
so far from being innate, or born with us, that I think it requires
great care and attention to form them right in our understandings.
They are so far from being brought into the world with us, so
remote from the thoughts of infancy and childhood, that I believe, upon examination it will be found that many grown men
want them.

4. If *identity* (to instance that alone) be a native impression,
and consequently so clear and obvious to us that we must needs
know it even from our cradles, I would gladly be resolved by any
one of seven, or seventy years old, whether a man, being a creature consisting of soul and body, be the same man when his body
is changed? Whether Euphorbus and Pythagoras, having had the
same soul, were the same men, though they lived several ages
asunder? Nay, whether the cock too, which had the same soul,
were not the same with both of them? Whereby, perhaps, it
will appear that our idea of *sameness* is not so settled and clear as
to deserve to be thought innate in us. . . .

LEIBNIZ—*I have stated sufficiently that what is natural to us is not known to us as such from the cradle; and even an idea can be known to us without our being able to decide at once all questions which can be formed thereupon. It is as if someone maintained that a child cannot know what a square is and what its diagonal is, because he will have difficulty in recognizing that the diagonal is incommensurable with the side of the square. . . .*

LOCKE [Book II, chapter i, "Of Ideas in General, and Their Original"] —

1. Every man being conscious to himself that he thinks; and that which his mind is applied about whilst thinking being the *ideas* that are there, it is past doubt that men have in their minds several ideas—such as are those expressed by the words *whiteness, hardness, sweetness, thinking, motion, man, elephant, army, drunkenness,* and others: it is in the first place then to be inquired, *How he comes by them?*

I know it is a received doctrine, that men have native ideas, and original characters, stamped upon their minds in their very first being. This opinion I have at large examined already; and, I suppose what I have said in the foregoing Book will be much more easily admitted, when I have shown whence the understanding may get all the ideas it has; and by what ways and degrees they may come into the mind—for which I shall appeal to every one's own observation and experience.

2. Let us then suppose the mind to be, as we say, white paper, void of all characters, without any ideas—How comes it to be furnished? Whence comes it by that vast store which the busy and boundless fancy of man has painted on it with an almost endless variety? Whence has it all the *materials* of reason and knowledge? To this I answer, in one word, from EXPERENCE. In that all our knowledge is founded; and from that it ultimately derives itself. Our observation employed either, about external sensible objects, or about the internal operations of our minds perceived and reflected on by ourselves, is that which supplies our understandings with all the *materials* of thinking. These two are the fountains of knowledge, from whence all the ideas we have, or can naturally have, do spring.

LEIBNIZ— . . . *Experience is necessary, I admit, in order that the soul be determined to such or such thoughts, and in*

*order that it take notice of the ideas which are in us; but by
what means can experience and the senses give ideas? Has the
soul windows, does it resemble tablets, is it like wax? It is
plain that all who so regard the soul, represent it as at bottom
corporeal. You will oppose to me this axiom which is received
among the philosophers,* that there is nothing in the soul which
does not come from the senses. *But you must except the soul
itself and its affections.* Nihil est in intellectu, quod non fuerit
in sensu, *excipe:* nisi ipse intellectus. *Now the soul includes
being, substance, the one, the same, cause, perception, reasoning,
and many other notions which the senses cannot give. This
view sufficiently agrees with your author of the Essay, who
seeks the source of a good part of the ideas in the mind's reflection upon its own nature.*

LOCKE—3. First, our Senses, conversant about particular
sensible objects, do convey into the mind several distinct perceptions of things, according to those various ways wherein
those objects do affect them. And thus we come by those *ideas*
we have of *yellow, white, heat, cold, soft, hard, bitter, sweet,*
and all those which we call sensible qualities; which when I say
the senses convey into the mind, I mean, they from external
objects convey into the mind what produces there those perceptions. This great source of most of the ideas we have, depending wholly upon our senses, and derived by them to the
understanding, I call SENSATION.

4. Secondly, the other fountain from which experience
furnisheth the understanding with ideas is—the perception of
the operations of our own mind within us, as it is employed
about the ideas it has got—which operations, when the soul
comes to reflect on and consider, do furnish the understanding
with another set of ideas, which could not be had from things
without. And such are *perception, thinking doubting, believing,
reasoning, knowing, willing,* and all the different actings of our
own minds—which we being conscious of, and observing in
ourselves, do from these receive into our understandings as
distinct ideas as we do from bodies affecting our senses. This
source of ideas every man has wholly in himself; and though it
be not sense, as having nothing to do with external objects, yet
it is very like it, and might properly enough be called *internal*

sense. But as I call the other Sensation, so I call this REFLEC—
TION, the ideas it affords being such only as the mind gets by
reflecting on its own operations within itself. By reflection
then, in the following part of this discourse, I would be understood to mean, that notice which the mind takes of its own
operations, and the manner of them, by reason whereof there
come to be ideas of these operations in the understanding.
These two, I say, viz. external material things, as the objects
of SENSATION, and the operations of our own minds within,
as the objects of REFLECTION, are to me the only originals
from whence all our ideas take their beginnings. The term
operations here I use in a large sense, as comprehending not
barely the actions of the mind about its ideas, but some sort
of passions arising sometimes from them, such as is the satis-
faction or uneasiness arising from any thought.

5. The understanding seems to me not to have the least
glimmering of any ideas which it doth not receive from one of
these two. *External objects* furnish the mind with the ideas of
sensible qualities, which are all those different perceptions they
produce in us; and *the mind* furnishes the understanding with
ideas of its own operations.

These, when we have taken a full survey of them, and their
several modes, combinations, and relations, we shall find to
contain all our whole stock of ideas; and that we have nothing
in our minds which did not come in one of these two ways. Let
any one examine his own thoughts, and thoroughly search into
his understanding; and then let him tell me, whether all the
original ideas he has there, are any other than of the objects of
his senses, or of the operations of his mind, considered as objects of his reflection. And how great a mass of knowledge so-
ever he imagines to be lodged there, he will, upon taking a strict
view, see that he has not any idea in his mind but what one of
these two have imprinted—though perhaps, with infinite variety
compounded and enlarged by the understanding, as we shall see
hereafter.

6. He that attentively considers the state of a child, at his
first coming into the world, will have little reason to think him
stored with plenty of ideas, that are to be the matter of his
future knowledge. It is *by degrees* he comes to be furnished

with them. And though the ideas of obvious and familiar qualities imprint themselves before the memory begins to keep a
register of time or order, yet it is often so late before some unusual qualities come in the way, that there are few men that
cannot recollect the beginning of their acquaintance with them.
And if it were worthwhile, no doubt a child might be so ordered
as to have but a very few, even of the ordinary ideas, till he
were grown up to a man. But all that are born into the world,
being surrounded with bodies that perpetually and diversely
affect them, variety of ideas, whether care be taken of it or not,
are imprinted on the minds of children. Light and colours are
busy at hand everywhere, when the eye is but open; sounds and
some tangible qualities fail not to solicit their proper senses, and
force an entrance to the mind—but yet, I think, it will be granted easily, that if a child were kept in a place where he never
saw any other but black and white till he were a man, he would
have no more ideas of scarlet or green, than he that from his
childhood never tasted an oyster, or a pineapple, has of those
particular relishes.

7. Men then come to be furnished with fewer or more simple ideas from without, according as the objects they converse
with afford greater or less variety; and from the operations of
their minds within, according as they more or less reflect on
them. For, though he that contemplates the operations of his
mind, cannot but have plain and clear ideas of them; yet, unless he turn his thoughts that way, and considers them *attentively*, he will no more have clear and distinct ideas of all the operations of his mind, and all that may be observed therein, than
he will have all the particular ideas of any landscape, or of the
parts and motions of a clock, who will not turn his eyes to it,
and with attention heed all the parts of it. The picture, or
clock may be so placed, that they may come in his way every
day; but yet he will have but a confused idea of all the parts
they are made up of, till he applies himself with attention, to
consider them each in particular.

8. And hence we see the reason why it is pretty late before
most children get ideas of the operations of their own minds;
and some have not any very clear or perfect ideas of the greatest
part of them all their lives. Because, though they pass there

continually, yet, like floating visions, they make not deep impressions enough to leave in their mind clear, distinct, lasting ideas, till the understanding turns inward upon itself, reflects on its own operations, and makes them the objects of its own contemplation. Children when they come first into it, are surrounded with a world of new things, which, by a constant solicitation of their senses, draw the mind constantly to them; forward to take notice of new, and apt to be delighted with the variety of changing objects. Thus the first years are usually employed and diverted in looking abroad. Men's business in them is to acquaint themselves with what is to be found without; and so growing up in a constant attention to outward sensations, seldom make any considerable reflection on what passes within them, till they come to be of riper years; and some scarce ever at all.

These selections from *An Essay Concerning Human Understanding,* by John Locke, edited, in 2 vols., by A. C. Fraser (Oxford: Clarendon Press, 1894), and *New Essays Concerning Human Understanding,* by Gottfried Wilhelm Leibniz, translated by A. G. Langley (New York: Macmillan, 1896), have been made, and Langley's translation of Leibniz extensively revised, by Robert Merrihew Adams, who is also responsible for the footnotes.

PART II

3

Where Do Our Ideas Come From?
—Descartes *vs.* Locke

ROBERT MERRIHEW ADAMS

The innatist-empiricist controversy of the seventeenth and eighteenth centuries is one of the most tangled and obscure, as well as one of the most famous, of philosophical debates. The issues are clouded by metaphorical talk about impressions on wax tablets and images in a *camera obscura,* and often were not clearly understood by the participants in the debate. It is not easy to see what—if anything—they were really disagreeing about.

In this essay I shall try to expose and clarify one disagreement between innatist and empiricist philosophers, and especially between Descartes and Locke, which seems to me to have been, in relation to the concerns of seventeenth- and eighteenth-century philosophy, the central disagreement in the controversy. It is a disagreement that can be expressed by saying that one party held that some (or all) of our ideas are innate, and the other party held that all our ideas are derived from experience. But that is not very informative. Both of the key terms—"derived from experience" as well as "innate"—need interpretation. It turns out that each of them is best understood in relation to doctrines that were stated with the use of the other term. In seeking the correct interpretation I believe it is most helpful to trace the development of the controversy, beginning with a pre-Cartesian empiricism.

In the first section of the paper I try to explain the sense in which Aristotelian scholastic empiricism held that all our ideas are derived from experience. In the second section I discuss why Descartes rejected Aristotelian empiricism, and in what senses he held that all and some of our ideas are innate. Locke partly revived, and partly abandoned, Aristotelian empiricism; this is discussed in the third section, and a disagreement between Locke and Descartes is defined. It is in large part a disagreement about what sorts of things our ideas can represent. Locke holds, and Descartes was committed to deny, that all our ideas either are, or are composed of, ideas of properties of bodies which we have experienced in sensation, or ideas of mental operations which we have experienced in ourselves. This disagreement has been thought important because philosophers have seen in such Lockean empiricism a basis for metaphysical economy, and in the opposing innatism a basis for metaphysical generosity. In the fourth section of the essay I note this point and argue that Lockean empiricism about ideas provides at most a very weak basis for empiricist metaphysical economy.

I shall be talking only about innate *ideas:* I shall not have anything to say about innate *beliefs* or innate *knowledge.* I do not claim that the issue to be discussed in this paper is the only interesting issue about ideas which was in dispute between innatists and empiricists in the seventeenth and eighteenth centuries. There are other disagreements between them about the ways in which concepts are formed which have attracted a good deal of attention lately,[1] but I will not be discussing them.

I

One point at which to begin in trying to understand the innatist-empiricist controversy in modern philosophy is the abandonment of the Aristotelian theory of perception. (When I say "Aristotelian" in this essay, I have chiefly in mind the Aristotelian scholasticism of the Middle Ages, which was familiar to seventeenth-century philosophers, rather than Aristotle himself.) The treatment of perception was an integral part of the fabric of Aristotelian natural science, an application of a very general theory of causality. According to this theory, efficient causality is a transaction in which a form is transmitted by something which has the form to something which did not have it, but had only the potentiality for it. Thus in the heating of a cold body it was thought that the form, heat, is transmitted from a warm body (which has it) to the cold body (which did not yet have it). Causality was regarded as a sort of process of contagion, in which one thing was, so to speak, infected with the properties of another.

Perception was interpreted as a transaction in which a form (the sensible form) is transmitted from the perceived object to the perceiver. Typically a medium (light, in the case of vision) is required, through which the form can pass on its way from the object to the perceiver. On reaching the sense organ (in the case of vision, the eye) the form transmitted from the object informs the organ, and is eventually received in the mind. This is a greatly simplified statement of the Aristotelian theory of perception. For our present purpose the most important point to grasp about it is that one and the same form, originally present in the object, is present also in the medium, the sense organ, and the mind. There is something (the sensible form) which literally comes into the mind from the object.

This theory of perception is the basis for the Aristotelian empiricist answer to the question, how we get our ideas. Platonist and Stoic doctrines, according to which certain ideas are in our minds since birth or before, are rejected. The human mind, at the beginning of its existence, is like a blank tablet. It has no ideas—that is, in Aristotelian scholastic terms, none of the sensible and intelligible forms by virtue of which it perceives, imagines, and understands things. Such forms first come into the mind from outside, in sense perception. These are, in the first instance, the sensible forms—for example, the forms by having which the mind is aware of sensing heat and cold, softness and hardness, and colors. But intelligible forms (such as those of body, apple, dog, and being) also come into the mind from outside, *in* the sensible forms. They are "abstracted" from the sensible forms by the intellect, and thus we understand things that we sense.

It is sometimes added that there are forms which neither come into the mind from outside nor are present in the mind from the beginning. These are the forms of the mind's own operations, of which it becomes aware as they occur. The mind is indirectly dependent on sensation for its possession of even these forms. For they are not actually present in it until it begins to operate, and it does not begin to operate until sensation provides it with other forms from outside, which are the first objects of its operation.[2]

It is important to see that in its Aristotelian context empiricism is a theory that is meant to have explanatory force. It is assumed that when the mind knows something, it does so by having in itself a likeness of the object—or more precisely, a form that is also present in the object. Then an explanation is needed for the presence of this form in the mind. On Aristotelian views of causality, the form must have come from something that had it. The empiricist theory, that all our ideas are (or are composed of) forms that first entered our awareness in experience of objects that had them, is an attempt to explain our possession of ideas in accordance with Aristotelian conceptions of causality.

II

Descartes agrees that the presence of an idea in one's mind requires an explanation. In fact he holds a causal principle very similar to that of the Aristotelians.

> But in order that an idea should contain some one certain objective reality rather than another, it must without doubt derive it from some cause in which there is at least as much formal reality as this idea contains of objective reality.[3]

The form or likeness of the thing known or thought about, as it exists in the mind, is what Descartes calls the "objective reality" of the idea by which we think about the thing. The thing or property represented, as it exists in the object independently of being thought about, is the corresponding "formal reality." Descartes makes an important modification in the Aristotelian principle. He does not demand that *the same* form be found in the cause of the idea as in the idea—in his terms, he does not demand that *the same* reality exist formally in the cause of the idea as exists objectively in the idea. What he demands is that *at least as much reality* exist formally in the cause as exists objectively in the idea. (We need not worry here about what is supposed to determine the quantity of reality.) One reason why Descartes is obliged to make this modification is that he believes that some of our ideas (for instance, the idea of a perfectly straight line) do not in fact derive their form or objective reality from something that has the same reality formally, but only from something (God) that has more reality formally. In spite of this modification, however, it is clear that Descartes retains an interest in tracing the form (or objective reality) of an idea to a source.

But he rejects the Aristotelian theory of perception, and with it the Aristotelian account of how we get our ideas. He says that "any man who rightly observes the limitations of the senses, and what precisely it is that can penetrate through this medium to our faculty of thinking must needs admit that no ideas of things, in the shape in which we envisage them by thought, are presented to us by the senses."[4] This position arises from Descartes's abandonment of the Aristotelian scheme of explanation in terms of infection by properties, in favor of a scheme of mechanical explanation. In Cartesian science all sensation must be explained in terms of the impact of other bodies (normally minute particles) on the organ of sensation, and the purely mechanical transmission of an impulse, by motions of the nerves, to the seat of consciousness (the pineal gland). At this point arises, of course, the famous Cartesian problem of how the motions of the pineal gland, or any other motions in the central nervous system, could cause the occurrence of ideas in the mind; but that problem need not concern us in the present argument.

The distinction between primary and secondary qualities is more important for an understanding of the argument. Like Galileo and Locke, Descartes believed that there are no properties of bodies which resemble our sensory ideas or perceptual images of colors, sounds, tastes, odors, heat and cold, softness and hardness, and tangible textures (the secondary qualities). In Aristotelian science it was supposed that there are properties of bodies which resemble our sensory ideas of these qualities. For in sense perception—in perception of secondary qualities as well as of primary qualities—a sensible form that is also present in the object of perception is present in the mind and is the image in the mind which represents the thing perceived. But the new physics of the seventeenth century had no use for properties of bodies which resemble our sensory ideas of secondary qualities. Everything in bodies was to be explained in terms of the sizes, shapes, positions, and motions (primary qualities) of portions of matter. The perception of secondary qualities was to be explained in terms of the size, shape, and velocity of particles striking the sense organs, and in terms of the motions of parts of the perceiver's body which transmit the signal to the brain. In the body perceived, the secondary quality is nothing but the power that it has, by virtue of its primary qualities, to cause certain ideas to occur in the mind of a perceiver; it is nothing that resembles those ideas. The form of our sensory idea of a secondary quality is present, therefore, neither in the body perceived nor in the intermediate causes between the body perceived and the perceiving mind. (For the intermediate causes are only motions.) Our sensory ideas of secondary qualities are not forms that enter the mind from outside in sense perception.

Descartes does not deny that bodies have properties that resemble our sensory ideas of their primary qualities. But he does deny that the motions in the body of the perceiver, which are the immediate corporeal cause of his sensory ideas, resemble the ideas of primary qualities which they cause. He concludes that the forms of our ideas of primary qualities, not being present in their immediate corporeal causes, do not come into the mind from outside in sense perception.

If our ideas of the primary and secondary qualities of bodies do not enter our minds from outside in sense perception, presumably no ideas enter that way at all. How do we get our ideas, then? Descartes can see no answer but that they must all be innate.

> ... in our ideas there is nothing which was not innate in the mind, or faculty of thinking, except only these circumstances which point to experience—the fact, for instance, that we judge that this or that idea, which we now have present to our thought, is to be referred to a certain extraneous thing, not that these extraneous things transmitted the ideas themselves to our minds through the organs of sense, but because they transmitted something which gave the mind occasion to form these ideas, by means of an innate faculty, at this time rather than at another. For nothing reaches our mind from external objects through the organs of sense beyond certain corporeal movements ... ; but even these movements, and the

figures which arise from them, are not conceived by us in the shape they
assume in the organs of sense, as I have explained at great length in my
Dioptrics. Hence it follows that the ideas of the movements and figures
are themselves innate in us. So much the more must the ideas of pain,
colour, sound, and the like be innate, that our mind may, on the occasion
of certain corporeal movements, envisage these ideas, for they have no
likeness to the corporeal movements.[5]

It is clear in this passage, of course, that what Descartes
thinks is innate, or born in us, in the case of ideas of sensible
qualities, is not the actual awareness or thought of the quality,
but a faculty or dispositional property of our minds. [We are
born with such a constitution that when our bodies are affected
with certain motions we will become aware of an idea of red,
when our bodies are affected with certain slightly different
motions we will become aware of an idea of orange, when our
bodies are affected with certain other motions we will become
aware of the idea of a triangular shape, and so forth. Given
the Cartesian theory of perception, it is not enough to suppose
that man is born with a general faculty of receiving sensible
forms from sensible objects—a faculty that could be compared
with the famous blank tablet on which nothing has yet been
written, ready to receive whatever forms the sensible objects
may impart to it. For according to Descartes, no forms come
to the mind from sensible objects. The mind must innately
have, not a faculty of receiving sensible forms in general, but
specific predispositions to form, on appropriate stimulation,
all the ideas of sensible qualities which it is capable of having.

There is an apparent contradiction in what Descartes says
about innateness of ideas. In the passage we have been considering, he argues that all our ideas are innate. But he commonly distinguishes innate ideas from others that he calls
"adventitious," and from still others that he calls "fictitious."[6]
I believe the contradiction here is only apparent. If an adventitious idea is an idea that comes into the mind from outside
in sensation, Descartes does not believe that we have any adventitious ideas. But he calls some ideas adventitious, meaning
that their occurrence in our minds is occasioned (or that we
judge it to be occasioned) by the action, on our sense organs,
of bodies that we perceive. Fictitious ideas are ideas that the
mind forms (or could have formed) voluntarily by combining

simpler ideas that do not imply each other. Descartes holds
that all our ideas are innate in us in the sense that we are born,
not with a capacity to receive them from outside, but with a
power to form each of them without receiving them from outside. He commonly calls some ideas innate in a narrower
sense, however, meaning that we need neither any particular
sensory stimulation, nor simpler component ideas, in order to
form them. (They are neither adventitious nor fictitious.) Such
ideas he evidently regarded as being part of our natural constitution in a more basic or fundamental way than others. It is
with this narrower sense of "innate" that we shall be primarily
concerned.

III

In many ways the resemblance between Locke's empiricism and Aristotelian scholastic empiricism is striking. Locke
denies that we have any innate ideas. He compares the human
mind, at the beginning of its existence, to "white paper, void
of all characters, without any ideas." Whence, then, does the
mind get its ideas? "From EXPERIENCE," Locke answers.[7]
⟨The first and principal source of our ideas is sensation of physical objects. The only other ultimate source of our ideas is
our awareness of the operations of our own mind; Locke agrees
with Aquinas that this source of ideas (which he calls *reflection)*
is dependent on sensation in that our minds do not have any
operations for us to be aware of until sensation has provided
them with ideas to operate about.[8] ⟨Locke does not claim that
all of our ideas come to us directly from sensation or reflection.
What he claims is that all of our *simple* ideas come directly
from sensation or reflection, and that all of our other ideas are
formed from simple ideas by the mental operations of com-
pounding, comparing, and abstracting. A doctrine of *abstraction,* whereby more general ideas are said to be extracted from
the ideas directly received in sensation and reflection, plays as
prominent a part in Locke's theory of the understanding as it
did in Aristotelian theories.

In all this Locke reproduces, in somewhat more modern
terminology, the structure of Aristotelian scholastic thought.

But in Locke the structure lacks its foundation in the theory of perception. Much of Locke's language is misleading on this point. He often speaks as if he thought of the simple ideas of sensation as forms that have literally come into the mind from outside, from physical objects that have them. The senses are said to "convey" ideas into the mind from external objects, which are said to "furnish the mind with the ideas of sensible qualities."[9] But these are metaphorical expressions. Locke's explicit explanation of what he means by saying that the senses "convey" ideas into the mind is plainly consistent with the view that what the senses transmit from physical objects to the mind is not a form that exists both in the object and in the mind, but only an influence that causes the idea to occur in the mind.

And thus we come by those *ideas* we have of *yellow, white, heat, cold, soft, hard, bitter, sweet,* and all those which we call sensible qualities; which when I say the senses convey into the mind, I mean, they from external objects convey into the mind what produces there those perceptions.[10]

And on a larger view it is clear that it is not Locke's doctrine that ideas, or sensible forms, literally come into the mind from outside in sense perception. Consistency would obviously require him to deny any such doctrine in the case of secondary qualities. For like Descartes, and unlike the Aristotelians, Locke denies that there is in bodies anything that resembles our sensory ideas of secondary qualities.[11]

He maintains, however, "that the ideas of primary qualities of bodies are resemblances of them, and their patterns do really exist in the bodies themselves."[12] But he is not in a position to hold that the forms of primary qualities literally travel from the bodies perceived to the mind (although he cannot definitely deny it as Descartes does). He advances no views about the question whether the forms of primary qualities perceived are present in the intermediate stages of the precess of perception, between the body perceived and the perceiving mind. For he explicitly declines to speculate about the physical causal processes involved in perception, or to examine "by what motions of our spirits or alterations of our bodies we come to have any *sensation* by our organs, or any *ideas* in our

understandings."[13] I take it to be Locke's position, therefore,
that the forms of our sensory ideas of secondary qualities do not
literally come into the mind from external material things because
they are not present in external material things at all, and that he
is not committed to the doctrine that the forms of our sensory
ideas of primary qualities literally come into the mind from external material things because he is not committed to any theory
about the physical causal process of sensation.

Seeing that Locke does not mean that sensible forms enter
our minds from outside in sensation, we may well wonder what he
does mean when he says that experience is the source of all our
ideas. Is he asserting anything that Descartes would deny? There
is an obvious analogy between Locke's classification of ideas as
simple and complex, and of simple ideas as ideas of sensation and
ideas of reflection, and Descartes's classification of ideas as fictitious, adventitious, and innate. Descartes's fictitious ideas correspond to Locke's complex ideas. Both are characterized as ideas
that the mind forms out of other, simpler ideas with which it is
already supplied. Descartes's adventitious ideas correspond to
Locke's ideas of sense. Both are characterized as being caused to
occur in the mind by appropriate sensory stimulation, although
they are not believed literally to come into the mind from outside.
But Descartes's innate ideas do not correspond at all closely to
Locke's ideas of reflection. An important disagreement between
the two philosophers is revealed at this point.

In order to understand this disagreement more clearly we can
formulate a thesis that Locke maintains and Descartes would deny:
"All our simple, nonsensory ideas are ideas of reflection." For
purposes of argument, let us ignore any differences there may be
between Locke and Descartes about what an idea is, what a simple (nonfictitious) idea is, and what a sensory (adventitious) idea
is. And let us ask what is being said about simple, nonsensory
ideas when it is claimed that they are ideas of reflection.

This looks like a claim about the *causes* of such ideas.
And so it is, in part. But if Locke were to say that (the first
conscious occurrences of) all our simple, nonsensory ideas are
caused by operations of our minds, that would be a trivial, uninteresting claim. For presumably every conscious occurrence
of any idea is caused, at least in part, by some operation of the

mind. Locke means to say more than that, however. He holds
that all our simple, nonsensory ideas arise from "our observation employed . . . about the internal operations of our minds
perceived and reflected on by ourselves." [14] It is not just *some*
operation of the mind which is needed as a cause of such ideas,
but reflection, self-awareness, *observation of* the operations of
our own minds. Locke holds that present or previous intro-
spective awareness of a certain operation of one's own mind is
a necessary condition (presumably a causally necessary condition)
of any conscious occurrence of a simple, nonsensory idea.

Locke's claim is also a claim about the *content* of simple,
nonsensory ideas. What is the operation of which one must
have been (or be) aware in one's own mind in order to have
such an idea? The operation that is represented by the idea,
of course—the operation *of* which it is an idea. Indeed Locke's
empiricism about ideas can be summed up in a thesis about
the content of our ideas, as follows: "All our ideas are either
simple or composed of simple ideas, and we cannot have a
simple idea which is an idea of anything but a property of
bodies which we have experienced in sensation or a mental
operation which we have experienced in ourselves." That is
certainly something which Descartes would deny.

Descartes held that we do have simple ideas that represent
things that we have not experienced in sensation or self-
awareness. The idea of God provides an important example.
Descartes and Locke agree that men have an idea of God as
an infinite substance, a being possessed of infinite degrees of
admirable and desirable qualities such as knowledge and power.
Descartes, however, holds that this idea is innate, and that the
idea of the infinite is not formed from that of the finite but
is prior to it. [15] For Descartes, the idea of infinite power is
a simple idea, although obviously infinite power is neither a
quality that we have experienced in bodies in sensation nor
an attribute that we have experienced in our own minds in
self-awareness. This account of the idea of God is inconsistent
with Locke's empiricism about ideas. Locke is obliged to
analyze the idea of God as a complex idea, formed by com-
pounding our idea of infinity with our ideas of knowledge,
power, etc. [16]—and to analyze the idea of infinity as compound-

ed of the idea of repetition with that of the negation of stop-
ping.[17]   He makes quite explicit that his empiricism about
ideas imposes restrictions on him with respect to the kind of
idea of God he can allow that we have.

This further is to be observed, that there is no idea we attribute to God,
bating infinity, which is not also a part of our complex idea of other
spirits. Because, being capable of no other simple ideas, belonging to
anything but body, but those which by reflection we receive from the
operation of our own minds, we can attribute to spirits no other but
what we receive from thence: and all the difference we can put between
them, in our contemplation of spirits, is only in the several extents and
degrees of their knowledge, power, duration, happiness, etc. [18]

IV

I believe that it is this issue, about what sorts of thing our
ideas can represent, which has usually seemed to philosophers
to be the most important issue in the controversy between
empiricism and innatism about ideas. For it has commonly
been supposed that empiricism would lead to metaphysical
economy and innatism would facilitate metaphysical generosity.
Locke's empiricist doctrine might be found to constitute a
reason for denying that we have any ideas at all of some things
that some philosophers (and perhaps not only philosophers)
have believed in (or somehow thought they believed in). And
that in turn might be a reason for denying that we can talk
intelligibly about such things. But if one holds an innatist
doctrine about ideas, then one can consistently maintain that
one has ideas of things even if those ideas neither are, nor are
analyzable into, ideas of sensible properties of bodies or ideas
of mental operations which one has experienced in oneself.
    This view of the controversy between empiricism and
innatism about ideas, and of its relevance to metaphysical
inquiry, is quite clearly to be found in eighteenth-century
sources, such as the following passage of Hume.

We have establish'd it as a principle, that as all ideas are deriv'd from
impressions, or some precedent *perceptions*, 'tis impossible we can have
any idea of power and efficacy, unless some instances can be produc'd
wherein this power *is perceiv'd* to exert itself. Now as these instances
can never be discover'd in body, the *Cartesians*, proceeding upon their
principle of innate ideas, have had recourse to a supreme spirit or deity,

whom they consider as the only active being in the universe, and as the immediate cause of every alteration in matter. But the principle of innate ideas being allow'd to be false, it follows, that the supposition of a deity can serve us in no stead, in accounting for that idea of agency, which we search for in vain in all the objects, which are presented to our senses, or which we are internally conscious of in our own minds. For if every idea be deriv'd from an impression, the idea of a deity proceeds from the same origin; and if no impression, either of sensation or reflection, implies any force or efficacy, 'tis equally impossible to discover or even imagine any such active principle in the deity. ... All ideas are deriv'd from, and represent impressions. We never have any impression, that contains any power or efficacy. We never therefore have any idea of power. [19]

I do not mean to say that empiricism about ideas is the only (nor perhaps even the most important) foundation of classical empiricist claims that we cannot talk intelligibly about certain putative things. There is also the Berkeleyan principle (important also to Hume, and more important than Lockean empiricism about ideas to Berkeley) that an idea cannot resemble anything but an idea. It is clear, nonetheless, that empiricism about ideas has been an important basis of empiricist metaphysical economy (or stinginess, depending on your point of view).

In its Lockean form, however, it is a somewhat shaky basis, because of the nature of the argument on which Locke has to rely for the establishment of his empiricist principle about ideas. In some way Aristotelian empiricism about ideas may have been in a stronger position, by virtue of its explanatory force and its connections with a general theory of causation. To the question, "Why can't we have ideas which neither are nor are composed of ideas of things which we have experienced?" the Aristotelian empiricist could reply, "Because ideas are sensible and intelligible forms which we must get from things that have them, and we do that by experiencing things that have them." Whether or not this would prove in the last analysis to be a very powerful argument, it is unavailable to Locke. Having abandoned the Aristotelian theories of perception and causation, and refusing to speculate about the causal process of sensation, he has in effect stripped his empiricism about ideas of its explanatory force, and must find other arguments to support it.

Locke doubtless believed that he had provided support for

empiricism by refuting innatism. If we assume that our possession of ideas must be explained in terms of the natural powers
of the human mind (and not, say, occasionalistically, in terms
of the miraculous intervention of God), then it follows that a
doctrine of innate ideas (in a certain sense of "innate ideas")
is the only alternative to empiricism about ideas. This follows,
however, only because "innate idea" can be defined as meaning,
in effect, an idea that we have a natural ability to form in
ways other than those that are countenanced by Lockean empiricism about ideas. An innate idea, in this sense, is one that
satisfies the following three conditions. (1) It is an idea that
we have a natural ability to form. (2) The exercise of the
ability to form it does not depend on any particular sort of
sensory stimulation, nor is the idea formed from other ideas
whose occurrence does depend on some particular sort of
sensory stimulation. (3) The formation of the idea does not
depend on the occurrence in one's own mind of a mental
operation that is the object of the idea, nor is the idea formed
from other ideas whose occurrence does depend on the occurrence of their objects in one's own mind. This definition of
"innate idea" does not do violence to the history of the term.
The sense that it gives to "innate idea" is at least very similar
to the sense in which, as we have seen, Descartes commonly
spoke of some (but not all) of our ideas as innate—though I
would not claim it is exactly the same sense.

If Locke can prove that we have no ideas that are innate
in the sense that they satisfy the three conditions stated in
the previous paragraph, that would strongly support his empiricism about ideas. But in this form the doctrine of innate ideas
is not clearly envisaged, let alone refuted, by Locke. He may
have refuted some other form of innatism. Perhaps he has
succeeded, in Book One of the Essay, in showing the implausibility of the doctrine that there are some ideas of which all
men have been conscious since birth. That doctrine, however, is
obviously not the only alternative to Locke's empiricism about
ideas. We may have the power to form ideas in ways other
than those in which Locke thinks we can form them, even if
there are no ideas of which we have always been conscious.

Against the theory that we have ideas that are innate

only in the sense that we have a natural power to form them in ways other than those admitted by Lockean empiricism, I do not see that Locke has any argument except the claim that all our ideas can in fact be accounted for on his principles. And in defense of this latter claim he really has nothing to say except that he has not found that men have any ideas which his empiricism cannot account for. Locke himself seems to recognize that this is the state of his argument. "I must appeal to experience and observation whether I am in the right," he says, with reference to the justification of his empiricism about ideas. [20]

To deal truly, this is the only way that I can discover, whereby the *ideas of things* are brought into the understanding. If other men have either innate ideas or infused principles, they have reason to enjoy them; and if they are sure of it, it is impossible for others to deny them the privilege that they have above their neighbours. I can speak but of what I find in myself, and is agreeable to those notions, which, if we will examine the whole course of men in their several ages, countries, and educations, seem to depend on those foundations which I have laid, and to correspond with this method in all the parts and degrees thereof. [21]

We can see now why Locke's theory of the origin of our ideas provides only a shaky basis for empiricist metaphysical economy (or stinginess). If he is confronted with someone who claims to have an idea which (it is agreed) cannot be accounted for on Lockean principles, Locke is not in a position to reply, "You don't really have such an idea, because I've proved you can't." In order to defend his principles Locke must determine independently that no one has such an idea. If his only justification for the empiricist principle is that he has not found any idea that fails to satisfy it, then the principle stands in danger of being refuted by the first counterexample, and cannot be used to prove that people do not really have ideas they think they have.

Perhaps it is not quite fair to say that Locke's theory stands in danger of being refuted by the first counterexample. If Locke has made careful investigation, and has found hitherto no idea in human beings which cannot be accounted for on his empiricist principles, that may be taken as evidence of some weight for the claim that his principles express universal laws of nature according to which all human ideas are formed. And it is sometimes reasonable to reject the claim that a counter-example has been found, in preference to giving up a theory about the laws of nature for which one has good evidence.

But this observation still leaves Locke with a weak basis for argument. His empiricism lacks explanatory force, as we have noted. It does not follow from more general theories about the workings of nature, but presents itself as an inductive generalization. Such simple generalizations (if they include a claim of strict, exceptionless universality) are more liable than most other theories to be overthrown by counterexamples— and rightly so. There are, after all, many generalizations that hold true about the world for the most part, but have a few exceptions. If there should be even one idea that cannot be accounted for on Locke's empiricist principles, but which most men who have thought carefully about the matter believe they have formed, surely then the conclusion that would be warranted by the evidence would be that while most ideas that men have may be such as can be accounted for on Lockean principles, there is at least one exception.

If there are only a few metaphysicians who claim to have a certain nonempirical idea, it may be reasonable for the Lockean empiricist to refuse to accept their claim. But it will not be the weight of evidence for empiricism that justifies his skeptical attitude. It will rather be that he agrees with the innatist that all men (of roughly similar intelligence) have basically the same abilities with regard to the formation of ideas. If, then, he finds that he, and many others whom he consults, seem to be unable to form a certain idea, that is a reason for suspecting that those who claim to have it are making some mistake. But in this case each of us must examine himself (with as little prejudice as possible) concerning each putative nonempirical idea, to determine whether he has that idea or not. And we cannot appeal to Lockean empiricist principles to settle the issue. Epistemologically, those principles are not prior but posterior to the question whether I have such an idea. If there is a nonempirical idea that it seems to most of us, after careful reflection, that we have, then we can reject Lockean empiricism about ideas with some confidence. [22]

NOTES

1. See, e.g., in this anthology, the essays by Chomsky, Putnam, Katz, and Harman.

2. Thomas Aquinas, *Summa Theologiae,* I, qu. 87, a. 3.

3. Descartes, Meditation III: *The Philosophical Works of Descartes,* trans. by E. S. Haldane and G. R. T. Ross, I (Cambridge: Cambridge University Press, 1911), 163 (hereafter cited as HR I).

4. "Notes Directed Against a Certain Programme": HR I, 442. As appears in a subsequent passage which I shall quote next, Descartes is not denying that we have sensory ideas (ideas occasioned by sensation). He is denying that the form of any of our ideas is preserved and transmitted in the corporeal process of sensation.

5. Ibid., HR I, 442-443.

6. For instance, in Meditation III: HR I, 160.

7. *Essay,* II. i. 2 *(An Essay Concerning Human Understanding,* ed. A. C. Fraser, Vol. I [Oxford: Clarendon Press, 1894], Book II, chapter i, section 2).

8. Ibid., II. i. 23-24.

9. Ibid., II. i. 3, 5.

10. Ibid., II. i. 3.

11. Ibid., II. viii. 15.

12. Ibid.

13. Ibid., Introduction, section 2. The "spirits" mentioned here, of course, are not incorporeal, but are subtle fluids in the body which figured in earlier theories of perception.

14. Ibid., II. i. 2.

15. See Meditation III: HR I, 166, 170 f.

16. *Essay,* II. xxiii. 33-36.

17. Ibid., II. xvii.

18. Ibid., II. xxiii. 36. "Spirits" here obviously is meant to refer to minds.

19. David Hume, *A Treatise of Human Nature,* ed. L. A. Selby-Bigge (Oxford: Clarendon Press, 1888), pp. 160-161. Hume says that the question whether all ideas are derived from impressions "is the same with what has made so much noise in other terms, when it has been disputed whether there be any *innate ideas,* or whether all ideas be derived from sensation and reflection" (ibid., p. 7).

20. *Essay,* II. xi. 15.

21. Ibid., II. xi. 16.

22. I am indebted to Marilyn McCord Adams for helpful comments on an earlier version of this essay.

4

Cartesian Linguistics:
Acquisition and Use of Language

NOAM CHOMSKY

The central doctrine of Cartesian linguistics is that the general features of grammatical structure are common to all languages and reflect certain fundamental properties of the mind. It is this assumption which led the philosophical grammarians to concentrate on *grammaire generale* rather than *grammaire particulière* and which expresses itself in Humboldt's belief that deep analysis will show a common "form of language" underlying national and individual variety. There are, then, certain language universals that set limits to the variety of human language. The study of the universal conditions that prescribe the form of any human language is "grammaire generale." Such universal conditions are not learned; rather, they provide the organizing principles that make language learning possible, that must exist if data is to lead to knowledge. By attributing such principles to the mind, as an innate property, it becomes possible to account for the quite obvious fact the speaker of a language knows a great deal that he has not learned.

In approaching the question of language acquisition and linguistic universals in this way, Cartesian linguistics reflects the concern of seventeenth-century rationalistic psychology with the contribution of the mind to human knowledge. Perhaps the earliest exposition of what was to become a major theme, throughout most of this century, is Herbert of Cherbury's *De Veritate*

Excerpted with the kind permission of Professor Chomsky from his *Cartesian Linguistics* (New York and London: Harper and Row, 1966), pp. 59-72.

(1624),[1] in which he develops the view that there are certain "principles or notions implanted in the mind" that "we bring to objects from ourselves . . . [as] . . . a direct gift of Nature, a precept of natural instinct" (p. 133). Although these Common Notions "are stimulated by objects," nevertheless, "no one, however wild his views, imagines that they are conveyed by objects themselves" (p. 126). Rather, they are essential to the identification of objects and the understanding of their properties and relations. Although the "intellectual truths" comprised among the Common Notions "seem to vanish in the absence of objects, yet they cannot be wholly passive and idle seeing that they are essential to objects and objects to them . . . It is only with their aid that the intellect, whether in familiar or new types of things, can be led to decide whether our subjective faculties have accurate knowledge of the facts" (p. 105). By application of these intellectual truths, which are "imprinted on the soul by the dictates of Nature itself," we can compare and combine individual sensations and interpret experience in terms of objects, their properties, and the events in which they participate. Evidently, these interpretive principles cannot be learned from experience in their entirety, and they may be independent of experience altogether. According to Herbert:

[They] are so far from being drawn from experience or observation that, without several of them, or at least one of them, we could have no experience at all nor be capable of observations. For if it had not been written in our soul that we should examine into the nature of things (and we do not derive this command from objects), and if we had not been endowed with Common Notions, to that end, we should never come to distinguish between things, or to grasp any general nature. Vacant forms, prodigies, and fearful images would pass meaninglessly and even dangerously before our minds, unless there existed within us, in the shape of notions imprinted in the mind, that analogous faculty by which we distinguish good from evil. From where else could we have received knowledge? In consequence, anyone who considers to what extent objects in their external relationship contribute to their correct perception; who seeks to estimate what is contributed by us, or to discover what is due to alien or accidental sources, or again to innate influences, or to factors arising from nature, will be led to refer to these principles. We listen to the voice of nature not only in our choice between what is good and evil, beneficial and harmful, but also in that external correspondence by which we distinguish truth from falsehood, we possess hidden faculties which when stimulated by objects quickly respond to them (pp. 105-106).

It is only by the use of these "inborn capacities or Common Notions" that the intellect can determine "whether our subjective faculties have exercised their perceptions well or ill" (p.87). This "natural instinct" thus instructs us in the nature, manner, and scope of what is to be heard, hoped for, or desired" (p. 132).

Care must be taken in determining what are the Common Notions, the innate organizing principles and concepts that make experience possible. For Herbert, the "chief criterion of Natural Instinct" is "universal consent" (p. 139). But two qualifications are necessary. First, what is referred to is universal consent among "normal men" (p. 105). That is, we must put aside "persons who are out of their minds or mentally incapable" (p. 139) and those who are "headstrong, foolish, weak-minded and imprudent" (p. 125). And although these faculties "may not ever be entirely absent," and "even in madmen, drunkards, and infants extraordinary internal powers may be detected which minister to their safety" (p. 125), still we can expect to find universal consent to Common Notions only among the normal, rational, and clear-headed. Second, appropriate experience is necessary to elicit or activate these innate principles; "it is the law or destiny of Common Notions and indeed of the other forms of knowledge to be inactive unless objects stimulate them" (p. 120). In this respect, the common notions are like the faculties of seeing, hearing, loving, hoping, etc., with which we are born and which "remain latent when their corresponding objects are not present, and even disappear and give no sign of their existence" (p. 132). But this fact must not blind us to the realization that "the Common Notions must be deemed not so much the outcome of experience as principles without which we should have no experience at all" and to the absurdity of the theory that "our mind is a clean sheet, as though we obtained our capacity for dealing with objects from objects themselves" (p. 132).

The common notions are "all intimately connected" and can be arranged into a system (p. 120); and although "an infinite number of faculties may be awakened in response to an infinite number of new objects, all the Common Notions which embrace this order of facts may be comprehended in a few propositions" (p. 106). This system of common notions is not

to be identified with "reason." It simply forms "that part of
knowledge with which we were endowed in the primeval plan
of Nature," and it is important to bear in mind that "it is the
nature of natural instinct to fulfil itself irrationally, that is to
say, without foresight." On the other hand, "reason is the process of applying Common Notions as far as it can" (pp. 120-
121).

In focusing attention on the innate interpretive principles
that are a precondition for experience and knowledge and in
emphasizing that these are implicit and may require external
stimulation in order to become active or available to introspection, Herbert expressed much of the psychological theory
that underlies Cartesian linguistics, just as he emphasized those
aspects of cognition that were developed by Descartes and, later,
by the English Platonists, Leibniz and Kant.[2]

The psychology that develops in this way is a kind of
Platonism without preexistence. Leibniz makes this explicit
in many places. Thus he holds that "nothing can be taught us
of which we have not already in our minds the idea," and he
recalls Plato's "experiment" with the slave boy in the *Meno* as
proving that "the soul virtually knows those things [i.e., truths
of geometry, in this case], and needs only to be reminded (ani-
madverted) to recognize the truths. Consequently, it possesses
at least the idea upon which these truths depend. We may say
even that it already possesses those truths, if we consider them
as the relations of the ideas" (sec. 26)[3]

Of course, what is latent in the mind in this sense may
often require appropriate external stimulation before it becomes
active, and many of the innate principles that determine the
nature of thought and experience may well be applied quite
unconsciously. This Leibniz emphasizes, in particular, throughout his *Nouveaux Essais.*

That the principles of language and natural logic are known
unconsciously and that they are in large measure a precondition
for language acquisition rather than a matter of "institution" or
"training" is the general presupposition of Cartesian linguistics.[4]
When Cordemoy, for example, considers language acquisition
(*op. cit.*, pp. 40 ff.), he discusses the role of instruction and
conditioning of a sort, but he also notices that much of what

children know is acquired quite apart from any explicit instruction, and he concludes that language learning presupposes possession of "la raison toute entiere; car enfin cette maniere d'apprendre à parler, est l'effet d'un si grand discernement, et d'une raison si parfaite, qu'il n'est pas possible d'en concevoir un plus merveilleux"[a] (p. 59).

Rationalist conclusions reappear with some of the romantics as well. Thus A. W. Schlegel writes that "on puorrait comparer la raison humaine à une matière infiniment combustible, mais qui néanmoins ne s'embrase d'elle même. Il faut qu'une étincelle soit jetée dans l'âme"[b] ("De l'étymologie en général," p. 127). Communication with an already formed intellect is necessary for reason to awaken. But external stimulation is only required to set innate mechanisms to work; it does not determine the form of what is acquired. In fact, it is clear "dass dieses Erlernen [of language] durch Mitteilung schon die Fähigkeit, Sprache zu erfinden, voraussetzt"[c] (*Kunstlehre,* p. 234). In a certain sense, language is innate to man; namely, "im echteren philosophischen Sinne, wo alles, was nach der gewöhnlichen Ansicht dem Menschen angeboren scheint, erst durch seine eigene Tätigkeit hervorgebracht werden muss"[d] *(ibid.,* p. 235). While Schlegel's precise intentions, with many such remarks, might be debated, in Humboldt the Platonism with respect to language acquisition is quite clear. For Humboldt, "die Erlernung ist . . . immer nur Wiedererzeugung"[e] *(op. cit.,* p. 126). Despite superficial appearances, a language "lässt sich . . . nicht eigentlich lehren, sondern nur im Gemüthe wecken; man kann ihr nur den Faden hingeben, an dem sie sich von selbst entwickelt";[f] thus languages are, in a sense, "Selbstschöpfungen der Individuen"[g] (p. 50):

Das Sprechenlernen der Kinder ist nicht ein Zumessen von Wörtern, Niederlegen im Gedächtniss, und Wiedernachlallen mit den Lippen, sondern ein Wachsen des Sprachvermögens durch Alter und Übung (p. 21).

Dass bei den Kindern nicht ein mechanisches Lernen der Sprache, sondern eine Entwickelung der Sprachkraft vorgeht, beweist auch, dass, da den haupsächlichsten menschlichen Kräften ein gewisser Zeitpunkt im Lebensalter zu ihrer Entwicklung angewiesen ist, alle Kinder unter den verschiedenartigsten Umständen ungefähr in demselben, nur innerhalb eines kurzen Zeitraums schwankenden, Alter sprechen und verstehen (p. 72).[h]

In short, language acquisition is a matter of growth and
maturation of relatively fixed capacities, under appropriate
external conditions. The form of the language that is acquired
is largely determined by internal factors; it is because of the
fundamental correspondence of all human languages, because of
the fact that "der Mensch überall Eins mit dem Menschen ist,"[i]
that a child can learn any language (pp. 72-73). The functioning of the language capacity is, furthermore, optimal at a certain "critical period" of intellectual development.

It is important to emphasize that seventeenth-century
rationalism approaches the problem of learning—in particular,
language learning—in a fundamentally nondogmatic fashion. It
notes that knowledge arises on the basis of very scattered and
inadequate data and that there are uniformities in what is
learned that are in no way uniquely determined by the data
itself. Consequently, these properties are attributed to the
mind, as preconditions for experience. This is essentially
the line of reasoning that would be taken, today, by a scientist
interested in the structure of some device for which he has
only input-output data. In contrast, empiricist speculation, particularly in its modern versions, has characteristically adopted
certain a priori assumptions regarding the nature of learning
(that it must be based on association or reinforcement, or on
inductive procedures of an elementary sort—e.g., the taxonomic
procedures of modern linguistics, etc.) and has not considered
the necessity for checking these assumptions against the observed
uniformities of "output"—against what is known or believed
after "learning" has taken place. Hence the charge of a priorism
or dogmatism often leveled against rationalistic psychology and
philosophy of mind seems clearly to be misdirected.

The strong assumptions about innate mental structure
made by rationalistic psychology and philosophy of mind eliminated the necessity for any sharp distinction between a theory
of perception and a theory of learning. In both cases, essentially the same processes are at work; a store of latent principles
is brought to the interpretation of the data of sense. There is,
to be sure, a difference between the initial "activation" of
latent structure and the use of it once it has become readily
available for the interpretation (more accurately, the determin-

ation) of experience. The confused ideas that are always latent
in the mind may, in other words, become distinct and at this
point they can heighten and enhance perception. Thus, for
example, a

skilful and expert limner will observe many elegancies and curiosities of
art, and be highly pleased with several strokes and shadows in a picture,
where a common eye can discern nothing at all; and a musical artist hearing a consort of exact musicians playing some excellent composure of many
parts, will be exceedingly ravished with many harmonical airs and touches,
that a vulgar ear will be utterly insensible of (Cudworth, p. 446).

It is the "acquired skill" that makes the difference; "the artists
of either kind have many inward anticipations of skill and art
in their minds" that enable them to interpret the data of sense
in a way that goes beyond the "mere noise and sound and clatt-
ter" provided by passive sense, just as the informed mind can
interpret the "vital machine of the universe" in terms of "inter-
ior symmetry and harmony in the relations, proportions, apti-
tudes and correspondence of things to one another in the great
mundane system" (*ibid.*). Similarly, in looking at and "judging
of" a picture of a friend, one makes use of a "foreign and adventitious" but preexistent idea (pp. 456-457). Once this distinction between learning and perception has been noted, however, the essential parallel between the cognitive processes that
are involved outweighs the relatively superficial differences,
from the point of view of this rationalist doctrine. For this
reason, it is often unclear whether what is being discussed is
the activity of the mind in perception or in acquisition—that is,
in selecting an already distinct idea on the occasion of sense, or
in making distinct what was before only confused and implicit.

Descartes's theory of cognition is clearly summarized in
his *Notes Directed against a Certain Program* (1647; Haldane and
Ross, pp. 442-443):

. . . any man who rightly observes the limitations of the senses, and what
precisely it is that can penetrate through this medium to our faculty of
thinking must needs admit that no ideas of things, in the shape in which
we envisage them by thought, are presented to us by the senses. So much
so that in our ideas there is nothing which was not innate in the mind, or
faculty of thinking, except only these circumstances which point to experience—the fact, for instance, that we judge that this or that idea, which we
now have present to our thought, is to be referred to a certain extraneous
thing, not that these extraneous things transmitted the ideas themselves to

our minds through the organs of sense, but because they transmitted
something which gave the mind occasion to form these ideas, by means
of an innate faculty, at this time rather than at another. For nothing
reaches our mind from external objects through the organs of sense beyond certain corporeal movements . . . but even these movements, and
the figures which arise from them, are not conceived by us in the shape
they assume in the organs of sense . . . Hence it follows that the ideas of
the movements and figures are themselves innate in us. So much the more
must the ideas of pain, color, sound, and the like be innate, that our
mind may, on occasion of certain corporeal movements, envisage these
ideas, for they have no likeness to the corporeal movements. Could anything be imagined more preposterous than that all common notions which
are inherent in our mind should arise from these movements, and should
be incapable of existing without them? I should like our friend to in-
struct me as to what corporeal movement it is which can form in our
mind any common notion, e.g., the notion that *things which are equal to
the same thing are equal to one another,* or any other he pleases; for
all these movements are particular, but notions are universal having no
affinity with the movements and no relation to them.

Rather similar ideas are developed at length by Cudworth.[5]
He distinguished the essentially passive faculty of sense from
the active and innate "cognoscitive powers" whereby men (and
men alone) "are enabled to understand or judge of what is
received from without by sense." This cognoscitive power is
not a mere storehouse of ideas, but "a power of raising intelligible ideas and conceptions of things from within itself"
(p. 425). The function of sense is "the offering or presenting
of some object to the mind, to give it an occasion to exercise
its own activity upon." Thus, for example, when we look into
the street and perceive men walking, we are relying, not merely
on sense (which shows us at most surfaces—i.e., hats and clothes
—and, in fact, not even objects), but on the exercise of the
understanding, applied to the data of sense (pp. 409-410). The
"intelligible forms by which things are understood or known,
are not stamps or impressions passively printed upon the soul
from without, but ideas vitally protended or actively exerted
from within itself." Thus prior knowledge and set play a large
role in determining what we see (e.g., a familiar face in a crowd)
(pp. 423-424). It is because we use intellectual ideas in perception "that those knowledges which are more abstract and
remote from matter, are more accurate, intelligible and demon-
strable,—than those which are conversant about concrete and
material things," as Aristotle has observed (p. 427).[6] This claim

is illustrated by a discussion of our conceptions of geometrical figures (pp. 455 f.). Obviously every sensed triangle is irregular, and if there were a physically perfect one, we could not detect this by sense; "and every irregular and imperfect triangle [is] as perfectly that which it is, as the most perfect triangle." Our judgments regarding external objects in terms of regular figures, our very notion of "regular figure" therefore have their source in the "rule, pattern and exemplar" which are generated by the mind as an "anticipation." The concept of a triangle or of a "regular proportionate and symmetrical figure" is not taught but "springs originally from nature itself," as does, in general, the human concept of "pulchritude and deformity in material objects"; nor can the a priori truths of geometry be derived from sense. And it is only by means of these "inward ideas" produced by its "innate cognoscitive power" that the mind is able to "know and understand all external individual things" (p. 482).

Descartes had discussed the same question in very similar terms, in his *Reply to Objections V:*

> Hence when first in infancy we see a triangular figure depicted on paper, this figure cannot show us how a real triangle ought to be conceived, in the way in which geometricians consider it, because the true triangle is contained in this figure, just as the statue of Mercury is contained in a rough block of wood. But because we already possess within us the idea of a true triangle, and it can be more easily conceived by our mind than the more complex figure of the triangle drawn on paper, we, therefore, when we see that composite figure, apprehend not it itself, but rather the authentic traingle (Haldane and Ross, *op. cit.*, II, 227-228.).

For Cudworth, the interpretation of sensory data in terms of objects and their relations, in terms of cause and effect, the relations of whole and part, symmetry, proportion, the functions served by objects and the characteristic uses to which they are put (in the case of all "things artificial" or "compounded natural things"), moral judgments, etc., is the result of the organizing activity of the mind (pp. 433 f.). The same is true of the unity of objects (or, for example, of a melody); sense is like a "narrow telescope" that provides only piecemeal and successive views, but only the mind can give "one comprehensive idea of the whole" with all its parts, relations, proportions, and

Gestalt qualities. It is in this sense that we speak of the intelligible idea of an object as not "stamped or impressed upon the
soul from without, but upon occasion of the sensible idea ex-
cited and exerted from the inward active and comprehensive
power of the intellect itself" (p. 439).[7]

Ideas of this sort regarding perception were common in
the seventeenth century but were then swept aside by the
empiricist current, to be revived again by Kant and the romantics. Consider, for example, Coleridge's remarks on active processes in perception:

> Instances in which a knowledge given to the mind quickens and
> invigorates the faculties by which such knowledge is attainable indepen-
> dently cannot have escaped the most ordinary observer, and this is equally
> true whether it be faculties of the mind or of the senses. . . . It is indeed
> wonderful both how small a likeness will suffice a full apprehension of
> sound or sight when the correspondent sound or object is foreknown and
> foreimagined and how small a deviation or imperfection will render the
> whole confused and indistinguishable or mistaken where no such previous
> intimation has been received. Hence all unknown languages appear to a
> foreigner to be spoken by the natives with extreme rapidity and to those
> who are but beginning to understand it with a distressing indistinction.[8]

> Does nature present objects to us without exciting any act on our
> part, does she present them under all circumstances perfect and as it were
> ready made? Such may be the notion of the most unthinking . . . not
> only must we have some scheme or general outline of the object to which
> we could determine to direct our attention, were it only to have the power
> of recognizing it.[9]

It is, once again, with Humboldt that these ideas are
applied most clearly to the perception and interpretation of
speech. He argues (*Verschiedenheit,* pp. 70-71) that there is a
fundamental difference between the perception of speech and
the perception of unarticulated sound. For the latter, "das
thierische Empfindungsvermögen"[j] would suffice. But human
speech perception is not merely a matter of "das blosse gegen-
seitige Hervorrufen des Lauts und des angedeuteten Gegenstandes."[k] For one thing, a word is not "ein Abdruck des
Gegenstandes an sich, sondern des von diesem in der Seele
erzeugten Bildes"[l] (p. 74). But, furthermore, speech perception
requires an analysis of the incoming signal in terms of the underlying elements that function in the essentially creative act of
speech production, and therefore it requires the activation of

the generative system that plays a role in production of speech as well, since it is only in terms of these fixed rules that the elements and their relations are defined. The underlying "Gesetze der Erzeugung"[m] must, therefore, function in speech perception. If it were not for its mastery of these, if it were not for its ability "jene Möglichkeit zur Wirklichkeit zu bringen,"[n] the mind would no more be able to deal with the mechanisms of articulated speech than a blind man is able to perceive colors. It follows, then, that both the perceptual mechanisms and the mechanisms of speech production must make use of the underlying system of generative rules. It is because of the virtual identity of this underlying system in speaker and hearer that communication can take place, the sharing of an underlying generative system being traceable, ultimately, to the uniformity of human nature.

In brief,

Es kann in der Seele nichts, als durch eigne Thätigkeit, vorhanden sein, und Verstehen und Sprechen sind nur verschiedenartige Wirkungen der nämlichen Sprachkraft. Die gemeinsame Rede ist nie mit dem Übergeben eines Stoffes vergleichbar. In dem Verstehenden, wie im Sprechenden, muss derselbe aus der eigenen, inneren Kraft entwickelt werden: und was der erstere empfängt, ist nur die harmonisch stimmende Anregung. . . . Auf diese Weise liegt die Sprache in jedem Menschen in ihrem ganzen Umfange, was aber nichts Anderes bedeutet, als dass jeder ein, durch eine bestimmt modificirte Kraft, anstossend und beschränkend, geregeltes Streben besitzt, die ganze Sprache, wie es äussere oder innere Veranlassung herbeiführt, nach und nach aus sich hervorzubringen und hervorgebracht zu verstehen.

Das Verstehen könnte jedoch nicht, so wie wir es eben gefunden haben, auf innerer Selbstthätigkeit beruhen, und das gemeinschaftliche Sprechen müsste etwas Andres, als bloss gegenseitiges Wecken des Sprachvermögens des Hörenden, sein, wenn nicht in der Verschiedenheit der Einzelnen die, sich nur in abgesonderte Individualitäten spaltende, Einheit der menschlichen Natur läge.[o]

Even in the case of perception of a single word, an underlying system of generative rules must be activated. It would be inaccurate, Humboldt maintains, to suppose that speaker and hearer share a store of clear and totally formed concepts. Rather the perceived sound incites the mind to generate a corresponding concept by its own means:

Die Menschen verstehen einander nicht dadurch, dass sie sich Zeichen der Dinge wirklich hingeben, auch nicht dadurch, dass sie sich gegenseitig bestimmen, genau und vollständig denselben Begriff hervorzubringen, sondern dadurch, dass sie gegenseitig in einander dasselbe Glied der Kette ihrer sinnlichen Vorstellungen und inneren Begriffserzeugungen berühren, dieselbe Taste ihres geistigen Instruments anschlagen, worauf alsdann in jedem entsprechende, nicht aber dieselben Begriffe hervorspringen (p. 213).[P]

In short, speech perception requires internal generation of a representation both of the signal and the associated semantic content.

Contemporary research in perception has returned to the investigation of the role of internally represented schemata or models[10] and has begun to elaborate the somewhat deeper insight that it is not merely a store of schemata that function in perception but rather a system of fixed rules for generating such schemata. In this respect too, it would be quite accurate to describe current work as a continuation of the tradition of Cartesian linguistics and the psychology that underlies it.

NOTES

1. Translated by M. H. Carre (1937), University of Bristol Studies, 6.

2. These developments are familiar except, perhaps, for seventeenth-century English Platonism. See A. O. Lovejoy, "Kant and the English Platonists," in *Essays Philosophical and Psychological in Honor of William James* (New York: Longmans, Green, 1908), for some discussion of English Platonism, in particular, of its interest in the "ideas and categories which enter into every presentation of objects and make possible the unity and inter-connectedness of rational experience." Lovejoy's account, in turn, is based heavily on G. Lyons, *L'idealisme en Angleterre au XVIIIe siècle* (Paris, 1888). See also J. Passmore, *Ralph Cudworth* (Cambridge: Cambridge University Press, 1951); L. Gysi, *Platonism and Cartesianism in the Philosophy of Ralph Cudworth* (Bern: Verlag Herbert Lang, 1962). Some relevant quotes from Descartes, Leibniz, and others are given in Noam Chomsky, *Aspects of the Theory of Snytax* (Cambridge, Mass.: MIT Press, 1965), chap. 1, sec. 8, where the relevance of this position to current issues is also briefly discussed.

See also Chomsky, *"Explanatory Models in Linguistics,"* in E. Nagel et al., eds., *Logic, Methodology and the Philosophy of Science* (Stanford, Calif.: Stanford University Press, 1962), and Jerrold J. Katz, *Philosophy of Language* (New York: Harper and Row, 1965), for discussion of an essentially rationalist approach to the problem of language acquisition and of the inadequacy of empiricist alternatives. In the same connection, see E. H. Lenneberg, "A Biological Perspective of Language," in E. H. Lenneberg, ed., *New Directions in the study of Language* (Cambridge, Mass.: M.I.T. Press, 1964), and *The Biological Bases for Language* (New York:

John Wiley, 1967); and sec.VI of J. Fodor and J. Katz, eds., *The Structure of Language: Readings in the Philosophy of Language* (Englewood Cliffs, N.J.: Prentice-Hall, 1964).

3. Leibniz, *Discourse on Metaphysics.* The quotations here are from the English translation by G. R. Montgomery (LaSalle, Ill. Open Court, 1902). With reference to Plato's theory, Leibniz insists only that it be "purged of the error of preexistence." Similarly, Cudworth accepts the theory of reminiscence without the doctrine of preexistence that Plato suggests as an explanation for the facts he describes: "And this is the only true and allowable sense of that old assertion, that knowledge is reminiscence; not that it is the rememberance of something which the soul had some time before actually known in a pre-existent state, but because it is the mind's comprehending of things by some inward anticipations of its own, something native and domestic to it, or something actively exerted from within itself" *(Treatise concerning Eternal and Immutable Morality,* p. 424; page references, here and below, are to the first American edition of works of Cudworth, vol. II, T. Birch, ed., 1838).

4. The typical Cartesian view would apparently have been that, although these principles may function unconsciously, they can be brought to consciousness by introspection.

5. On the relation between Cudworth and Descartes, see Passmore, *op. cit.;* Gysi, *op. cit.;* and for more general background, S. P. Lamprecht, "The Role of Descartes in Seventeenth-century England," *Studies in the History of Ideas,* vol. III, edited by the Department of Philosophy of Columbia University (New York: Columbia University Press, 1935), pp. 181-242. Passmore concludes (*op. cit.,* p. 8) that, despite some divergence, "it is still not misleading to call Cudworth a Cartesian, so great was their agreement on so many vital issues."

6. However, "the cogitations that we have of corporeal things [are] usually both noematical and phantasmatical together." This accounts for the fact that geometricians will rely on diagrams and that "in speech, metaphors and allegories do so exceedingly please" (pp. 430, 468).

7. In a similar way, Cudworth arrives at the typical rationalist conclusion that our knowledge is organized as a kind of "deductive system" by which we arrive at "a descending comprehension of a thing from the universal ideas of the mind, and not an ascending perception of them from individuals by sense" (p. 467).

8. Quoted in A. D. Snyder, *Coleridge on Logic and Learning* (New Haven: Yale University Press, 1929), pp. 133-134.

9. Quoted *ibid.,* p. 116.

10. See, for example, D. M. MacKay, "Mindlike Behavior in Artefacts," *British Journal for Philosophy of Science,* 2 (1951), 105-121. J. S. Bruner, "On Perceptual Readiness," *Psychological Review,* 64 (1957), 123-152, "Neural Mechanisms in Perception," *Psychological Review,* 64 (1957), 340-358. For a review of many of the findings relating to central processes in perception, see H. L. Teuber, "Perception," in the *Handbook of Physiology—Neurophysiology* III, ed. J. Field, H. S. Magoun, V. E. Hall, (Washington, D.C.: American Physiological Society, 1960), chap. LXV.

TRANSLATION NOTES

[a] "reason in its entirety, because, in the end, this manner of learning to speak is the result of a discrimination so great, and of a reason so perfect that it is impossible to conceive of one more marvelous."

[b] "one could compare human reason to an infinitely combustible material, which does not, however, ignite by itself. A spark must be thrown into the soul"

[c] "that this learning [of language] through communication already presupposes the ability to invent languages"

[d] "in the truer philosophical sense, where everything which appears to be innate according to the usual view of man must in fact be produced through his own activity."

[e] "learning is . . . never anything but regeneration."

[f] "cannot be actually . . . taught; rather it must be awakened in the mind. One can only provide the initial impetus which will provoke it into further development"

[g] "spontaneous creations of individuals"

[h] "A child's acquisition of speech is not a meting out of words, a storing up in his memory and parroting back with the lips. No, the acquisition of speech is the growth of the total language capacity through age and practice.

That children learn to speak by unfolding their linguistic capacity, and not by the mechanical memorization of constantly repeated phrases is further demonstrated by the fact that, since each of the primary human skills is acquired during a specified period in a child's development, all children learn to speak and understand at approximately the same stage of their development, in spite of the most diverse of circumstances.

[i] "man is everywhere one with mankind,"

[j] "an animal's perceptive faculty"

[k] "the mere connecting of a sound with an indicated object."

[l] "a representation of the object itself; it is a representation of the picture which the object creates on the soul"

[m] "generative laws"

[n] "to turn a potentiality into a reality."

[o] Nothing can be in the soul except what is there through the soul's own activity; and understanding and speaking are only different aspects of the same language ability. A conversation cannot ever be regarded as a simple exchange of subject matter. Both the listener and the speaker must generate the content out of their own inner power; what the former receives is but a harmonically sounding impulse. Thus language resides in its totality in each human being; but this means nothing else than that each person possesses a natural drive, modified by a certain both prodding and limiting power, to gradually evoke and have evoked out of himself the totality of speech, be it through external or internal stimulation.

However, as we have just seen, comprehension could not derive from spontaneous inner activity. Communal speech would have to be something other than a simple mutual arousing of the speech capacity of the listener, if it were not the case that the unity of all human nature resided in the diversity of individuals, a unity which was merely split among separate persons.

P Humans understand each other not because they really offer to each other signs standing for things, or because they cause each other to produce the exactly and completely identical concepts, but because they touch in each other the same link in the chain of their sense perceptions and inner conceptual representations, because they touch the same key of their mental instruments, whereupon corresponding, but not identical, concepts are produced in each person.

PART III

5

Innate Ideas
and A Priori Knowledge

W. D. HART

Suppose we knew that we have some innate ideas. Would that solve the problem of a priori knowledge? Not on your tintype.

Let us first mention one approach only to dismiss it. Consider the positivist style scheme of explanation on which a person A can know a priori that p because the (or every) statement that p is analytic. Suppose, for the sake of implausibility, that the idea of a bachelor is innate and recall the late, lamented doctrine that a man could not (or could not be said to) have the idea of a bachelor unless he knew that all bachelors are unmarried. Putting all this together, what do we get? At least this: it may seem puzzling how we can explain a priori knowledge by appealing to at least quasi-linguistic knowledge should it be thought to require experience of some sort to acquire such ideas as that of a bachelor; if that idea were innate, this puzzle would be solved. But this is a solution only to a pseudo-problem. For the real problem was how one could know that all bachelors are unmarried without experience *of bachelors;* and that problem is "solved" (if at all) by analyticity and our late, lamented doctrine, not by the innateness of the idea of a bachelor. Here, innateness does no work, and the problem of a priori knowledge is at best only fouled by analyticity.

We would perhaps do well to begin again by asking just what the problem of a priori knowledge is. Here, a number of traditional analyses of traditional notions are relevant because we are interested in connections *between* two traditional notions, those of innate ideas and a priori knowledge.

On the traditional analysis of the form "A knows that p", it is required that:

(a) A believes that p;
(b) It is true that p;
(c) A is justified in believing that p.

Most difficulties center around (c). The epistemological task is often to describe for some substituent or substituents for "p", just *how* A is justified in believing that p. (Of course, objections like the Gettier Problem have been raised against [c]. But these do not seem to require eliminating it so much as strengthening it, which would not reduce the pressure of the epistemological tasks.)

For the traditional category of empirical knowledge, it was said that A knows *a posteriori* that p if A can only be justified by experience in believing that p. Even recalling the ancient and honorable problems about specifying experience (e.g., sense data versus intersubjective, repeatable experiment and observation) and about explaining how experience justifies some empirical beliefs but not others (the problem of induction), still this traditional account of a posteriori knowledge does seem to yield at least a partial, schematic solution to the epistemological task of explaining how a person's empirical knowledge is justified.

But what is a priori knowledge? If, as seems traditional, we define a priori knowledge as knowledge which is not a posteriori (and if we assume that there is a priori knowledge), then A knows a priori that p if A knows that p but A's belief that p can be (and in the interesting case is) justified otherwise than by experience. The problem of a priori knowledge is then to explain *how,* otherwise than by experience, A's belief *is* justified.

Can we explain it by appeal to innate ideas? Abstracting in a Cartesian vein from distinctions between such mental phenomena as ideas and beliefs, suppose that we tried to explain how A's a priori knowledge that p is justified by stating that A's belief that p is innate. The trouble is that (without Descartes' God) innateness does not guarantee or even make

probable truth; why could not A have been born believing that
2 + 2 = 69? But if the innateness of a belief in no way af-
fects the chances that it is true, then it is foolish to try to
explain how A's a priori knowledge that p is justified by saying
that his belief that p is innate; for to explain how something
is justified ought at the very least to involve an attempt to
argue for its truth. To put the point another way, talk of
innateness is appropriate in a context of discovery (of perhaps
a peculiar sort), but *not* in a context of justification; yet the
problem of a priori knowledge is posed wholly within contexts
of justification. (As some seem recently to have suggested,
these twain contexts may sometimes meet, but there is as yet
no reason to suppose that they meet on the shaky ground of
innate ideas.)

   Lastly, suppose it were suggested in a final fit of madness
that a man has innate justifications for his a priori knowledge.
(It seems somehow odder to suppose innateness for justifications than for ideas or even beliefs.) The trouble with this
suggestion is that nothing is a justification just *because* it is
innate. That is, we have still not explained *what* justifies a
priori knowledge in even the sketchy way we said that experience justifies a posteriori knowledge. We have not yet infor-
matively specified a genuine variety of justification peculiar
to a priori knowledge as experience is peculiar to a posteriori
knowledge; why should we not go on just as well to suppose
innate justifications for empirical knowledge?

   In short, for the problem of a priori knowlege, innate
ideas are an inane solution.

6

Innate Knowledge

ALVIN I. GOLDMAN

If there were true innate beliefs, would there also be innate *knowledge?* Much of the controversy over innate ideas, both historical and contemporary, has focused on two questions: (1) whether allegedly innate cognitive elements are supposed to be actual concepts or beliefs, or merely latent capacities to acquire concepts or beliefs under appropriate stimulus conditions; and (2) whether such cognitive elements, occurrent or dispositional, really are innate. But let us set these traditional problems aside. Assume, for the sake of argument, that an organism is born with certain beliefs, and that these beliefs are true. A further epistemological problem then arises: Do these true beliefs constitute *knowledge?* This question has been raised recently by W. D. Hart, Thomas Nagel, and R. Edgely. [1] The existence of innate cognitive elements, even true ones, it is pointed out, does not ensure the existence of innate knowledge. Whether or not innate beliefs may be counted as knowledge depends on what knowledge is; in particular, it depends on what further conditions must be satisfied by an item of true belief in order for it to be an item of knowledge.

According to the traditional analysis of knowing, S knows that p if and only if (i) S believes that p, (ii) p is true, and (iii) S is justified in believing that p. Edmund Gettier has shown that (i), (ii), and (iii) are not jointly sufficient for "S knows that p," and most writers now maintain that condition (iii) must be strengthened. On the other hand, most epistemologists continue to maintain that (iii) is at least a *necessary* condition of knowledge, and if so, then it may be argued that the mere possession of innate true belief gives one no title to knowledge. For how does innateness provide a *justification* for one's belief?

This argument, however, depends on the assumption that justification is at least a necessary condition of knowing, and I find this assumption dubious. I do not deny, of course, that *many* of the propositions one knows satisfy the justification condition. But I think that there are *some* propositions one knows which one cannot be said to be justified in believing. If this is correct, then the fact that innateness does not confer justification does not preclude the possibility of innate knowledge.

Rejection of the justification condition, however, is only part of the job of vindicating innate knowledge. It must certainly be acknowledged that true belief per se is not knowledge. If innate true beliefs are to be items of knowledge, there must be some further condition or conditions that they satisfy. But what would such further conditions be? If we reject justification as an additional requirement for knowledge, what should be substituted in its place? And if we can find such a substitute, can it be shown that innate true beliefs can satisfy this substitute condition?

In a previous paper, entitled "A Causal Theory of Knowing,"[2] I argued that a necessary and sufficient condition of "S knows that p," at least where p is a contingent proposition, is that there be an appropriate *causal* connection between the fact that p and S's belief that p. Without reviewing the causal theory in detail, we can quickly see the plausibility of a causal requirement by examining three cases.

1. Suppose that holography has been so perfected that when a hologram of a vase is placed at a distance of, say, ten feet from a person, it looks to him exactly as if there were a vase, say, fifteen feet in front of him. Now suppose that there actually is a vase fifteen feet in front of S, but that S's view of the vase is blocked by a holographic photograph of another vase. Since the hologram makes it *appear* as if there is a vase in front of him, however, S forms the belief that there is one in front of him, S is clearly justified in believing that there is

a vase in front of him—at any rate, he is *as* justified in believing this as he is on many other occasions when we would credit him with knowledge. Moreover, his belief is true. In this case, however, we would not be willing to say that S *knows* that there is a vase in front of him. The reason for this concerns the causal process by which S's belief is formed. There simply is no causal connection here between the fact that there is a vase in front of him and S's belief that there is a vase in front of him. Certainly there is no *appropriate* causal connection between this fact and S's belief.

2. S witnesses the occurrence of x at time t_1, but at time t_2 S has an accident that obliterates his memory of this occurrence. At time t_3 S's friend Brown, who is unaware that S witnessed x or even that x actually occurred, hypnotizes S into seeming to remember, and into believing, that he witnessed the occurrence of x. At time t_3 S does not *know* that x occurred. But the reason why he cannot be said to know this fact has nothing to do with his justification for believing it. In the case imagined S has the same memory-impressions, and the same evidence, as he would if he had genuinely remembered the occurrence of x. (Assume that X has no evidence about his accident or about his hypnosis.) So if in the case of genuine memory S would be justified in believing that x occurred, then he is also justified in the present case. The correct explanation of why S does not *know* that x occurred has nothing to do with his justification, but rather with the causal process that results in his believing, at t_3, that x occurred. The reason why S cannot be credited with *knowledge* is that there is no appropriate causal connection linking the fact that x occurred with S's belief of this fact. In a genuine case of memory there is an appropriate causal connection, but in the example described here such a causal connection is lacking.[3]

3. S perceives that there is solidified lava in various parts of the countryside. On the basis of this belief S concludes that a nearby mountain erupted many centuries ago. Suppose, however, that although the mountain did erupt centuries ago, the lava that S sees was not spewed forth, as S assumes it was, by that mountain. Rather, what happened was this. A century after the eruption a man came along and removed all the lava.

Another century later another man, not knowing that there
had ever been any lava in the vicinity, decided to make it look
as if there had been a volcano, and therefore put lava in the
appropriate places. In this case, S does not *know* that the
mountain erupted. He may have good evidence for this, but
he does not *know* it. And the reason for his lack of knowledge
clearly has something to do with the nature of the causal
process that resulted in his belief. In this case, indeed, there is
no causal connection at all between the fact that the mountain
erupted and his belief that the mountain erupted.

The above three cases are intended to provide an intuitive
rationale—though, of course, not a complete defense—for a
causal account of knowing. But these cases do not disprove the
contention that justification is a necessary condition of knowing. Against this contention I wish to adduce two different
cases (many similar ones could be added).[4]

1. A professional chicken-sexer looks at a chick and forms
the true belief that it is male. The chicken-sexer is unaware
of the process by which he tells the sex of the chick, but, as
always, he is correct in his judgment. Although the chicken-
sexer is ignorant of *how* he tells the sex of the chick, most of
us would say that he *knows* it is male.

2. Jones has a rheumatic condition that is affected by
atmospheric pressure, so that whenever rain is in the offing he
suffers pains in his joints. Jones does not *notice* the correlation between his aches and the onset of rain, but whenever it
is going to rain (and only then) his joints start to ache, and
whenever his joints start to ache this produces in Jones the
belief that it is going to rain. Here too we would say, I think,
that Jones *knows* that it is going to rain on each of these
occasions.[5]

In both of these cases a person *knows* a certain proposition without being *justified* in believing it. Under the usual
interpretation, S is "justified" in believing a proposition p only
if either (a) p is self-warranting or self-justifying for S, or (b)
there are some other propositions S knows which are good
reasons or good grounds for believing that p. In neither of
these cases is p a self-warranting or self-justifying proposition.
But, equally, in neither of these cases are there any propositions

known by S which constitute good reasons or good grounds for believing that p. In particular, there are no propositions S could cite which would justify his belief that p. If asked to justify the belief that it is going to rain, the rheumatic could only say that he "feels" or "intuits" that it is going to rain. These responses would hardly constitute an adequate justification for the belief in question. A man who has no training whatever in chickensexing, for example, might also genuinely say that a chick "looks" like a male to him. But this would not incline us to say that he is *justified* in believing that it is a male. A similar point can be made in the rain-predicting case.

Perhaps we have not done justice to the nature of the justification of the chicken-sexer and of the rain-predictor. It might be argued that each man's justification does not depend simply on the proposition that he has an "intuition" about the proposition he believes, but on this proposition *conjoined* with the proposition that his intuitions on these matters have generally been right in the past. For example, the chicken-sexer's justification is not merely that the chick "looks" like a male to him. His justification consists in the conjunction of this proposition with the proposition (which he knows) that, generally, when a chick "looks" like a male to him it turns out actually to *be* a male.

But this defense is inadequate. Suppose that we falsely persuade the chicken-sexer that his chicken-sexing performance in the recent past has been very bad, that his intuitions have been turning out wrong of late. If he is persuaded by this story, the chicken-sexer is no longer justified in relying on his intuition. He can no longer appeal to the premise that his intuition is generally a reliable guide, for he himself no longer believes (or knows) this premise. Nevertheless, if the chicken-sexer actually does make correct judgments about each chick, and in fact shows no loss in his ability to form correct beliefs simply by looking at the chick, then we would be forced to admit to ourselves that he really does know the sex of the chicks. Despite the fact that he (no longer) has *justification* for these judgments, he must be credited with *knowledge*. An analogous argument can be developed for the rain-predictor case.

Why, then, are we inclined to credit knowledge to the
chicken-sexer and the rain-predictor? The answer, I suggest, is
given by the causal theory of knowing. In each of these cases
there is a certain kind of causal connection between the fact that
p and S's belief that p. In each case there is a certain kind of
causal process that produces in S a true belief. In the chicken-
sexing case the fact that the chick is male causes S to believe
that it is male. And in the rain-predicting case the fact that it
will rain and S's belief that it will rain are causally connected
in virtue of sharing a *common* cause, viz., the drop in atmospheric pressure.[6] To be sure, the causal theory of knowing
does not say that *any* causal connection between the fact that
p and S's belief that p yields knowledge; the theory requires
that the causal connection be an "appropriate" one. But in
order for a particular causal connection to be appropriate, it is
sufficient, I think, that it be an instance of a kind of process
which *generally* leads to true beliefs of the sort in question.
Now in our two cases this requirement is satisfied. In the case
of the chicken-sexer there is a certain kind of causal process
that always results in his having a true belief about the sex of
the chick examined. And in the case of the rheumatic, there
is a kind of causal process that always leads to true beliefs
about the onset of rain. In other words, both the chicken-sexer
and the rain-predictor *have reliable techniques* for forming beliefs about their respective subject matters, even though neither
has any idea what his technique *is,* and even though neither may
know that his technique is perfectly reliable.

It might be argued that whenever a person has a reliable
"technique" for telling when it will rain, or for telling the sex
of a chick, etc., then he is "justified" in holding beliefs that are
formed by the use of this technique. Of course, it is open to
us to interpret the phrase "S is justified in believing that p" in
this way. But two comments would be in order. First, it
should be noted that this is not the usual epistemological interpretation of the phrase. Secondly, under this interpretation the
justification requirement may well turn out to be virtually equivalent to the causal requirement I have been defending. And
if this is so, then it is not clear that the justification requirement stands in the way of the possibility of innate knowledge.

It is time to turn to the problem of innate knowledge. Granting the correctness of the causal theory of knowing, how could it be argued that an innate belief can be an item of knowledge? In order for an innate belief to qualify as an item of knowledge, it must be causally related in an appropriate way to the fact to which it corresponds. But what might such a causal connection be like? What sort of causal process might this be? The answer, I suggest, is *evolutionary adaptation.* Suppose there is a general fact p about the environment of a certain animal species, or about the relationship between members of the species and their environment. This fact p, let us suppose, has great survival value for the members of the species. In particular, recognition or apprehension of this fact by a member of the species is a crucial factor in ensuring its survival. Under these conditions, it would not be surprising if, by a process of natural selection, the members of this species eventually come to be born with the belief that p. If this does occur, then there is a causal connection between the fact that p and the belief that p which is innately present in each individual of this species. Moreover, it seems reasonable to say that the causal connection is an "appropriate" one, for the process of natural selection is presumably a kind of process that will generally produce *true* beliefs, if it produces beliefs at all. According to our causal theory of knowing, therefore, we could say of each member of this species not merely that it innately *believes* that p, but that it innately *knows* that p.

A detailed example would be helpful at this juncture. Let us take an example not from the species *Homo sapiens* but from another animal species. A problem with any such example is that it is usually difficult to decide when members of such species are to be credited with *beliefs.* But let us be generous on this point. Consider Eckhard H. Hess's description of the common tick, in the context of his discussion of innate behavioral mechanisms.[7]

Instinctive behavior, in particular, is evoked in response to only a few of the stimuli in an animal's environment; these stimuli are called *sign stimuli,* or *releasers* of the behaviors which they elicit.

An example of these facts is to be found in the behavior of the common tick, which was described in detail by von Uexküll (1909). The tick does not respond to the sight of a host, but when an odor of butyric

acid from a mammal strikes the tick's sensory receptors, the tick drops
from the twig to the host, finds a spot on the skin which is about 37°
centigrade, and begins to drink blood. Only a few stimuli elicit the tick's
behavior, this behavior being without doubt innate.

But the simplicity of releasers can sometimes lead animals into grave
situations. For instance, a patient tick climbs up a slippery twig to waylay
its prey, a nice, juicy mammal. When it has reached the end of the twig,
it is above a rock on which a fat, perspiring man has been sitting. The
rock therefore emanates the typical odor of butyric acid, and is just the
right temperature. So the tick jumps, and lands on the rock—whereupon,
in trying to suck from the rock, it breaks it proboscis.

It seems plausible to ascribe at least two beliefs to our tick.
First, it believes that there is a good place to suck blood just
below the twig on which it has been sitting. Second, it believes
that, in general, a certain odor (of butyric acid) and a certain
temperature (about 37° centigrade) are signs of a good place to
suck blood. The first of these two beliefs is neither innate nor
a piece of knowledge. It is not innate inasmuch as it is formed
as the result of certain current stimuli that the tick experiences.
It is not knowledge because, in the case described, it is false.
The second belief, however, has good claim to being both innate
and an item of knowledge. According to Hess's assessment of
the evidence, the tick has an *innate* propensity to suck blood
at spots from which the odor of butyric acid emanates and
which are about 37° centigrade. If this behavioral propensity
justifies us in ascribing a *belief* to the tick, then we must surely
say that this belief is innate. Moreover, there is good reason to
say that this innate belief of the tick is an item of knowledge.
First, it is clearly a *true* belief. It is true that, in general, the
odor of butyric acid and a temperature of about 37° centigrade
are signs of a good spot (for a tick) to suck blood. Second, it
is very probable that there is a causal connection, indeed, an
appropriate causal connection, between the tick's belief and the
fact that such spots are good for sucking blood. In particular,
it is probable that the innate propensity of the tick to suck
blood under these stimulus conditions is attributable to a process of natural selection based on the fact that such spots *are*
good for sucking blood. The causal theory of knowing, therefore, would vindicate the claim that the tick not only has innate
true belief, but that it has innate knowledge.

Analogous cases pertaining to human beings are less easy

to find. Although empirical evidence clearly shows that certain kinds of behavioral responses and perceptual preferences are innate,[8] these facts do not readily support ascriptions of "beliefs" or "cognitions." But let us suppose, as seems plausible,[9] that babies also have innate propensities to interpret various facial or vocal expressions in specific ways, e.g., to interpret smiling as a sign of affection. Here it seems reasonable to say that the organism has an innate *belief* (or disposition to believe) that smiling is a sign of affection, and clearly (judging by independent criteria of affection) this belief is true. The question then arises whether this true belief can be classified as *knowledge.* As before, the causal theory of knowing enables us to vindicate such a claim. If there is an innate propensity to interpret smiling as a signal of affection, it is quite probable that the genesis of this propensity is attributable to a process of natural selection which is based on the fact that smiling *is* a signal of affection. Thus, there may well obtain an "appropriate" sort of causal connection between the innate belief and the fact to which it corresponds. If so, an ascription of "knowledge" would be sanctioned by the causal theory.

Needless to say, it is not the purpose of this paper to argue for the actual existence of innate knowledge, nor to speculate about its extent; such theses could only be fully defended by appeal to detailed empirical investigation, most of which still remains to be done. The point of the present discussion is simply to defend the possibility of innate knowledge against epistemological attack, i.e., against the claim that the concept of knowing precludes the possibility of innate knowledge. What I have tried to show is that the possibility of innate knowledge is fully compatible with an adequate analysis of the concept of knowing.

NOTES

1. W. D. Hart, "Innate Ideas and A Priori Knowledge," *this volume*; Thomas Nagel, in "Linguistics and Epistemology," in Sidney Hook, ed., *Language and Philosophy* (New York: New York University Press, 1969); and

R. Edgely, in "Innate Ideas," *Knowledge and Necessity*, Royal Institute of
Philosophy Lectures, vol. 3 (London: Macmillan, 1970).

2. "A Causal Theory of Knowing," *The Journal of Philosophy*,
LXIV, 12 (June 22, 1967), 357-372; reprinted in Michael Roth and Leon
Galis, eds., *Knowing* (New York: Random House, 1970).

3. Cases of this sort are discussed by Max Deutscher and C. B.
Martin, in "Remembering," *The Philosophical Review*, Vol. LXXV (1966).

4. Another example used to make the same point is given by Peter
Unger, in "Experience and Factual Knowledge," *The Journal of Philosophy*,
LXIV, 5 (March 16, 1967), 152-173. I find Unger's example of the
crystal-ball-gazing gypsy a bit too fanciful to be convincing, however.

5. This example is due to Ronald de Sousa, "Knowing, Consistent
Belief, and Self-consciousness," *The Journal of Philosophy*, LXVII, 3
(February 12, 1970), 66-73.

6. According to my causal theory of knowing, the causal connection
between the fact that p and S's belief that p can either be one in which
the fact that p *causes* (or is one of the causal ancestors of) S's belief that
p or one in which the fact that p and S's belief that p have a *common*
cause. For details see "A Causal Theory of Knowing," *op. cit.*

7. "Ethology: An Approach Toward the Complete Analysis of
Behavior," in Roger Brown et al., *New Directions in Psychology* (New
York: Holt, Rinehart and Winston, 1962), p. 179.

8. See William Kessen, "Sucking and Looking: Two Organized Con-
genital Patterns of Behavior in the Human Newborn," and Robert L. Fantz,
"Visual Perception and Experience in Early Infancy: A Look at the
Hidden Side of Behavior Development," both in H. W. Stevenson, E. H.
Hess, and H. L. Rheingold, eds., *Early Behavior, Comparative and Develop-
mental Approaches* (New York: John Wiley, 1967).

9. See I. Eibl-Eibesfeldt, "Concepts of Ethology and Their Significance in the Study of Human Behavior," ibid., especially pp. 142-143.

7

Recent Contributions to the
Theory of Innate Ideas

NOAM CHOMSKY

I think that it will be useful to separate two issues in the discussion of our present topic—one is the issue of historical interpretation, namely, what in fact was the content of the classical
doctrine of innate ideas, let us say, in Descartes and Leibniz;
the second is the substantive issue, namely, in the light of the
information presently available, what can we say about the
prerequisites for the acquisition of knowledge—what can we
postulate regarding the psychologically a priori principles that
determine the character of learning and the nature of what is
acquired.

These are independent issues; each is interesting in its own
right, and I will have a few things to say about each. What I
would like to suggest is that contemporary research supports a
theory of psychological a priori principles that bears a striking
resemblance to the classical doctrine of innate ideas. The sep-
arateness of these issues must, nevertheless, be kept clearly in
mind.

The particular aspect of the substantive issue that I will be
concerned with is the problem of acquisition of language. I
think that a consideration of the nature of linguistic structure
can shed some light on certain classical questions concerning the
origin of ideas.

To provide a framework for the discussion, let us consider

Reprinted with the kind permission of Professor Chomsky and the copyright holder from *Synthese* 17 (Dordrecht, Holland: D. Reidel Publishing
Company, 1967), pp. 2-11.

the problem of designing a model of language-acquisition, an
abstract 'language acquisition device' that duplicates certain aspects of the achievement of the human who succeeds in acquiring linguistic competence. We can take this device to be an
input-output system

$$\text{data} \rightarrow \boxed{\text{LA}} \rightarrow \text{knowledge}$$

   To study the substantive issue, we first attempt to determine the nature of the output in many cases, and then to
determine the character of the function relating input to output. Notice that this is an entirely empirical matter; there is
no place for any dogmatic or arbitrary assumptions about the
intrinsic, innate structure of the device LA. The problem is
quite analogous to the problem of studying the innate principles that make it possible for a bird to acquire the knowledge
that expresses itself in nest-building or in song-production. On
a priori grounds, there is no way to determine the extent to
which an instinctual component enters into these acts. To study
this question, we would try to determine from the behavior of
the mature animal just what is the nature of its competence,
and we would then try to construct a second-order hypothesis
as to the innate principles that provide this competence on the
basis of presented data. We might deepen the investigation by
manipulating input conditions, thus extending the information
bearing on this input-output relation. Similarly, in the case of
language-acquisition, we can carry out the analogous study of
language-acquisition under a variety of different input conditions, for example, with data drawn from a variety of languages.
   In either case, once we have developed some insight into
the nature of the resulting competence, we can turn to the investigation of the innate mental functions that provide for the
acquisition of this competence. Notice that the conditions of
the problem provide an upper bound and a lower bound on the
structure that we may suppose to be innate to the acquisition
device. The upper bound is provided by the diversity of resulting competence—in our case, the diversity of languages. We
cannot impose so much structure on the device that acquisition
of some attested language is ruled out. Thus we cannot suppose

that the specific rules of English are innate to the device and these alone, since this would be inconsistent with the observation that Chinese can be learned as readily as English. On the other hand, we must attribute to the device a sufficiently rich structure so that the output can be attained within the observed limits of time, data and access.

To repeat, there is no reason for any dogmatic assumptions about the nature of LA. The only conditions we must meet in developing such a model of innate mental capacity are those provided by the diversity of language, and by the necessity to provide empirically attested competence within the observed empirical conditions.

When we face the problem of developing such a model in a serious way, it becomes immediately apparent that it is no easy matter to formulate a hypothesis about innate structure that is rich enough to meet the condition of empirical adequacy. The competence of an adult, or even a young child, is such that we must attribute to him a knowledge of language that extends far beyond anything that he has learned. Compared with the number of sentences that a child can produce or interpret with ease, the number of seconds in a lifetime is ridiculously small. Hence the data available as input is only a minute sample of the linguistic material that has been thoroughly mastered, as indicated by actual performance. Furthermore, vast differences in intelligence have only a small effect on resulting competence. We observe further that the tremendous intellectual accomplishment of language acquisition is carried out at a period of life when the child is capable of little else, and that this task is entirely beyond the capacities of an otherwise intelligent ape. Such observations as these lead one to suspect, from the start, that we are dealing with a species-specific capacity with a largely innate component. It seems to me that this initial expectation is strongly supported by a deeper study of linguistic competence. There are several aspects of normal linguistic competence that are crucial to this discussion.

I. CREATIVE ASPECT OF LANGUAGE USE

By this phrase I refer to the ability to produce and interpret new sentences in independence from "stimulus control"—i.e., external stimuli or independently identifiable internal states. The normal use of language is "creative" in this sense, as was widely noted in traditional rationalist linguistic theory. The sentences used in everyday discourse are not "familiar sentences" or "generalizations of familiar sentences" in terms of any known process of generalization. In fact, even to speak of "familiar sentences" is an absurdity. The idea that sentences or sentence-forms are learned by association or conditioning or "training" as proposed in recent behaviorist speculations, is entirely at variance with obvious fact. More generally, it is important to realize that in no technical sense of these words can language use be regarded as a matter of "habit" or can language be re-graded as "a complex of dispositions to respond."

A person's competence can be represented by a *grammar,* which is a system of rules for pairing semantic and phonetic interpretations. Evidently, these rules operate over an infinite range. Once a person has mastered the rules (unconsciously, of course), he is capable, in principle, of using them to assign semantic interpretations to signals quite independently of whether he has been exposed to them or their parts, as long as they consist of elementary units that he knows and are composed by the rules he has internalized. The central problem in designing a language acquisition device is to show how such a system of rules can emerge, given the data to which the child is exposed. In order to gain some insight into this question, one naturally turns to a deeper investigation of the nature of grammars. I think real progress has been made in recent years in our understanding of the nature of grammatical rules and the manner in which they function to assign semantic interpretations to phonetically represented signals, and that it is precisely in this area that one can find results that have some bearing on the nature of a language-acquisition device.

II. ABSTRACTNESS OF PRINCIPLES OF SENTENCE INTERPRETATION

A grammar consists of syntactic rules that generate certain underlying abstract objects, and rules of semantic and phono-

logical interpretation that assign an intrinsic meaning and an
ideal phonetic representation to these abstract objects.

Concretely, consider the sentence 'The doctor examined
John'. The phonetic form of this sentence depends on the
intrinsic phonological character of its minimal items ('The',
'doctor', 'examine', 'past tense', 'John'), the bracketing of the
sentence (that is, as [[[the] [doctor]] [[examined] [John]]]),
and the categories to which the bracketed elements belong
(that is, the categories 'Sentence', 'Noun-Phrase', 'Verb-Phrase',
'Verb', 'Noun', 'Determiner', in this case). We can define the
'surface structure' of an utterance as its labeled bracketing,
where the brackets are assigned appropriate categorial labels
from a fixed, universal set. It is transparent that grammatical
relations (e.g., 'Subject-of', 'Object-of', etc.) can be defined in
terms of such a labeled bracketing. With terms defined in this
way, we can assert that there is very strong evidence that the
phonetic form of a sentence is determined by its labeled bracketing by phonological rules that operate in accordance with certain very abstract but quite universal principles of ordering
and organization.

The meaning of the sentence 'the doctor examined John'
is, evidently, determined from the meanings of its minimal
items by certain general rules that make use of the grammatical
relations expressed by the labeled bracketing. Let us define the
'deep structure' of a sentence to be that labeled bracketing that
determines its intrinsic meaning, by application of these rules
of semantic interpretation. In the example just given, we would
not be far wrong if we took the deep structure to be identical
with the surface structure. But it is obvious that these cannot
in general be identified. Thus consider the slightly more complex sentences: 'John was examined by the doctor'; 'someone
persuaded the doctor to examine John'; 'the doctor was persuaded to examine John'; 'John was persuaded to be examined
by the doctor'. Evidently, the grammatical relations among
doctor, examine, and *John,* as expressed by the deep structure,
must be the same in all of these examples as the relations in
'the doctor examined John'. But the surface structures will
differ greatly.

Furthermore, consider the two sentences:

  someone expected the doctor to examine John
  someone persuaded the doctor to examine John.

It is clear, in this case, that the similarity of surface structure
masks a significant difference in deep structure, as we can see,
immediately, by replacing 'the doctor to examine John' by
'John to be examined by the doctor' in the two cases.

  So far, I have only made a negative point, namely, that
deep structure is distinct from surface structure. Much more
important is the fact that there is very strong evidence for a
particular solution to the problem of how deep and surface
structures are related, and how deep and surface structures are
formed by the syntactic component of the grammar. The details of this theory need not concern us for the present. A
crucial feature of it, and one which seems inescapable, is that
it involves formal manipulations of structures that are highly
abstract, in the sense that their relation to signals is defined by
a long sequence of formal rules, and that, consequently, they
have nothing remotely like a point by point correspondence to
signals. Thus sentences may have very similar underlying structures despite great diversity of physical form, and diverse underlying structures despite similarity of surface form. A theory of
language acquisition must explain how this knowledge of abstract underlying forms and the principles that manipulate them
comes to be acquired and freely used.

III. UNIVERSAL CHARACTER OF LINGUISTIC STRUCTURE

  So far as evidence is available, it seems that very heavy
conditions on the form of grammar are universal. Deep structures seem to be very similar from language to language, and
the rules that manipulate and interpret them also seem to be
drawn from a very narrow class of conceivable formal operations.
There is no a priori necessity for a language to be organized in
this highly specific and most peculiar way. There is no sense
of 'simplicity' in which this design for language can be intel-
libibly described as 'most simple'. Nor is there any content
to the claim that this design is somehow 'logical'. Furthermore,
it would be quite impossible to argue that this structure is

simply an accidental consequence of 'common descent'. Quite apart from questions of historical accuracy, it is enough to point out that this structure must be rediscovered by each child who learns the language. The problem is, precisely, to determine how the child determines that the structure of his language has the specific characteristics that empricial investigation of language leads us to postulate, given the meagre evidence available to him. Notice, incidentally, that the evidence is not only meagre in scope, but very degenerate in quality. Thus the child learns the principles of sentence formation and sentence interpretation on the basis of a corpus of data that consists, in large measure, of sentences that deviate in form from the idealized structures defined by the grammar that he develops.

Let us now return to the problem of designing a language acquisition device. The available evidence shows that the output of this device is a system of recursive rules that provide the basis for the creative aspect of language use and that manipulate highly abstract structures. Furthermore, the underlying abstract structures and the rules that apply to them have highly restricted properties that seem to be uniform over languages and over different individuals speaking the same language, and that seem to be largely invariant with respect to intelligence and specific experience. An engineer faced with the problem of designing a device meeting the given input-output conditions would naturally conclude that the basic properties of the output are a consequence of the design of the device. Nor is there any plausible alternative to this assumption, so far as I can see. More specifically, we are led by such evidence as I have mentioned to suppose that this device in some manner incorporates: a phonetic theory that defines the class of possible phonetic representations; a semantic theory that defines the class of possible semantic representations; a schema that derives the class of possible grammars; a general method for interpreting grammars that assigns a semantic and phonetic interpretation to each sentence, given a grammar; a method of evaluation that assigns some measure of 'complexity' to grammars.

Given such a specification, the device might proceed to acquire knowledge of a language in the following way: the given schema for grammar specifies the class of possible hypotheses; the method of interpretation permits each hypothesis to be tested against the input data; the evaluation measure selects the highest valued grammar compatible with the data. Once a hypothesis—a particular grammar—is selected, the learner knows the language defined by this grammar; in particular, he is capable of pairing semantic and phonetic interpretations over an indefinite range of sentences to which he has never been exposed. Thus his knowledge extends far beyond his experience and is not a 'generalization' from his experience in any significant sense of 'generalization' (except, trivially, the sense defined by the intrinsic structure of the language acquisition device).

Proceeding in this way, one can seek a hypothesis concerning language acquisition that falls between the upper and lower bounds, discussed above, that are set by the nature of the problem. Evidently, for language learning to take place the class of possible hypotheses—the schema for grammar—must be heavily restricted.

This account is schematic and idealized. We can give it content by specifying the language acquisition system along the lines just outlined. I think that very plausible and concrete specifications can be given, along these lines, but this is not the place to pursue this matter, which has been elaborately discussed in many publications on transformational generative grammar.

I have so far been discussing only the substantive issue of the prerequisites for acquisition of knowledge of language, the a priori principles that determine how and in what form such knowledge is acquired. Let me now try to place this discussion in its historical context.

First, I mentioned three crucial aspects of linguistic competence: (1) creative aspect of language use; (2) abstract nature of deep structure; (3) apparent universality of the extremely special system of mechanisms formalized now as transformational grammar. It is interesting to observe that these three aspects of language are discussed in the rationalist philosophy of the seventeenth century and its aftermath, and that the linguistic theories that were developed within the framework of this discussion are, in essence, theories of transformational grammar.

Consequently, it would be historically accurate to describe the views regarding language structure just outlined as a rationalist conception of the nature of language. Furthermore, I employed it, again, in the classical fashion, to support what might fairly be called a rationalist conception of acquisition of knowledge, if we take the essence of this view to be that the general character of knowledge, the categories in which it is expressed or internally represented, and the basic principles that underlie it, are determined by the nature of the mind. In our case, the schematism assigned as an innate property to the language acquisition device determines the form of knowledge (in one of the many traditional senses of 'form'). The role of experience is only to cause the innate schematism to be activated, and then to be differentiated and specified in a particular manner.

In sharp contrast to the rationalist view, we have the classical empiricist assumption that what is innate is (1) certain elementary mechanisms of peripheral processing (a receptor system), and (2) certain analytical machanisms or inductive principles or mechanisms of association. What is assumed is that a preliminary analysis of experience is provided by the peripheral processing mechanisms and that one's concepts and knowledge, beyond this, are acquired by application of the innate inductive principles to this initially analyzed experience. Thus only the procedures and mechanisms for acquisition of knowledge constitute an innate property. In the case of language acquisition, there has been much empiricist speculation about what these mechanisms may be, but the only relatively clear attempt to work out some specific account of them is in modern structural linguistics, which has attempted to elaborate a system of inductive analytic procedures of segmentation and classification that can be applied to data to determine a grammar. It is conceivable that these methods might be somehow refined to the point where they can provide the surface structures of many utterances. It is quite inconceivable that they can be developed to the point where they can provide deep structures or the abstract principles that generate deep structures and relate them to surface structures. This is not a matter of further refinement, but of an entirely different approach to the question. Similarly, it is difficult to imagine how

the vague suggestions about conditioning and associative nets
that one finds in philosophical and psychological speculations
of an empiricist cast might be refined or elaborated so as to
provide for attested competence. A system of rules for generating deep structures and relating them to surface structures,
in the manner characteristic of natural language, simply does
not have the properties of an associative net or a habit family;
hence no elaboration of principles for developing such structures can be appropriate to the problem of designing a language
acquisition device.

I have said nothing explicit so far about the doctrine that
there are innate ideas and innate principles of various kinds
that determine the character of what can be known in what may
be a rather restricted and highly organized way. In the traditional view a condition for these innate mechanisms to become
activated is that appropriate stimulation must be presented.
This stimulation provides the occasion for the mind to apply
certain innate interpretive principles, certain concepts that proceed from 'the power of understanding' itself, from the faculty
of thinking rather than from external objects. To take a typical example from Descartes (Reply to Objections, V): ". . .
When first in infancy we see a triangular figure depicted on
paper, this figure cannot show us how a real triangle ought to
be conceived, in the way in which geometricians consider it,
because the true triangle is contained in this figure, just as the
statue of Mercury is contained in a rough block of wood. But
because we already possess within us the idea of a true triangle,
and it can be more easily conceived by our mind than the more
complex figure of the triangle drawn on paper, we, therefore,
when we see the composite figure, apprehend not it itself, but
rather the authentic triangle" (Haldane and Ross, II, 227). In
this sense, the idea of triangle is innate. For Leibniz what is
innate is certain principles (in general, unconscious), that "enter into our thoughts, of which they form the soul and the
connection." "Ideas and truths are for us innate as inclinations
dispositions, habits, or natural potentialities." Experience
serves to elicit, not to form, these innate structures. Similar
views are elaborated at length in rationalist speculative psychology.

It seems to me that the conclusions regarding the nature of language acquisition, discussed above, are fully in accord with the doctrine of innate ideas, so understood, and can be regarded as providing a kind of substantiation and further development of this doctrine. Of course, such a proposal raises nontrivial questions of historical interpretation.

What does seem to me fairly clear is that the present situation with regard to the study of language learning, and other aspects of human intellectual achievement of comparable intricacy, is essentially this. We have a certain amount of evidence about the grammars that must be the output of an acquisition model. This evidence shows clearly that knowledge of language cannot arise by application of step-by-step inductive operations (segmentation, classification, substitution precedures, 'analogy' association, conditioning, and so on) of any sort that have been developed or discussed within linguistics, psychology, or philosophy. Further empiricist speculations contribute nothing that even faintly suggests a way of overcoming the intrinsic limitations of the methods that have so far been proposed and elaborated. Furthemore, there are no other grounds for pursuing these empiricist speculations, and avoiding what would be the normal assumption, unprejudiced by doctrine, that one would formulate if confronted with empirical evidence of the sort sketched above. There is, in particular, nothing known in psychology or physiology that suggests that the empiricist approach is well-motivated, or that gives any grounds for skepticism concerning the rationalist alternative sketched above.

8

The "Innateness Hypothesis" and Explanatory Models in Linguistics

HILARY PUTNAM

I. THE INNATENESS HYPOTHESIS

The "innateness hypothesis" (henceforth, the I.H.) is a daring—or apparently daring; it may be meaningless, in which case it is not daring—hypothesis proposed by Noam Chomsky. I owe a debt of gratitude to Chomsky for having repeatedly exposed me to the I.H.; I have relied heavily in what follows on oral communications from him; and I beg his pardon in advance if I misstate the I.H. in any detail, or misrepresent any of the arguments for it. In addition to relying upon oral communications from Chomsky, I have also relied upon Chomsky's paper "Explanatory Models in Linguistics," in which the I.H. plays a considerable role.

    To begin, then, the I.H. is the hypothesis that the human brain is "programmed" at birth in some quite *specific* and *structured* aspects of human natural language. The details of this programming are spelled out in some detail in "Explanatory Models in Linguistics." We should assume that the speaker has "built in"[1] a function which assigns weights to the grammars G_1, G_2, G_3, ... in a certain class Σ of transformational grammars. Σ is not the class of all *possible* transformational grammars; rather all the members of Σ have some quite strong similarities. These similarities appear as "linguistic universals"—i.e., as characteristics of *all* human natural languages. If intelligent non-terrestrial life—

Reprinted with the kind permission of Professor Putnam and the copyright holder from *Synthese* 17 (Dordrecht, Holland: D. Reidel Publishing Company, 1967), pp. 12-22.

say, Martians—exists, and if the "Martians" speak a language
whose grammar does not belong to the subclass Σ of the class of
all transformational grammars, then, I have heard Chomsky
maintain, humans (except possibly for a few geniuses or linguistic experts) would be unable to learn Martian; a human
child brought up by Martians would fail to acquire language;
and Martians would, conversely, experience similar difficulties
with human tongues. (Possible difficulties in *pronunciation*
are not at issue here, and may be assumed *not* to exist for
the purposes of this argument.) As examples of the similarities that all grammars of the subclass Σ are thought to possess
(above the level of phonetics), we may mention the *active-passive*
distinction, the existence of a *nonphrase-structure* portion of the
grammar, the presence of such major categories as *concrete noun,
verb taking an abstract subject,* etc. The project of delimiting the
class Σ may also be described as the project of defining a *normal
form for grammars.* Conversely, according to Chomsky, any nontrivial normal form for grammars, such that correct and perspic-
uous grammars of all human languages can an should be written in
the normal form, "constitutes, in effect, a hypothesis concerning
the innate intellectual equipment of the child."[2]

Given such a highly *restricted* class Σ of grammars (highly
restricted in the sense that grammars not in the class are perfectly conceivable, not more "complicated" in any absolute sense
than grammars in the class, and may well be employed by nonhuman speakers, if such there be), the performance of the
human child in learning his native language may be understood
as follows, according to Chomsky. He may be thought of as
operating on the following "inputs"[3] : a list of utterances,
containing both grammatical and ungrammatical sentences; a
list of corrections, which enable him to classify the input utterances *as* grammatical or ungrammatical; and some information
concerning which utterances count as *repetitions* of earlier utterances. Simplifying slightly, we may say that, on this model,
the child is supplied with a list of grammatical sentence *types*
and a list of ungrammatical sentence *types.* He then "selects"
the grammar in Σ compatible with this information to which
his weighting function assigns the highest weight. On this
scheme, the general *form* of grammar is not learned from ex-

perience, but is "innate," and the "plausibility ordering" of grammars compatible with given data of the kinds mentioned is likewise "innate."

So much for a statement of the I.H. If I have left the I.H. vague at many points, I believe that this is no accident—for the I.H. seems to me to be *essentially* and *irreparably* vague—but this much of a statement may serve to indicate *what* belief it is that I stigmatize as irreparably vague.

A couple of remarks may suffice to give some idea of the role that I.H. is supposed to play in linguistics. Linguistics relies heavily, according to Chomsky, upon "intuitions" of grammaticality. But *what* is an intuition of "grammaticality" an intuition *of?* According to Chomsky, the sort of theory-construction programmatically outlined above is what is needed to give this question the only answer it can have or deserves to have. Presumable, then, to "intuit" (or assert, or conjecture, etc.) that a sentence is grammatical is to "intuit" (or assert, or conjecture, etc.) that the sentence is generated by the highest-valued G_i in the class Σ which is such that it generates all the grammatical sentence types with which we have been supplied by the "input" and none of the ungrammatical sentence types listed in the "input."[4]

Chomsky also says that the G_i which receives the highest value must do *more* than agree with "intuitions" of grammaticality; it must account for certain ambiguities, for example.[5] At the same time, unfortunately, he lists no semantical information in the input, and he conjectures[6] that a child needs semantical information only to "provide motivation for language learning," and not to arrive at the *formal* grammar of its language. Apparently, then, the fact that a grammar which agrees with a sufficient amount of "input" must be in the class Σ to be "selected" by the child is what rules out grammars that generate all and only the grammatical sentences of a given natural language, but fail to correctly "predict"[7] ambiguities (cf. E. M. in L., p. 533).

In addition to making clear what it *is* to be grammatical, Chomsky believes that the I.H. confronts the linguist with the following tasks: To *define* the normal form for grammars described above, and to *define* the weighting function. In *Syntactic Structures* Chomsky, indeed, gives this as an objective for linguistic theory: to give an *effective* procedure for choosing between rival grammars.

Lastly, the I.H. is supposed to justify the claim that what the linguist provides is "a hypothesis about the innate intellectual equipment that a child brings to bear in language learning."[8] Of course, even if language is *wholly* learned, it is still true that linguistics "characterizes the linguistic abilities of the mature speaker,"[9] and that a grammar "could properly be called an explanatory model of the linguistic intuition of the native speaker."[10] However, one could with equal truth say that a driver's manual "characterizes the car-driving abilities of the mature driver" and that a calculus text provides "an explanatory model of the calculus-intuitions of the mathematician." Clearly, it is the idea that *these* abilities and *these* intuitions are close to the human *essence*, so to speak, that gives linguistics its "sex appeal," for Chomsky at least.

II. THE SUPPOSED EVIDENCE FOR THE I.H.

A number of empirical facts and alleged empirical facts have been advanced to support the I.H. Since limitations of space make it impossible to describe all of them here, a few examples will have to suffice.

(a) The *ease* of the child's original language learning. "A young child is able to gain perfect mastery of a language with incomparably greater ease [*than an adult*—H.P.] and without any explicit instruction. Mere exposure to the language, and for a remarkably short period, seems to be all that the normal child requires to develop the competence of the native speaker."[11]

(b) The fact that reinforcement, "in any interesting sense," seems to be unnecessary for language learning. Some children have apparently even learned to speak without *talking*,[12] and then displayed this ability at a relatively late age to startled adults who had given them up for mutes.

(c) The ability to "develop the competence of the native speaker" has been said not to depend on the intelligence level. Even quite low I.Q.'s "internalize" the grammar of their native language.

(d) The "linguistic universals" mentioned in the previous

section are allegedly accounted for by the I.H.

(e) Lastly, of course, there is the "argument" that runs *"what else* could account for language learning?" The task is so incredibly complex (analogous to learning, at least implicitly, a complicated physical theory, it is said), that it would be miraculous if even one tenth of the human race accomplished it without "innate" assistance. (This is like Marx's "proof" of the Labour Theory of Value in *Capital,* Vol. III, which runs, in essence, *"What else* could account for the fact that commodities have different value *except* the fact that the labor-content is different?")

III. CRITICISM OF THE ALLEGED EVIDENCE

A. The Irrelevance of Linguistic Universals

1. Not surprising on any theory. Let us consider just how surprising the "linguistic universals" cited above really are. Let us assume for the purpose a community of Martians whose "innate intellectual equipment" may be supposed to be as different from the human as is compatible with their being able to speak a language at all. What could we expect to find in their language?

If the Martians' brains are not vastly richer than ours in complexity, then they, like us, will find it possible to employ a practically infinite set of expressions only if those expressions possess a "grammar"—i.e., if they are built up by recursive rules from a limited stock of basic forms. Those basic forms need not be built up out of a *short* list of phonemes— the Martians might have vastly greater memory capacity than we do—but if Martians, like humans, find rote learning difficult, it will not be surprising if they too have *short* lists of phonemes in their languages.

Are the foregoing reflections argument *for* or *against* the I.H.? I find it difficult to tell. If belief in "innate intellectual equipment" is *just* that, then how *could* the I.H. be false? How could something with *no* innate intellectual equipment *learn* anything? *To be sure,* human "innate intellectual equipment" is relevant to language learning; if this means that such parameters as memory span and memory capacity play a crucial role.

But what rank Behaviorist is supposed to have ever denied
this? On the other hand, that a particular mighty arbitrary set
Σ of grammars is "built in" to the brain of *both* Martians and
Humans is *not* a hypothesis we would have to invoke to account
for *these* basic similarities.

But for what similarities above the level of phonetics,
where constitutional factors play a large role for obvious reasons,
would the I.H. have to be invoked *save* in the trivial sense that
memory capacity, intelligence, needs, interests, etc., are all
relevant to language learning, and all depend, in part, on the
biological makeup of the organism? If Martians are such strange
creatures that they have no interest in physical objects, for
example, their language will contain no concrete nouns; but
would not this be *more*, not *less* surprising, on any *reasonable*
view, than their having an interest in physical objects? (Would
it be surprising if Martian contained devices for forming truth-
functions and for quantification?)

Two more detailed points are relevant here. Chomsky has
pointed out that no natural language has a phrase structure
grammar. But this too is not surprising. The sentence "John
and Jim came home quickly" is not generated by a phrase-
structure rule, in Chomsky's formalization of English grammar.
But the sentence "John came home quickly and Jim came home
quickly" *is* generated by a phrase-structure rule in the grammar
of mathematical logic, and Chomsky's famous "and-transfor-
mation" is just an abbreviation rule. Again, the sentence "That
was the lady I saw you with last night" is not generated by a
phrase-structure rule in English, or at least not in Chomsky's
description of English. But the sentence "That is $\imath x$ (x is a lady
and I saw you with x last night)" is generated by a phrase-
structure rule in the grammar of mathematical logic. And again
the idiomatic English sentence *can* be obtained from its phrase-
structure counterpart by a simple rule of abbreviation. Is it
really surprising, does it really point to anything more interesting than *general intelligence*, that these operations which
break the bounds of phrase-structure grammar appear in every
natural language?[13]

Again, it may appear startling at first blush that such
categories as noun, verb, adverb, etc. have "universal" applica-

tion. But, as Curry has pointed out, it is too easy to multiply "facts" here. If a language contains nouns—that is, a phrase-structure category which contains the proper names—it contains noun phrases, that is, phrases which occupy the environments of nouns. If it contains noun phrases it contains verb phrases—phrases which when combined with a noun phrase by a suitable construction yield sentences. If it contains verb phrases, it contains adverb phrases—phrases that, when combined with a verb phrase yield a verb phrase. Similarly, adjective phrases, etc., can be defined in terms of the *two* basic categories "noun" and "sentence." Thus the existence of nouns is all that has to be explained. And this reduces to explaining two facts: (1) The fact that all natural languages have a large phrase structure portion in their grammar, in the sense just illustrated, in spite of the effect of what Chomsky calls "transformations." (2) The fact that all natural languages contain proper names. But (1) is not surprising in view of the fact that phrase-structure rules are extremely simple algorithms. Perhaps Chomsky would reply that "simplicity" is subjective here, but this is just not so. The fact is that all the natural measures of complexity of an algorithm—size of the machine table, length of computations, time, and space required for the computation—lead to the same result here, quite independently of the detailed structure of the computing machine employed. Is it surprising that algorithms which are "simplest" for virtually any computing system we can conceive of are also simplest for naturally evolved "computing systems"? And (2)—the fact that all natural languages contain proper names—is not surprising in view of the utility of such names, and the difficulty of always finding a definite description that will suffice instead.

Once again, "innate" factors are relevant *to be sure*—if choosing *simple* algorithms as the basis of the grammar is "innate," and if the need for identifying persons rests on something innate—but what Behaviorist would or should be surprised? Human brains are computing systems and subject to some of the constraints that effect all computing systems; human beings have a natural interest in one another. If *that* is "innateness," well and good!

2. Linguistic universals could be accounted for, even if surprising, without invoking the I.H. Suppose that language-using human beings evolved *independently* in two or more places. Then, if Chomsky were *right,* there should be two or more *types* of human beings descended from the two or more original populations, and normal children of each type should fail to learn the languages spoken by the other types. Since we do not observe this, since there is only *one* class Σ built into *all* human brains, we have to conclude (if the I.H. is true) that language-using is an evolutionary "leap" that occurred only *once.* But in that case, it is overwhelmingly likely that all human languages are descended from a single original language, and that the existence today of what are called "unrelated" languages is accounted for by the great lapse of time and by countless historical changes. This is, indeed, likely even if the I.H. is false, since the human race itself is now generally believed to have resulted from a single evolutionary "leap," and since the human population was extremely small and concentrated for millennia, and only gradually spread from Asia to other continents. Thus, even if language using was learned or invented rather than "built in," or even if only some general dispositions in the direction of language using are "built in,"[14] it is likely that some one group of humans first developed language as we know it, and then spread this through conquest or imitation to the rest of the human population. Indeed, we do know that this is just how *alphabetic* writing spread, In any case, I repeat, this hypothesis—a single origin for human language—is certainly *required* by the I.H., but much weaker than the I.H.

But just this *consequence* of the I.H. is, in fact, enough to account for "linguistic universals"! For, if all human languages are descended from a common parent, then just such highly useful features of the common parent as the presence of some kind of quantifiers, proper names, nouns, and verbs, etc., would be expected to survive. Random variation may, indeed, alter many things; but that it should fail to strip language of proper names, or common nouns, or quantifiers, is not *so* surprising as to require the I.H.

B. The "ease" of Language Learning is not clear

Let us consider somewhat closely the "ease" with which children do learn their native language. A typical "mature" college student seriously studying a foreign language spends three hours a week in lectures. In fourteen weeks of term he is thus exposed to forty-two hours of the language. In four years he may pick up over 300 hours of the language, very little of which is actual listening to native informants. By contrast, direct method teachers estimate that 300 hours of direct-method teaching will enable one to converse fluently in a foreign language. Certainly 600 hours—say, 300 hours of direct-method teaching and 300 hours of reading—will enable any adult to speak and read a foreign language with ease, and to use an incomparably larger vocabulary than a young child.

It will be objected that the adult does not acquire a perfect accent. So what? The adult has been speaking one way all of his life, and has a huge set of habits to unlearn. What can equally well be accounted for by learning theory should not be cited as evidence for the I.H.

Now the child by the time it is four or five years old has been exposed to *vastly* more than 600 hours of direct-method instruction. Moreover, even if "reinforcement" is not necessary, most children are consciously and repeatedly reinforced by adults in a host of ways—e.g., the constant repetition of simple one-word sentences ("cup," "doggie") in the presence of babies. Indeed, any foreign adult living with the child for those years would have an incomparably better grasp of the language than the child does. The child indeed has a better accent. Also, the child's grammatical mistakes, which are numerous, arise not from carrying over previous language habits, but from not having fully acquired the first set. But it seems to me that this "evidence" for the I.H. stands the facts on their head.

C. Reinforcement another Issue

As Chomsky is aware, the evidence is today slim that *any* learning requires reinforcement "in any interesting sense." Capablanca, for example, learned to play chess by simply watch-

ing adults play. This is comparable to Macaulay's achievement
in learning language without speaking. Nongeniuses normally
do require practice both to speak correctly and to play chess.
Yet probably anyone *could* learn to speak *or* to play chess
without practice if muffled, in the first case, or not allowed to
play, in the second case, with sufficiently prolonged observation.

D. *Independence of Intelligence Level an Artifact*

Every child learns to speak the native language. What does
this mean? If it means that children do not make serious grammatical blunders, even by the standards of descriptive as opposed to prescriptive grammar, this is just not true for the young
child. By nine or ten years of age this has ceased to happen,
perhaps (I speak as a parent), but nine or ten years is enough
time to become pretty darn good at *anything.* What is more
serious is what "grammar" *means* here. It does not include
mastery of vocabulary, in which even many adults are deficient,
nor ability to understand *complex* constructions, in which many
adults are *also* deficient. It means purely and simply the ability
to learn what every *normal* adult learns. Every normal adult
learns what every normal adult learns. What this "argument"
reduces to is "Wow! How complicated a skill every normal
adult learns. What else could it be but *innate.*" Like the preceding argument, it reduces to the "What Else" argument.

But what of the "What Else?" argument? Just how impressed should we be by the failure of current learning theories
to account for complex learning processes such as those involved
in the learning of language? If Innateness were a *general* solution, perhaps we should be impressed. But the I.H. *cannot,* by
its very nature, *be* generalized to handle all complex learning
processes. Consider the following puzzle (called "jump"):

```
        *  *  *
        *  *  *
  *  *  *  *  *  *  *
  *  *  *  O  *  *  *
  *  *  *  *  *  *  *
        *  *  *
        *  *  *
```

To begin with, all the holes but the center one are filled. The object of the game is to remove all the pegs but one by "jumping" (as in checkers) and to end with the one remaining peg in the center. A clever person can get the solution in perhaps eight or ten hours of experimentation. A not so clever person can get a "near-solution"—two pegs left—in the same time. No program exists, to my knowledge, that would enable a computer to solve even the "near solution" problem without running out of both time and space, even though the machine can spend the equivalent of many human lifetimes in experimentation. When we come to the discovery of even the simplest mathematical theorem the situation is even more striking. The theorems of mathematics, the solutions to puzzles, etc., cannot on *any* theory be *individually* "innate"; what must be "innate" are heuristics, i.e., learning strategies. In the absence of any knowlege of what *general multipurpose learning strategies* might even look like, the assertion that such strategies (which absolutely must exist and be employed by all humans) cannot account for this or that learning process, that the answer or an answer schema must be "innate," is utterly unfounded.

I will be told, of course, that *everyone* learns his native language (as well as everyone does), and that not everyone solves puzzles or proves theorems. But everyone does learn pattern recognition, automobile driving, etc., and everyone in fact can solve many problems that no computer can solve. In conversation Chomsky has repeatedly used precisely such skills as these to support the idea that humans have an "innate conceptual space." Well and good, if true. *But that is no help. Let a complete seventeenth-century Oxford University education be innate if you like;* still the solution to "jump" was not innate; the Prime Number Theorem was not innate; and so on. *Invoking "Innateness" only postpones the problem of learning; it does not solve it.* Until we understand the strategies which make general learning possible—and vague talk of "classes of hypotheses" and "weighting functions" is utterly useless here—no discussion of the *limits* of learning can even begin.

NOTES

1. What "built in" means is highly unclear in this context. The

weighting function by itself determines only the relative ease with which various grammars can be learned by a human being. If a grammar G_1 can be learned more easily than a grammar G_2, then doubtless this is "innate" in the sense of being a fact about human learning *potential,* as opposed to a fact about what has been learned. But this sort of fact is what learning theory tries to account for; *not* the explanation being sought. It should be noticed that Chomsky has never offered even a schematic account of the sort of device that is supposed to be present in the brain, and that is supposed to do the job of selecting the highest weighted grammar compatible with the data. But only a description, or at least a theory, of such a device could properly be called an innateness *hypothesis* at all.

2. Noam Chomsky, "Explanatory Models in Linguistics" (hereafter cited as E. M. in L.,), p. 550.

3. E. M. in L., pp. 530-531.

4. I doubt that the child really is told which sentences it hears or utters are *ungrammatical.* At most it is told which are *deviant* – but it may not be told which are deviant for *syntactical* and which for *semantical* reasons.

5. Many of these—e.g., the alleged "ambiguity" in "the shooting of the elephants was heard"—*require coaching to detect.* The claim that grammar "explains the ability to recognize ambiguities" thus lacks the impressiveness that Chomsky believes it to have. I am grateful to Paul Ziff and Stephen Leeds for calling this point to my attention.

6. E. M. in L., p. 531, n. 5.

7. A grammar "predicts" an ambiguity, in Chomsky's formalism, whenever it assigns two or more structural descriptions to the same sentence.

8. E. M. in L., p. 530.

9. E. M. in L., p. 530.

10. E. M. in L., p. 533.

11. E. M. in L., p. 529.

12. Macaulay's *first* words, it is said, were: "Thank you, Madam, the agony has somewhat abated" (to a lady who had spilled hot tea on him).

13. Another example of a transformation is the "active-passive" transformation (cf. *Syntactic Structures).* But (a) the presence of this, if it *is* a part of the grammar, is not surprising—why should not there be a systematic way of expressing the *converse* of a relation?—and (b) the argument for the existence of such a "transformation" at all is extremely slim. It is contended that a grammar which "defines" active and passive forms separately (this can be done by even a phrase-structure grammar) fails to represent something that every speaker knows, *viz.* that active and passive forms are *related.* But why must every *relation* be mirrored by *syntax?* Every "speaker" of the canonical languages of mathematical logic is aware that each sentence $(x) (Fx \supset Gx)$ is related to a sentence (x) $(Gx \supset Fx)$; yet the definition of "well formed formula" fails to mirror "what every speaker knows" in this respect, and is not inadequate on that account.

14. It is very difficult to account for such phenomena as the spontaneous babbling of infants without *this* much "innateness." But this is not to say that a class Σ and a function f are "built in," as required by the I.H.

9

Innate Ideas

JERROLD J. KATZ

Rationalists such as Plato, Descartes, Leibniz, and Kant argued
that men are born with a stock of ideas which determine to a very
large extent both the form and content of their mature knowledge, while empiricists like Hobbes, Locke, Berkeley, and Hume
argued that at birth men are a virtual *tabula rasa* on which experience writes its lessons according to the principles of associative
learning. The rationalists claimed that our concepts originate in
principles that form the inborn constitution of the mind, and the
empiricists claimed that all our ideas come originally from experience. The controversy is fundamentally a conflict between two
opposed hypotheses to account for how conceptual knowledge is
built up from experience by the operation of innate principles of
mental functioning. The basis for the controversy is not, as it is
often conceived in popular discussions, that empiricists fail to
credit the mind with any innate principles, but rather that the
principles which are accorded innate status by empiricists do not
place any substantive restrictions on the ideas that can qualify as
components of complex ideas or any formal restrictions on the
structure of associations which bond component ideas together to
form a complex idea. On the empiricist's hypothesis, the innate
principles are purely combinatorial devices for putting together
items from experience. So these principles provide only the machinery for instituting associative bonds. Experience plays the

Excerpted with the kind permission of Professor Katz from Jerrold J. Katz,
The Philosophy of Language (New York and London: Harper and Row,
1966), pp. 240-256 and 268-278.

selective role in determining which ideas may be connected by association, and principles of association are, accordingly, unable to exclude any ideas as, in principle, beyond the range of possible intellectual acquisition.

Thus, the empiricist's account of how conceptual knowledge develops is essentially this. Experience provides examples of things of a certain kind which are somehow copied by the mind to form a simple idea of such things. Empiricists differ among themselves about the sort of things that are represented as simple ideas, but this has no bearing on the present discussion. Simple ideas are combined to form complex ideas, and these are combined to form still more complex ideas, without any limit on the level of complexity that may be reached. Such combinations are dictated by the regularities exhibited in experience. The network of associative bonds instituted to form a complex idea from simpler ones is itself a copy of the pattern of regularities which connect items in experience, where these regularities are represented as associative bonds. Since the associative machinery does not place restrictions either on the intrinsic characteristics of the items from experience to determine which of them can be represented as simple ideas or on the structure of the complex ideas resulting from the process of combining ideas, any logically possible concepts can, given the appropriate experience, be realized in the mind in the form of some simple or complex idea. Since any simple ideas whatever are possible, since any simple ideas can become the elements associated in the formation of a complex idea, and since any complex idea is just a network of associative bonds whose ultimate elements can be nothing other than simple ideas derived from experience, it follows that the empiricist's principles of mental operation are, as it were, neutral with respect to which ideas from the totality of all logically possible ones are chosen for use in making sense of our actual experience. In this regard, these principles defer to experience to provide a basis for choice among the totality. To explain how this choice is made, empiricists introduce the doctrine that the causally effective factor in learning is the frequency of presentations of spatially and temporally contiguous items together with perhaps other precipitating factors such as drive reduction.[1] The components of every complex idea are bonded together by links forged by the operation of enumerative

techniques of inductive generalization from frequently repeated
instances of contiguously occurring items in experience.

Contrary to this, rationalists claim that the principles of
mental operation with which man is innately equipped place
quite severe restrictions on what a simple idea can be and on
what ways simple ideas can combine with one another and with
complex ideas in the production of complex ideas. To account
for the attainment of conceptual knowledge, such restrictions
are incorporated in the rationalist hypothesis in the form of a
system of innately fixed conceptual forms which sharply limit
the set of those ideas which the mind is capable of acquiring to
a very small subset of the set of all logically possible ideas.
These innate conceptual forms, or innate ideas, contribute
directly to our stock of abstract concepts and indirectly organize the content of experience by serving as models for the
construction of particular concepts, which, accordingly, have
the structure of the abstract concepts on which they are modeled. For example, an abstract concept such as our concept of
an object with spatially and temporally contiguous parts is not
learned by copying experienced objects but is manifested as a
functional component of our conceptual knowledge under
precipitating sensory conditions. Similarly, experience does
not present instances of a particular concept such as that of
a stone or animal which the mind copies without the benefit
of a template. Experience sets off a process in which such
particular concepts are manufactured from the same innately
fixed conceptual form which gives rise to the abstract concept
that determines the category to which those particular concepts
belong.

Hence, the rationalist is no more claiming that all our ideas
arise from innate forms in a way that is wholly independent
of a selective effect of experience than the empiricist is claiming that there are no innate principles of mental operation.
"Necessary truths," wrote Leibniz, ". . . must have principles
whose proof does not depend on examples, nor consequently upon the testimony of the senses, although without the senses it
would never have occurred to us to think of them." According
to the rationalists, conceptual knowledge is a joint product of
the mind and the senses, in which sense experience serves to

realize the innately fixed form of mature conceptual knowledge.
Leibniz phrased this point in terms of a particularly revealing
analogy. He wrote, ". . . I have taken as illustration a block of
veined marble, rather than a block of perfectly uniform marble
or than empty tablets, that is to say, what is called by philosophers *tabula rasa.* For if the soul were like these empty
tablets, truths would be in us as the figure of Hercules is in a
block of marble, when the block of marble is indifferently
capable of receiving this figure or any other. But if there were
in the stone veins, which should mark out the figure of Hercules
rather than other figures, the stone would be more determined
towards this figure, and Hercules would somehow be, as it
were, innate in it, although labor would be needed to uncover
the veins and to clear them by polishing and thus removing
what prevents them from being fully seen. It is thus that ideas
and truths are innate in us, as natural inclinations, dispositions,
habits or powers, and not as activities. . . ."[2]   The rationalist
thus denies the empiricist contention that all of our ideas come
from sense experience, arguing instead that sense experience
serves to activate such natural inclinations, dispositions, habits
or powers, i.e., to transform the latent unperceived ideas with
which men are innately equipped into clearly perceived, actual
ideas. The senses, to return to Leibniz's analogy, play the role
of the sculptor who by polishing and clearing away extraneous
marble reveals the form of Hercules.

Rationalists claim that the set of possible ideas from which
experience selects those that are actually acquired by us is a
far narrower set than those which it is possible to imagine or
formulate. Consequently, in denying the empiricist's contention
that all our ideas come from experience, the rationalist is putting forth a stronger hypothesis about the innate contribution
to conceptual knowledge. The controversy is, then, whether
some version of this stronger hypothesis or the empiricist's
weaker one best explains how a conceptual system of the sort
that mature humans possess is acquired on the experience they
have accumulated.

We make no effort here to review the traditional arguments of empiricists and rationalists. Instead we shall consider
the form that the issue over innate ideas takes in the case of

language acquisition. The reason for thus narrowing the issue is
that in doing so we deal with the crux of the issue in terms of a
case about which enough is now known in the theory of language
to afford a substantial basis for deciding between the empiricist
and rationalist hypotheses.

   The major fact to be explained by the contending hypotheses
is that a child who undergoes the transition from nonverbal infant to fluent speaker of a natural language on the basis of an
exposure to a sample of speech has acquired an internal representation of the rules that determine how sentences are constructed,
used, and understood. These internally represented rules constitute his competence in his native language. Thus, at the final
stage of the nonverbal infant's transformation into fluent speaker,
the product of the process of language acquisition is an internal
representation of a linguistic description. This internal representation is, then, the object whose acquisition has to be explained
by the contending empiricist and rationalist hypotheses. Accordingly, we may conceive of the nonverbal infant as initially equipped with a language acquisition device of undetermined constitution,

(D)

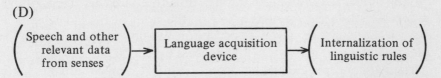

and we may think of the empiricist and rationalist hypotheses
as hypotheses about its constitution. Since the input to (D) is
a sample of utterances over a certain maturational period, and
perhaps other linguistically relevant sensory information as
well, and its output is an internalization of the rules of the
language from which the sample was drawn, the best hypothesis about (D) is that hypothesis which accounts in the most
revealing way for how such an output is produced on the basis
of such an input. Therefore, our approach to deciding whether
the empiricist or rationalist hypothesis is best will be to study
the properties of the input and output of (D) to determine the
kind of mechanism that can convert an input with the properties that the input to (D) is found to have into an output with
the properties that the output of (D) is found to have. Which-

ever hypothesis thus provides the most fruitful model of the internal structure of the language acquisition device will be accepted as the best hypothesis.

The empiricist hypothesis claims that the language acquisition device operated essentially by principles of inductive generalization which associated observable features of utterances with one another and with other relevant sensory information to obtain an internalization of the rules of a linguistic description. These principles have been given a precise statement in various, from our point of view, equivalent forms in the work of taxonomic linguistics in the Bloomfieldian tradition and learning theorists in the tradition of American behaviorist psychology.[3] Such statements are attempts to work out a simulation model of the device (D). On the other hand, the rationalist hypothesis, which attributes a far richer structure to the device (D), has never been expressed in a precise enough form for it to receive serious consideration as a competing explanation. The rationalist hypothesis claims that the language acquisition device contains a stock of innate ideas that jointly specify the necessary form of language (realized in any actual natural language) and thus the necessary form of a speaker's internal representation of the rules of his language. But no rationalist has given a precise formulation of these innate ideas, or an exact account of the process by which abstract and particular concepts are created from the interaction of innate conceptual forms and sensory stimulation. Thus, one might even say that there is no definite rationalist hypothesis, but just a general notion about the character of such a hypothesis. These difficulties with the formulation of the rationalist hypothesis have been one major factor which has discouraged cultivation of such an alternative to the empiricist conception of intellectual acquisitions. Another difficulty is the somewhat greater initial plausibility that the empiricist hypothesis has by virtue of its apparent greater simplicity. Consequently, we consider the empiricist hypothesis first, and ask whether there are fundamental inadequacies in it that force us to resort to the rationalist's apparently more complicated account of language acquisition and to take on the burden of trying to give their account a more precise formulation. This means that we shall examine the output and input to (D) to find out if an empiricist model of associative learning can provide an account of how the input is transformed into the output which squares with what is known about them.

For a predetermined output from an input-output device, there is a functional relationship between the input and the richness of the internal structure of the device. Namely, the weaker the input in structural organization, the richer the internal structure of the device must be in order to give the fixed output from the input, i.e., in order to make up for the poverty of the input. Let us take a rather mundane example. A very intelligent person can obtain the solutions to certain mathematical problems (the output) given just the barest formulation of the problems (the input) whereas a very unintelligent person might have to be virtually told the solutions before he gets them. Thus, we often infer the poverty of someone's intellect from how much has to be given him at the outset for him to arrive at the solution to a problem. Similarly, here we will try to show that the input to the language acquisition device would be too impoverished for it to be able to produce an internalization of the rules of a linguistic description were it to be constructed in accord with the empiricist hypothesis. That is, we shall try to establish that operations of inductive generalization and association cannot produce an internalization of a linguistic description from the kind of speech and other data that is available to the child.

One fundamental assumption of any associative theory of learning is that what is learned can be broken down into elements which have been each associated with observable and distinguishable constituents of the input in the following sense. The elements of the input which can have something associated with them must be distinguishable in terms of the discriminative and analytic capacities of the perceptual mechanism that codes the input into discrete parts and analyzes those parts as units within one or another category. Thus, limitations on the perceptual mechanism based on the discriminative and analytic distinctions it can make are also limitations on the richness of the information which the input provides for the associative machinery. Similarly, insufficiencies in the input itself are also limitations on the richness of the information with which the associative machinery can work. Therefore, if the associationist theory is to successfully explain the case of language learning, the physical speech sounds, or utterances, from which the child acquires his knowledge of the rules of the linguistic description must contain, or be analyzable into, observable and distinguishable elements such that for each constituent of the meaning of an utterance whose meaning has been acquired there is an observable and distinguishable component of its phonetic shape with which that semantic constituent can be associated. Since learning the meanings of the sentences of a language is conceived of as a process of associating semantic elements of some kind with observable features of the phonetic shape of the sentences to which the child is exposed, these observable features must provide a rich enough basis of distinct elements for each semantic component of the meaning of such sentences to have a distinct phonetic element(s) with which it can be correlated by association. If, therefore, we can show that this fundamental assumption is false—that there are, in the case of certain essential semantic elements, literally no observable features of the phonetic shape of sentences with which these semantical elements can be associated—then we will have established that the input to (D) is structurally too impoverished for the rules of a linguistic description to be derived from it by principles of inductive generalization and association. That is what we shall now attempt to establish.

To show this, we first define two notions, that of the *observable grammatical features of a sentence* and that of the *unobservable grammatical features of a sentence*. To define the first of these notions, we refer back to our earlier discussion of final derived phrase markers. It will be recalled that these phrase markers are the objects on which the phonological rules, the rules that determine the pronunciation of sentences, operate. These rules map phonetic interpretations onto final derived phrase markers. Since it is only the speech sounds represented by such phonetic interpretations which the child encounters in acquiring his fluency in the language—since, that is, this is the only data about the language that he can observe, it is natural to define the notion of observable grammatical features in terms of properties of final derived phrase markers, along with properties of their phonological interpretations where these are relevant. *Thus, we define the observable grammatical features of the sentence S to be any features of S which can be predicted directly from its final derived phrase marker or any feature that can be predicted directly from its phonological representation, and nothing else.* Anything that requires information from other sources, such as the rules of the linguistic description or other phrase markers of the sentence, in order to be predicted is *ipso facto* not an observable grammatical feature. . . .

Note that this definition of a sentence's observable grammatical features, although it seems natural in the sense that it permits us to count anything that we would intuitively regard as an observable grammatical feature as such, is nonetheless, overly generous to the empiricist. That is, it is overly liberal in the sense that it counts much more information about the grammar of a sentence as observable than a nonverbal child could be expected to be able to inductively extract from the sounds he actually encounters. For one thing, it is quite obvious that the child is in no sense given a classification of the constituents of a sentence into their syntactic categories. Furthermore, the essentially inductive techniques of data cataloguing devised by taxonomic linguists in order to provide a mechanical discovery procedure for final derived phrase markers on the basis of their phonological representation have always proved a dismal failure, not because there was little skill employed in their development, but because, without the general definitions of the grammatical properties they were to identify in particular cases, they lacked the conceptual apparatus to do their job.[4] For another thing, and perhaps more significantly, it has been found in recent work in acoustic phonetics that the physical sounds of speech do not themselves provide a complete basis for identifying the significant phonological units of sentences. These two points are by themselves a strong argument against the empiricist hypothesis about language acquisition, but we shall not develop them here. If on the basis of this overly liberal definition of an observable grammatical feature we can show that the observable features of sentences are insufficient to enable a child to acquire the rules of his

language by operations of inductive generalization and association, then we have an adequate refutation of the empiricist
conception of language learning. . . .

Final derived markers do not, and could not, adequately
specify all the information about the syntactic structure of
sentences. This means that the syntactic structure of a sentence
is not given by a single phrase marker which segments it into
continuous constituents and labels these segments but must
be given by other phrase markers also. These other phrase
markers are connected with the final derived phrase marker by
a system of transformational rules which convert underlying
phrase markers into derived phrase markers, and these into
still further derived phrase markers, until the final one is
reached. The underlying phrase markers may be thought of, in
contrast to the final derived phrase markers, as reconstructing
the unobservable, theoretically inferred, features of sentences.

Now, in terms of the underlying phrase markers, we can
define the notion unobservable grammatical feature of a senten-
tense. *An unobservable grammatical feature of S is any syntactic feature of S which can be predicted directly from its
underlying phrase marker but cannot be predicted from its
final derived phrase marker.* In general, if we compare final
derived phrase markers with their corresponding underlying
phrase markers, we find that the unobservable grammatical
features of sentences form quite an impressive collection. The
occurrence of a 'you' subject in normal English imperative
sentences is one example of an unobservable grammatical
feature. . . .

Such features cannot be detected in the perceptible or
physically definable properties of the data in the sample of the
language which a language learner encounters, but, nevertheless,
they must, as we have already shown, be theoretically posited
by the linguist as part of the structure of sentences in order that
his linguistic description successfully explain observable grammatical features. Thus, the unobservable features of a sentence as
well as its observable features must be considered as information
that a speaker utilizes to produce it on the appropriate occasion
and to understand it when it is produced by other speakers.

That unobservable grammatical features of sentences bear

semantic content which makes an essential contribution to the meaning of sentences, i.e., that the meaning of sentences having such features is not complete without the semantic contribution made by them, is obvious from the examples we have already given. Thus, it follows that any hypothesis to explain how the rules of a language are acquired must explain how the semantic content contributed by unobservable grammatical features becomes part of the full meaning of sentences. Otherwise, the hypothesis fails to explain how a speaker knows what sentences with unobservable grammatical features mean. Now, the empiricist hypothesis claims that the meanings of sentences are learned by a conditioning process in which inductive generalization and association provide the steps of language acquisition. Since such steps must proceed exclusively from observable features of the utterances to which the child is exposed, the empiricist hypothesis is claiming that the meaning of sentences can be learned solely on the basis of operations of associating semantic elements with observable grammatical features of sentences. But this is simply false. First, the observable grammatical features account for only a small fraction of the semantic content of sentences; and, second, on the empiricist hypothesis, there is no means of associating the semantic content of unobservable grammatical features with the sentences whose meaning contains that semantic content. We conclude, then, that the empiricist hypothesis is, in principle, incapable of accounting for the acquisition of a natural language, where by acquisition is meant mastery of rules that provide the full meaning of any sentence in the language.

To put the matter another way, since the observable structure of sentences is often quite severely impoverished from the point of view of semantic interpretation and since principles of inductive generalization and association add nothing structural or substantive to these structures on which they operate, it follows that such principles cannot account for the full range of semantic, as well as syntactic, properties on which the interpretation of sentences, essential to communication with them, depends.

The above arguments show that the empiricist hypothesis attributes far too little internal structure to the language acquisition device (D). The obvious moral to draw is that we need a stronger hypothesis if we are to successfully explain the output of (D) in terms of its input. This hypothesis must be strong enough to fully determine the output, given the input, but not so strong that it determines an output having properties that conflict with what is known about the ways in which natural languages can diverge. For example, the internal structure attributed to (D) by the hypothesis cannot be so rich that it incorporates the rules for English phonological structure, since, then, the hypothesis would predict that every natural language sounds like English. Within the known limits of richness, we wish to find a hypothesis that is rich enough as an explanatory hypothesis, rather than to find a hypothesis that is weak enough to satisfy empiricist preconceptions about the insignificance of innate contributions to knowledge. The empiricist falsely identifies his preconceptions about the paucity of the innate contribution with simplicity as a methodological canon and then argues that simplicity considerations favor his hypothesis. He overlooks the fact that simplicity is a consideration in choosing between competing hypotheses only when the hypotheses can afford an equally plausible basis on which to explain the available evidence.

A hypothesis strong enough to account for what we know about the product of language acquisition will be rationalistic in that it will be designed to introduce into the language acquisition device, as part of its internal constitution, all those facets of natural languages which must be taken as innate equipment to explain how a child's earliest linguistic experience enable him to arrive at an internalization of the rules of a linguistic descriptions. The hypothesis we suggest (to be referred to as the "rationalist hypothesis") is this: *The language acquisition device contains, as innate structure, each of the principles stated within the theory of language.* That is, the language acquisition device contains,

   (i)   the linguistic universals which define the form of a linguistic description,

  (ii)   the form of the phonological, syntactic, and semantic components of a linguistic description,

 (iii)   the formal character of the rules in each of these components,

 (iv)   the set of universal phonological, syntactic, and semantic constructs out of which particular rules in particular descriptions are formulated,

(v)   a methodology for choosing optimal linguistic descriptions.

It should be noted that this hypothesis is open-ended in the sense that it asserts that anything which, for good empirical reasons, is found to be part of the theory of language is *ipso facto* part of the language acquisition device, and hence part of the child's native language-forming apparatus, his innate ideas about language. But, even with this open-endedness, there is no indefiniteness about what is thus given the status of innate ideas. What the hypothesis asserts to be part of the language acquisition device is just what the theory of language specifies as universals, and these are established on the basis of definite empirical evidence from the analysis of natural languages. Hence, any particular claim that something is or is not an innate idea can be justified or refuted within the same methodological framework that serves this purpose in other sciences. The theory of language formulates its principles with scientific precision, so that the characterization of the set of innate ideas is itself explicitly specified. This makes up for the vagueness of classical rationalist attempts to put forth their doctrine. Thus, the principle defect of the rationalist position is removed. Note, finally, that innate ideas are conceived of as components of a device for internally representing linguistic rules and as constituents of the particular rules acquired by the operation of this device. Accordingly, the question as to what are innate ideas can be answered by saying that innate ideas are parts of a system of principles for organizing experience whose existence has been hypothetically inferred from the linguistic performance of speakers in their acquisition and use of language.

Adopting the rationalist hypothesis enables us to explain why every natural language has the features attributed to it by the principles of the theory of language. Why, that is, natural languages that have been investigated and those that will be investigated conform to the linguistic universals in the theory of language. We may assume that the generalizations in the theory of language which formulate the linguistic universals are true over the set of natural languages and ask, with respect to this assumption, why these generalizations hold. We are thus asking why the facts that they express are the way these generalizations say they are. We are seeking a more comprehensive and deeper explanation for the facts than is provided by laws that express them. We seek an explanation of those laws.[5] The explanatory power of the rationalist hypothesis lies in its ability to provide such an explanation.

We cannot assume that the presence of some feature in every natural language is merely as accidental correlation, such as the proverbial correlation between rum sales and preacher's salaries. We must provide a more scientifically plausible account. We must find something in the context in which natural languages are acquired which is invariant from one such context to another and can be plausibly regarded as the *causal antecedent* for the existence of common features in different natural languages. (Accordingly, we ignore such invariants as the fact that all speakers of a natural language live close to the earth's surface, that all breathe air, that all walk on two legs, etc., since these invariants cannot plausibly count as causally sufficient for the acquisition of a natural language.) This context includes, besides a nonverbal infant and fluent speakers of a natural language speaking their language, geographical, cultural, psychological, and sociological factors. When we compare communities in which languages such as English, Chinese, Croatian, Urdu, Mohawk, Norwegian, Arabic, Hebrew, Greek, etc., are spoken to determine if any environmental factors are invariably present in contexts where natural languages are acquired, it is obvious that no such factors qualify. The psychology, sociology, and anthropology differ from case to case as much as does the geography and climate. In child rearing patterns, mores, traditions, properties, rituals, artifacts, political and social structure, etc., there is no sufficiently strong cross-community regularity that could account for the impressive fact, that all languages which human children acquire have those features which the generalizations in the theory of language prescribe. Moreover, we must also rule out every aspect of the psychology of infants and adult speakers which constitutes a respect in which one individual can differ normally from another, i.e., unique past experience, system of beliefs, morals, attitudes, emotional make-up, intelligence, disposition toward special ability or talent, etc. For, even within a given language community, children and adult speakers differ markedly from

one another in these respects and yet normal children acquire
essentially the same linguistic fluency so long as they are exposed to an adequate sample of speech. Hence, by this process
of elimination, the only thing left that can provide the invariant condition that we want to connect with the universal
features of language as their causal antecedent is the common
innate endowment of human language learners, i.e., some component of their specifically human nature. This is not only
the one constant feature amid all the differences among the
participants in language acquisition situations and between
the behavioral and contextual aspects of these situations, but
it is also the differentia between language at the human level
and its absence at lower levels of the animal kindom. We thus
conclude that the genetic endowment of a human being *qua*
human being is the only invariant feature of language acquisition contexts which can causally account for nonverbal infants
achieving a successful internalization of languages having the
universal properties described in the theory of language. This
gives us the regularity that whenever such languages are acquired
there is the antecedent condition that the language learner
possessed the genetic endowment of a member of the human
species.

Now, if we bring in the rationalist hypothesis, we can
obtain an explanation of this regularity. This hypothesis says
that part of the genetic endowment of a human being is the
full set of linguistic universals (i)–(v) and that these universals
constitute the internal structure of the device which the nonverbal infant utilizes to become a fluent speaker on exposure
to a sample of the utterances of a language. Since the innately
given language acquisition device incorporates the linguistic
universals, we can explain why the linguistic universals are
necessary features of any language that is spoken by a human
being. Namely, the linguistic universals are found in each and
every natural language because, in acquiring a language, they
are emplanted in the speaker's internalization of the rules of
his language by the device that accomplishes its acquisition. The
very mechanism which the child uses to acquire fluency in a
natural language introduces them as the framework in which his
linguistic experience is organized in the form of linguistic rules.

This explanation, it should be noted, is neither vacuous
nor a *petitio principii.* To say that the language spoken by
any human has the universal features of natural languages because the rules that define his linguistic competence are modeled
on inborn archetypical representations of these features would
be vacuous if there were no independently arrived at formal
statement of these archetypical representations. But there is
such a statement. Thus, this explanation is not vacuous because
it is formulated in terms of the independently arrived at specification of the linguistic universals given in the theory of language.
On the other hand, this explanation is not circular because the
justification of the theory of language nowhere presupposes it.
Note also that, although no account of the origin of such innate
ideas is given, there is no question to be begged because there is
no account of the origin of the principles of associative learning
which the empiricist takes as inborn.

To exhibit the explanatory power of the rationalist hypothesis, we must describe a model which specifies just how the universal features of language are imparted to speakers' internal representation of the rules of particular languages. Such a model
will be the alternative to the empiricist model in which such
rules are conceived of as acquired by inductive generalization
and association, and it will provide an account, not provided
by classical rationalist discussions, of the steps by which these
rules become part of a person's linguistic competence.

Chomsky has offered a conception of such a model.[6] He
conceives of language acquisition as a process of implicit theory
construction similar in character to theory construction in
science but without the explicit intellectual operations of the
latter. According to Chomsky's conception, the child formulates hypotheses about the rules of the linguistic description of
the language whose sentences he is hearing, derives predictions
from such hypotheses about the linguistic structure of sentences
he will hear in the future, checks these predictions against the
new sentences he encounters, eliminates those hypotheses that
are contrary to the evidence, and evaluates those that are not
eliminated by a simplicity principle which selects the simplest
as the best hypothesis concerning the rules underlying the
sentences he has heard and will hear. This process of hypothesis

construction, verification, and evaluation repeats itself until the child matures past the point where the language acquisition device operates.[7]

Chomsky's conception can be combined with the rationalist hypothesis to yield the model of language acquisition we require. The theory of language contains essentially four types of universals, as we indicated above. First, there are *formal universals*. These specify the form of the system of rules that comprise a linguistic description, the form of the rules of the phonological, syntactic, and semantic components, and the form of the rules within each of these components. Second, there are *substantive universals*. These specify the theoretical vocabulary to be employed in formulating particular rules of the form prescribed by the formal universals. The formal and substantive universals together permit the construction of a set of possible hypotheses about the linguistic description of a language. This set contains the systems of rules for each actual, natural language as well as systems for indefinitely many possible, but not actual, natural languages. Thus, we can regard this set of hypotheses, which we may refer to as "initial hypotheses," as those from which the child selects in arriving at his internalization of the rules of his language. But, so far, we have provided no conception of the mechanism by which the utterances in the input to the language acquisition device are utilized to produce a system of rules of the prescribed form and employing the prescribed constructs, i.e., no way to select among the initial hypotheses. To accomplish this, we must consider the other two types of principles in the theory of language. In the methodology for choosing optimal linguistic descriptions is a *simplicity metric* which evaluates alternative systems of rules of the proper kind to determine which is preferable on the basis of the sort of methodological considerations appropriate to the choice of one hypothesis as the best of those equally well supported by a body of evidence. This metric is a function F such that the value $F(H_i)$, where H_i is one of the initial hypotheses, is an integer assigned to H_i determining its preference ranking with respect to $H_1, H_2, \ldots, H_{i-1}, H_{i+1}, \ldots$, where the lower the integer, the higher the position of H_i on the ranking. Since the rationalist hypothesis states that each principle in the theory of language is represented in the structure of the language acquisition device, this simplicity metric is also part of the innate language forming equipment of the child. With this metric the child can rank the set of initial hypotheses prior to any linguistic experience, and thus can obtain a best hypothesis or set of best hypotheses given no evidence about the language community he is in. Fourth, and finally, there is, also in the methodology for choosing an optimal linguistic description, a *structure assignment algorithm* which converts the derivations of sentences that can be constructed from syntactic rules into phrase markers. The structure assignment algorithm provides the language acquisition device with a means of deriving predictions about sentences from the highest ranked initial hypotheses: each such hypothesis contains syntactic rules which generate derivations and these can be converted into phrase markers by the algorithm. If the device also has a method by which it can decide whether the observable structure of input sentences verifies or refutes the predictions made by the phrase markers constructed by the algorithm, it can eliminate initial hypotheses that do not predict correctly.[8] Note that the predictions about an input sentence are not confined to syntactic predictions, any more than the syntactic predictions are confined to those made by the final derived phrase markers. For, given the underlying and final derived phrase marker for a sentence, predictions about its semantic and phonological properties can be obtained without the aid of a further algorithm because the rules of the semantic and phonological components operate directly on the phrase markers that result from the application of the structure assignment algorithm. The child's internalization of the rules of a language *at any given time* is the maximally simplest hypothesis all of whose predictions are compatible with the facts about the linguistic structure of the sentences available to him from his experience *up to that time*.

NOTES

1. E.g., the law of effect or pattern of presentations, as in C. B. Ferster and B. F. Skinner, *Schedules of Reinforcement* (New York: Appleton-Century-Crofts, 1957).

2. G. W. Leibniz, *New Essays Concerning Human Understanding,* trans. and ed., A. C. Langley (La Salle. Ill., Open Court, 1949).

3. Cf. N. Chomsky, "Current Issues in Linguistic Theory" and "A Transformational Approach to Syntax," in J. A. Fodor and J. J. Katz, eds, *The Structure of Language: Readings in the Philosophy of Language* (Englewood Cliffs, N. J.: Prentice-Hall, 1964); also P. M. Postal, *Constituent Structure,* provides a discussion of taxonomic linguistics; for behaviorist learning theory, a convenient survey is provided by W. K. Estes et al., *Modern Learning Theory* (New York: Appleton-Century-Crofts, 1954).

4. Cf. Noam Chomsky, *Syntactic Structures* (The Hague: Mouton, 1957), nn. 3 and 7 of chap. 6.

5. In the sense in which N. Campbell, *What is Science?* (New York: Dover Publications, 1952) speaks of the explanation of laws.

6. N. Chomsky, "A Review of B. F. Skinner's *Verbal Behavior"* in J. A. Fodor and J. J. Katz, eds. *The Structure of Language: Readings in the Philosophy of Language.*

7. The ability to acquire a language in the effortless, natural way in which children do appears to terminate at about puberty, after which the more rote-like method of learning familiar to those who have to learn a second language as an adult is required to produce fluency. Thus, this ability of the child's is much like the abilities of various animals described as 'imprinting' with respect to the existence of a 'critical period.' Cf. C Schiller, ed., *Instinctive Behavior* (New York: International Universities Press, 1957), especially the papers by Lorenz and Tinbergen.

8. Thus, the role of experience is primarily to provide the data against which predictions and thus hypotheses are judged. Experience serves not to provide the things to be copied by the mind, as in the empiricist's account, but to help eliminate false hypotheses about the rules of a language.

10

Psychological Aspects of the Theory of Syntax

GILBERT H. HARMAN

Noam Chomsky contends that the theory of transformational grammar has important implications for certain psychological and philosophical issues. In particular, he attempts to show what these implications are for the theory of what it is to know a language and for the dispute between "rationalism" and "empiricism" taken as theories of how one learns a language. Part I of this paper discusses his claim that in describing what it is to know a language we must make use of the notion of linguistic "competence." Part II discusses his claim that "empiricists" cannot give an adequate explanation of language learning. In both parts I try to show that Chomsky's claims rest on serious confusions and cannot be accepted as they stand.

I

Chomsky distinguishes a person's linguistic *competence* from his *performance*. Competence is "the speaker-hearer's knowledge of his language." Performance is "the actual use of language in concrete situations" (4). Now, there are two senses in which a person may be said to have knowledge of a language.

* In writing this paper I have benefited from suggestions of Richard Jeffrey and Thomas Nagel.

Following Chomsky, I use the word "grammar" in a wide sense to include not only syntax but also phonology and semantics. Page references in the text are to Chomsky, *Aspects of the Theory of Syntax* (Cambridge, Mass.: MIT Press, 1965).

Reprinted with the kind permission of Professor Harman and the editor from *The Journal of Philosophy* LXIV (February 2, 1967), 75-87.

A typical speaker, call him "Smith," knows how to understand other speakers of his language and to communicate with them, although he cannot describe his language very well. Smith has knowledge of the language in one sense. A linguist, Jones, knows about the language, knows that it is described by certain rules, etc. Jones has knowledge of the language in a second sense. Is competence supposed to be what Smith has or what Jones has?

Chomsky says, "A grammar of a language purports to be a description of the ideal speaker's intrinsic competence" (4). He also says that a grammar is *descriptively adequate* to the extent that it correctly describes the intrinsic competence of the native speaker" (24). How can a grammar describe Smith's competence? If competence is knowing how to speak and understand a language and if the grammar describes that language, then the grammar indirectly describes Smith's competence as "the competence to speak and understand the language described by this grammar." But Chomsky does not refer only to such indirect description of Smith's competence. He also takes a grammar to describe competence as the knowledge that the language is described by the rules of the grammar. Since a speaker can rarely, if ever, say what the rules of his language are, Chomsky introduces a theory of *unconscious* knowledge about the language:

Obviously every speaker of a language has mastered and internalized a generative grammar that expresses his knowledge of the language. This is not to say that he is aware of the rules of the grammar or even that he can become aware of them, or that his statements about his intuitive knowledge are necessarily accurate. Any interesting generative grammar will be dealing, for the most part, with mental processes that are far beyond the level of actual or even potential consciousness (8).

Thus he says a grammar is "a theory of linguistic intuition" (19, 24, 26-27), where linguistic intuition is taken to be the same as "tacit competence" (26-27). A grammar specifies a speaker's "tacit knowledge" (19,11,27) or his "intuitive knowledge" (21). A speaker has "internalized" a grammar (8,21,24); i.e., he has "developed an internal representation of a system of rules" (25); he "has developed and internally represented a generative grammar (25); he has arrived "at an internal representation of a generative system" (46).

Chomsky does not intend these remarks to be taken overly literally; and it is important to see this. Taken literally, he would be saying that we are to explain how it is that Smith knows how to speak and understand a language by citing his knowledge of another more basic language in which he has (unconsciously) "internally represented" the rules of the first language. (It does not seem to make sense to assume that Smith can represent rules without representing them in some language.) The main problem with such a literal interpretation of these remarks would be the implausibility of the resulting view. How for example, would Smith understand the more basic language? In order to avoid either an infinite regress or a vicious circle, one would have to suppose that Smith can understand at least one language directly, without unconsciously knowing the rules for that language. But if this is admitted, there is no reason why Smith cannot know directly the language he speaks. Thus, literally interpreted, Chomsky's theory would almost certainly be false.

Similarly, on a literal interpretation of what Chomsky says about learning language, Wittgenstein's remark about Augustine would apply to Chomsky's theory.

And now, I think we can say: Augustine describes the learning of human language as if the child came into a strange country and did not understand the language of the country; that is, as if it already had a language, only not this one.[1]

Thus Chomsky says that the child learns a language on the basis of certain "primary linguistic data" (25). He proposes that

... the child approaches the data with the presumption that they are drawn from a language of a certain antecedently well defined type, his problem being to determine which of the (humanly) possible languages is that of the community in which he is placed (27). ... On the basis of such data, the child constructs a grammar. ... To learn a language, then, the child must ... possess a linguistic theory that specifies the form of a grammar of a possible human language (25). ... What are the initial assumptions that the child brings to language learning [?] (27). ... A child who is capable of language learning must have ... a technique for representing input signals ... a way of representing structural information about those signals (30).

Taken literally, Chomsky would be proposing that, before he learned any language, Smith had made a presumption about certain data; he had set himself a task; he possessed a theory; he made assumptions; he had techniques of representation. This would be possible only on the absurd assumption that before he learned his first natural language Smith already knew another language. So we could not accept Chomsky's proposal if it were to be taken literally.

In order to see just how Chomsky's remarks are to be interpreted, we must first understand how he conceives a theory of linguistic performance. He thinks there is a connection between theories of linguistic performance and "performance models":

To my knowledge, the only concrete results that have been achieved and the only clear suggestions that have been put forth concerning the theory of performance, outside of phonetics, have come from studies of performance models that incorporate generative grammars of specific kinds. . . . (10) In general it seems that the study of performance models incorporating generative grammars may be a fruitful study; furthermore, it is difficult to imagine any other basis on which a theory of performance might develop (15).

Such a model would be a device that duplicates certain aspects of the performance of what is modeled. Chomsky wants a theory of performance to describe how a model functions, but he does not require that the theory specify a physical realization of the model. Similarly, one might describe a computer by its program or flow chart without having to say whether it had vacuum tubes or transistors. Because of the abstract nature of the description of performance models and also because of a contrast he wants to make with "behavioristic theories," Chomsky calls theories incorporating performance models "mentalistic." His way of putting the point just made is:

The mentalist . . . need make no assumptions about the possible physiological basis for the mental reality that he studies. In particular, he need not deny that there is such a basis. One would guess, rather, that it is the mentalistic studies that will ultimately be of greatest value for the investigations of neurophysiological mechanisms, since they alone are concerned with determining abstractly the properties that such mechanisms must exhibit and the functions they must perform (193).

Similarly, Chomsky identifies a theory of language learning with the construction of a language "acquisition model":

To facilitate the clear formulation of deeper questions, it is useful to consider the abstract problem of constructing an "acquisition model" for language, that is, a theory of language learning or grammar construction (24-25).

Furthermore, it would seem that Chomsky intends the psychological remarks he makes about a child's learning of language to be interpreted as about such a model. The sentence immediately following that just cited is:

clearly, a child who has learned a language has developed an internal representation of a system of rules that determine how sentences are to be formed, used, and understood (25).

A few pages later he is more explicit:

Let us consider with somewhat greater care just what is involved in the construction of an "acquisition model" for language. A child who is capable of language learning must have . . . a technique for representing input signals [etc.] (30).

Sometimes Chomsky speaks of what the child must do. At other times he speaks of what a "language acquisition device" must do. For example,

This device must search through the set of possible hypotheses . . . and must select grammars that are compatible with the primary linguistic data (32).

Therefore, it seems reasonable to interpret Chomsky's psychological remarks as remarks about psychological models: models of linguistic performance and models of linguistic acquisition.

A model is a device duplicating certain aspects of behavior. But whose behavior, and what aspects? Chomsky speaks of a permformance model and a linguistic-acquisition model. These must be models of speakers rather than of linguists, of Smith rather than of Jones. Thus a performance model must duplicate something of what Smith does as an adult speaker, his communicating with others, etc., rather than something of what Jones does as a linguist, his giving analyses of particular sentences, etc. A language-acquisition model must duplicate Smith's ability, as a child, to learn a language after being exposed to it, rather than Jones's ability, as an adult, to discover a grammar of a language after some study of it.

An ideal performance model would be able to participate in

conversations with human speakers. If linguistic behavior includes appropriate responses to perception, such as answering questions about what is seen, and if it also includes following orders, then a performance model would have to duplicate a considerable amount of a person's behavior. Furthermore, since most thinking is in language and is made possible by language, we might expect a linguistic-performance model to duplicate the kind of intelligent behavior that depends on such thought. In that case, there will be little difference between a linguistic-performance model and a general psychological model of a person.

Chomsky sometimes speaks as if a speaker-hearer, like Smith, knows (unconsciously) the grammatical rules of his language, although in fact typically only a linguist, like Jones, would know what these rules are. Chomsky also suggests that in learning his language Smith made use of a linguistic theory, although in fact only someone like Jones would have such a theory. Can such remarks be interpreted in terms of psychological models? Do we want the models to contain grammatical or linguistic theories?

It is clear that no good model of performance or linguistic acquisition will produce structural descriptions of sentences or grammatical theories of language as final output meant to duplicate Smith's linguistic behavior. But models might produce such things internally in the process of duplicating Smith's linguistic behavior. In interpreting sentences, the performance model might use rewrite rules to form structural descriptions of sentences to be interpreted. Such a performance model would contain a representation of the rules of the grammar. When Chomsky says the speaker has internalized a representation of grammatical rules, we may interpret him to mean that a performance model contains such a representation. Similarly, a linguistic-acquisition model must duplicate language-learning behavior. Such a model would be a device that, when exposed to a particular language, comes to be a performance model of a speaker of that language. Now, since we have taken the performance model to contain a representation of the relevant rules, the language-acquisition device must in part produce a representation of the relevant grammar when the device is exposed to a natural language.

A very general sketch of a performance model might be as in figure I. Reasoning, etc., would be carried out in such a model using semantically interpreted structural descriptions (s.d.'s) of sentences rather than the sentences themselves. I have artificially separated things, e.g., by distinguishing perceptual input from phonetic input, in order to bring out some of the places where representations of grammatical rules might appear in such a model. This is somewhat misleading in that it

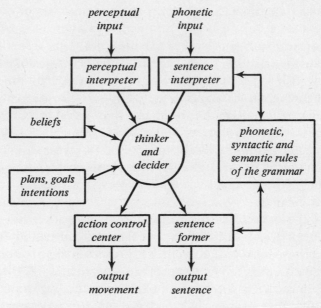

Figure I

disguises the influence of language on perception and thought, but this artificiality does not affect the following discussion.

Some of Chomsky's remarks about a speaker-hearer can now be interpreted. When he says a speaker has "an internal representation of a system of rules" (25), etc., he means that a performance model contains such a representation. (It is not obvious that every conceivable performance model need contain such a representation; but we have seen how a very natural performance model would.) Nevertheless, it is still not clear how to make sense of Chomsky's talk about linguistic competence, the speaker-hearer's "intuitive knowledge" of the rules of the grammar of his language. Should we say that the performance model, or some physical realization of the performance model, has tacit or intuitive knowledge of certain rules? What would that mean? Perhaps it would mean only that these rules are represented in the model.

In this connection it is useful to compare a linguistic-performance model with a model of a bicycle rider. The cyclist must keep balanced on the bicycle. Exactly what he needs to do in order to retain his balance will be dictated by certain principles of mechanics that he himself is unaware of. We might imagine that a model of a cyclist would contain representations of the relevant principles of mechanics and that it uses these principles in calculating what needs to be done so as to retain balance. Then, following Chomsky's model, we might say that the cyclist has an internal representation of the principles of mechanics. Should we go on to say that every cyclist has an intuitive or tacit knowledge of the principles of mechanics? This does not seem an illuminating way of talking about cyclists; and Chomsky's remarks about "tacit competence" (26-27) do not seem to provide an illuminating way of talking about speakers of a language.

I believe that Chomsky's notion of linguistic competence is best seen as the result of two separate but interacting factors. First Chomsky's use of the phrase 'tacit competence' betrays a confusion between the two sorts of knowledge of a language. Competence is knowledge in the sense of knowing how to do something; it is ability. It is not the sort of knowledge that can properly be described as "tacit." Tacit knowledge must be knowledge that something is the case. Second, and this abets the above confusion, speakers of a language do have something that might be thought of as tacit knowledge about the language. Thus, speakers can be brought to judge that certain sentences are ambiguous, that certain sentences are paraphrases of each other, or that certain strings of words are not grammatically acceptable. Such judgments are often taken as representing a speaker-hearer's "linguistic intuition"; and it is true, as Chomsky says, that for all practical purposes "there is no way to avoid the traditional assumption that a speaker-hearer's linguistic intuition is the ultimate standard that determines the accuracy of any proposed grammar, linguistic theory, or operational test" (21), *provided that 'linguistic intuition' refers to the intuitive judgments of speakers.* But notice that this sort of intuitive or unconscious knowledge is not the knowledge of particular rules of a transformational grammar. It is, as it were, knowledge about the output of such a grammar. Chomsky's tacit competence is, however, supposed to be knowledge of the particular rules of the grammar, the rules that are explicitly represented in a performance model. Therefore, linguistic competence cannot be identified with that type of unconscious knowledge speakers actually have. And it is only by identifying these two quite different things that Chomsky has been able to disguise his confusion between the two ways of knowing a language.

Thus, Chomsky's use of the phrase "linguistic competence" embodies at least two confusions. He confuses knowing how with knowing that; and he confuses knowing that certain sentences are grammatically unacceptable, ambiguous, etc., with knowing the rules of the grammar by virtue of which sentences are unacceptable, ambiguous, etc. It follows that he has not shown the need for a notion resembling his "linguistic competence."

II

For philosophers, Chomsky's most interesting claim is that facts about language support what he calls a "rationalist" theory of language learning as against an "empiricist" theory. In particular, he claims that transformational linguistics is incompatible with "empiricism." Unfortunately, much of his discussion of language learning is infected with his confusion about "linguistic competence." When these confusions are straightened out, it becomes clear that Chomsky gives us no reason to accept his claim about "empiricism."

For Chomsky, a theory of language learning concerns the linguistic-acquisition device. This device enables a potential performance model to become the performance model of a given language (e.g., as in figure I) when exposed to people speaking that language. The device does this by seeing that the appropriate grammatical rules become represented in the performance model. How does the device do this?

According to Chomsky the device has available to it what he calls "primary linguistic data." The device considers various hypotheses about the grammar of the language, selecting the hypothesis best confirmed by the data.

This device must search through the set of possible hypotheses and must select grammars that are compatible with the primary linguistic data. . . . The device would then select one of these potential grammars by [what Chomsky calls] the evaluation measure (32).

So the linguistic-acquisition device, as it were, *infers* that a certain grammar is the grammar of the language, given that the device has certain primary linguistic data.

This is, of course, highly oversimplified. Chomsky notes:

Obviously, to construct an actual theory of language learning, it would be necessary to face several other very serious questions involving, for example, the gradual development of an appropriate hypothesis, simplification of the technique for finding a compatible hypothesis, and the continual accretion of linguistic skill and knowledge and the deepening of the analysis of language structure that may continue long after the basic form of the language has been mastered. What I am describing is an idealization in which only the moment of acquisition of the correct grammar is considered (202).

But even with this qualification, there is little to be said for the view that the machine's problem is that of inferring something from data. Consider, for example, what these data must be. As we shall see, Chomsky speaks as if the data were sample sentences of the language and possibly some other information. This is clearly wrong. Chomsky elsewhere in the book correctly points out: "A record of natural speech will show numerous false starts, deviations from rules, changes of plan in mid-course and so on" (4). The "data" a linguistic-acquisition device has will include "a record of natural speech" plus information about how the device can get along in conversation, etc., with the provisional rules it has. It is hard to think of the device as making an inference unless one acknowledges that it not only infers what the grammar is but also infers a general theory of performance. What can be inferred from such data must provide an explanation of the data. And a hypothesis about grammar will not be sufficient for such an explanation. However, we have not envisioned the device as ever containing any representation of a theory of performance. We have envisioned it as coming to contain only a representation of grammatical rules.

To "infer" the grammar from what "data" it really has, the device must already "know" something about the theory of performance. That is, the device must already have detailed information about the model represented in figure I, above, excepting information about the actual grammatical rules represented in such a model. Since the device is taken as attached to a performance model, we may think of what it needs as "self-knowledge." Given a knowledge of its structure or of the structure of the performance model to which it is attached, given the information that models of other speakers of the language have the same structure, and given the "primary linguistic data," its problem is to discover the rules of grammar represented in the models of these other speakers.

This is certainly an artificial way of looking at the linguistic-acquisition device. We have seen in part I how misleading it is to say that a model has *knowledge* of those principles or statements represented in the model. What can it mean to ascribe "knowledge" to such a device, if we cannot even say that the knowledge in question is represented anywhere in the device? Perhaps we ought to suppose that the structure of the attached potential performance model itself represents the fact that performance models have such structure. Or perhaps we ought to suppose that the linguistic-acquisition device has an explicit representation of the structure of performance models. Chomsky does not even consider this problem. In any event, there is no reason to suppose any reasonable linguistic-acquisition device need make use of such representations. Surely it is more accurate to think of the device as a feedback mechanism that adjusts the rules represented in the attached potential performance model so as to maximize the way in which the resulting model gets along in conversation, etc.

Nevertheless, we must think of the linguistic-acquisition device as making inferences if there is to be any possibliity of making sense of Chomsky's argument against "empiricism." Let us assume, then, that to say the device has information available to it is to say this information is explicitly represented in the device. Chomsky characterizes two positions on language as follows. The "empiricist" believes that the linguistic-acquisition device can arrive at correct grammatical rules by inductive inference from the primary linguistic data. The "rationalist" denies this and holds that the linguistic-acquisition device requires further "information in addition to the primary linguistic data. Such further information consists of what Chomsky calls "innate ideas and principles" (48).

Whether or not empiricism, so defined, is defensible depends upon what is to count as inductive inference. On some interpretation of "inductive inference," empiricism can be ruled out directly, without appeal to transformational linguistics. On other interpretations, empiricism would not be incompatible with transformational linguistics. However, there does not seem to be any reasonable interpretation on which empiricism survives direct and relatively a priori refutation but is refuted by the appeal to tranformational linguistics.

For example, suppose that inductive inference is taken as a process of generalization sharply to be distinguished from "theoretical inference." Suppose this distinction is made in such a way that, from primary linguistic data ("a record of natural speech," etc.) induction permits only rather weak generalization about unobserved speech and does not permit any inference about the theory of performance. Now, the linguistic-acquisition device must have information about the theory of performance if it is to infer the grammar from the primary linguistic data. The empiricist's device, by definition, does not have this information built into it, so it must infer a theory of performance from the data it has. If "induction" does not permit this inference, then the empiricist's device cannot even begin to discover the rules of grammar and is ruled out even before any appeal is made to the facts of trasformationsl linguistics.

Chomsky must permit the empiricist's device at some point to have information about the structure of a performance model, given that he wants the failure of the device to be due to the facts of transformational linguistics. So, he must either (a) allow "induction" to include at least some theoretical inference or (b) maintain a strict distinction between induction and theoretical inference but permit the empiricist's device some initial information about performance models. Alternative (b) is not very promising. Where would one draw the line between what information the device can have and what it cannot have? Furthermore, given the emphasis in contemporary empiricism on the importance of theories in science, it would be quite unrealistic to define the empiricist's linguistic-acquisition device such that it could not make use of theoretical inference. Thus, Chomsky identifies Quine (47, 51) as one of the empiricists he has in mind; and Quine has certainly belabored the role of theory in any adequate account of human knowledge. Therefore, the empiricist device must be allowed to infer the truth of theories as well as generalizations, where this is appropriate, appropriateness being determined by certain principles of induction in a wide sense of "induction."

The same conclusion follows whether or not one agrees that it is necessary for the device to infer a whole theory of performance. In any event the device will need principles of theoretical inference. Weak principles of generalization would not even permit the inference of a corpus of sentences from a record of natural speech. Given the "data" possessed by the device, the notion of *sentence* is a theoretical notion.

Everything now depends on exactly what the principles of induction turn out to be. Empiricism cannot be refuted until they are specified. A resourceful empiricist, knowing some inductive logic, will deny that information from linguistics refutes his theory; instead he will take this information to reveal something about the correct set of inductive procedures. We know from Goodman's "New Riddle of Induction"[2] that any consistent set of inductive principles must favor certain generalizations over others. Therefore, one cannot support rationalism by showing that only languages with certain types of grammar (e.g., tranformational grammar) are learnable, since an empiricist could reply that this shows only that the principles of induction used (which must be biased in favor of some hypotheses) are biased in favor of grammars of the designated types.

Chomsky's statement of his argument proceeds without mention of any of the complexities we have been considering. He asks "can the inductive procedures (in the empiricist case)...

succeed in producing grammars within the given constraints of time and access, and within the range of observed uniformity of output?" (54) The answer to this question must depend on what counts as a legitimate inductive procedure. There is an enormous philosophical literature on induction. Chomsky ignores this literature. Instead he says,

The only proposals that are explicit enough to support serious study are those that have been developed within taxonomic linguistics. It seems to have been demonstrated beyond any reasonable doubt that, quite apart from any question of feasibility, methods of the sort that have been studied in taxonomic linguistics are intrinsically incapable of yielding the systems of grammatical knowledge that must be attributed to the speaker of a language (54)

In this argument Chomsky muddles together all the things we have been concerned to distinguish.

First, the procedures of taxonomic linguistics are not relevant here. As Chomsky notes (52), taxonomic procedures are designed to determine the grammar of a language from a corpus of sentences of that language. But primary linguistic data do not consist in such a corpus. They contain a "record of natural speech" plus information about how the performance model has been getting along in conversations, etc., given its provisional grammatical rules. There is no way to apply taxonomic procedures to this sort of data.

Second, "taxonomic principles of segmentation and classification" (47) represent an anti-theoretical position in linguistics, a position that would sharply distinguish inductive generalization from theoretical "speculation" so as to do without the latter. As we have seen, if an empiricist is taken to deny the role of theory, the empiricist's linguistic-acquisition device cannot even get started, since its first task must be to formulate a theory of performance. This means the empiricist can be refuted without the need of any appeal to the facts of transformational linguistics.

Third, Chomsky thinks that taxonomic methods cannot yield correct grammars because they yield only "taxonomic," i.e., phrase-structure, grammars, and because the theory of phrase-structure grammar has supposedly been refuted by transformational linguistics.[3] But it is unclear to me that taxonomic principles of segmentation and classification would work even if

the theory of phrase-structure grammar were right. I suspect
the principles would not work. The only connection I can see
between taxonomic procedures and phrase-structure grammar is
a tenuous historical one. People who have suggested taxonomic
procedures are among those Chomsky takes to subscribe to
the theory of phrase-structure grammar.

Fourth, it is not clear that taxonomic principles of segmentation and classification are the only empiricist proposals
"explicit enough to support serious study" (54). Harris and
Hiż's method of exploiting co-occurrence relationships is similar
in spirit to the taxonomic procedures Chomsky is talking about;
yet the method of co-occurrence cannot be associated with the
theory of phrase-structure grammar. If anything, it must be
associated with the theory of transformational grammar.[4]

Fifth, even if taxonomic procedures were of the relevant
sort, if no other explicit empiricist procedures had been proposed, and if Chomsky could demonstrate the inadequacy of
taxonomic procedures, that would not be enough to refute
empiricism. Chomsky would have to show that no explicit
empiricist procedure could be adequate. But, given the resourceful empiricist mentioned above, it does not seem possible that
Chomsky could show any such thing, no matter what the facts
about language turned out to be.

In short, Chomsky's discussion of rationalism and empiricism is as confused as his discussion of linguistic competence.
He has certainly not shown that the facts of transformational
linguistics defeat an empiricist theory of language learning.

NOTES

1. Ludwig Wittgenstein, *Philosophical Investigations* (New York:
Macmillan, 1953), pp. 15-16.
2. Nelson Goodman, *Fact, Fiction, and Forecast* (Cambridge, Mass.:
Harvard University Press, 1955).
3. I do not believe in this refutation. See my articles: "Generative
Grammars without Transformation Rules," *Language,* XXXIX (1963),
597-616; and "The Adequacy of Context-free Phrase-structure Grammars,"
to appear in *Word.*
4. Zellig S. Harris, "Co-occurrence and Transformation in Linguistic

Structure," *Language,* XXXIII (1957), 293-340. Henry Hiż, "Congrammaticality, Batteries of Transformations and Grammatical Categories," in Jakobson, ed., *Structure of Language and Its Mathematical Aspects, Proceedings of the Twelfth Symposium in Applied Mathematics* (Providence, R.I.: American Mathematical Society, 1961), pp. 43-50.

11

Linguistics and Philosophy

NOAM CHOMSKY

One might adopt the following research strategy for the study of cognitive processes in humans. A person is presented with a physical stimulus that he interprets in a certain way. Let us say that he constructs a certain "percept" that represents certain of his conclusions (unconscious, in general) about the source of stimulation. To the extent that we can characterize this percept, we can proceed to investigate the process of interpretation. We can, in other words, proceed to develop a model of perception that takes stimuli as inputs and assigns percepts as "outputs," a model that will meet certain given empirical conditions on the actual pairing of stimuli with interpretations of these stimuli. For example, the person who understands sentences

　　(1) John is certain that Bill will leave

and

　　(2) John is certain to leave

knows (whether he is aware of it or not) that in the case of (2) it is a proposition that is certain and in the case of (1) it is a person who is certain of something, in a very different sense of "certain." If we are interested in studying perception of language, specifically, the process by which sentences are understood, we can begin by describing the percepts in such a way as to bring out this difference, as we did in proposing that

(1") $[_S[_{NP}$ John] $[_{VP}$ is $[_{AP}$ certain $[_S$ that $[_{NP}$ Bill] $_{VP}$ will leave]]]]]

and

(2") $[_S[_{NP}$ John] $[_{VP}$ is $[_{AP}$ certain] $[_{VP}$ to leave]]],

interpreted in the suggested manner, are essential components of the percept. We can then ask how these percepts are constructed by the hearer, given the input stimuli (1) and (2).

A perceptual model that relates stimulus and percept might incorporate a certain system of beliefs, certain strategies that are used in interpreting stimuli, and other factors—for example, organization of memory. In the case of language, the technical term for the underlying system of beliefs is "grammar," or "generative grammar." A grammar is a system of rules that generates an infinite class of "potential percepts," each with its phonetic, semantic, and syntactic aspects, the class of structures that constitutes the language in question. The percepts themselves are first-order constructs; we determine their properties by experiment and observation. The grammar that underlies the formation of percepts is a second-order construct. To study it, we must abstract away from the other factors that are involved in the use and understanding of language, and concentrate on the knowledge of language[1] that has been internalized in some manner by the language user.

Concentrating on this system, we can then inquire into the means by which it was acquired and the basis for its acquisition. We can, in other words, attempt to construct a second model, a learning model, which takes certain data as input and gives, as "output," the system of beliefs that is one part of the internal structure of the perceptual model. The "output," in this case, is represented in the "final state" of the organism that has acquired this system of beliefs; we are asking, then, how this final state was achieved, through the interplay of innate factors, maturational processes, and organism-environment interaction.

In short, we can begin by asking "what is perceived" and move from there to a study of perception. Focusing on the role of belief (in our case, knowledge of language) in perception, we can try to characterize "what is learned" and move from

there to the study of learning. One might, of course, decide to
study some other topic, or to proceed in some different manner.
Thus much of modern psychology has decided, for reasons that
do not impress me, to limit itself to the study of behavior and
control of behavior. I do not want to pursue the matter here,
but I will merely state my own opinion: that this approach has
proven quite barren, and that it is irrational to limit one's ob-
jectives in this way. One cannot hope to study learning or
perception in any useful way by adhering to methodological
strictures that limit the conceptual apparatus so narrowly as to
disallow the concept "what is perceived" and the concept "what
is learned."

I think that interesting conclusions can be reached when
one studies human language along the lines just outlined. In
the areas of syntax and phonetics at least, a plausible general
account can be given of the system of representation for percepts in any human language. Furthermore, there has been substantial progress in constructing generative grammars that express the knowledge of language that is the "output" of a
learning model and a fundamental component of a perceptual
model. There is, I believe, good evidence that a generative
grammar for a human language contains a system of base rules
of a highly restricted sort, a set of grammatical transformations
that map the deep structures formed in accordance with base
rules onto surface structures, and a set of phonological rules
that assign phonetic interpretations, in a universal phonetic
alphabet, to surface structures. Furthermore, there is also good
evidence that certain highly restrictive principles determine
the functioning of these rules, conditions of ordering and organization of a complex and intricate sort. There is a considerable literature dealing with these matters, and I will not try to
review it here. I only wish to emphasize that there is no a
priori necessity for a language to be organized in the highly
specific manner proposed in these investigations. Hence if this
theory of linguistic structure is correct, or near correct, some
nontrivial problems arise for the theory of human learning.
Specifically, we must ask how on the basis of the limited data
available to him, the child is able to construct a grammar of
the sort that we are led to ascribe to him, with its particular
choice and arrangement of rules and with the restrictive principles of application of such rules. What, in other words, must

be the internal structure of a learning model that can duplicate
this achievement. Evidently, we must try to characterize innate
structure in such a way as to meet two kinds of empirical conditions. First, we must attribute to the organism, as an innate
property, a structure rich enough to account for the fact that
the postulated grammar is acquired on the basis of the given
conditions of access to data; second, we must not attribute to
the organism a structure so rich as to be incompatible with the
known diversity of languages. We cannot attribute knowledge
of English to the child as an innate property, because we know
that he can learn Japanese as well as English. We cannot attribute to him merely the ability to form associations, or to apply
the analytic procedures of structural linguistics, because (as is
easy to show when these proposals are made precise) the structures they yield are not those that we must postulate as generative grammars. Within the empirical bounds just stated, we
are free to construct theories of innate structure and to test
them in terms of their empirical consequences. To say this is
merely to define the problem. Substantive questions arise only
when a specific theory is proposed.

By investigating sentences and their structural descriptions,
speech signals and the percepts to which they give rise, we can
arrive at detailed conclusions regarding the generative grammar
that is one fundamental element in linguistic performance, in
speech and understanding of speech. Turning then to the next
higher level of abstraction, we raise the question of how this
generative grammar is acquired. From a formal point of view,
the grammar that is internalized by every normal human can be
described as a theory of his language, a theory of a highly intricate and abstract form that determines, ultimately, a connection between sound and meaning by generating structural descriptions of sentences ("potential percepts"), each with its
phonetic, semantic, and syntactic aspects. From this point of
view, one can describe the child's acquisition of knowledge of
language as a kind of theory construction. Presented with
highly restricted data, he constructs a theory of the language
of which this data is a sample (and, in fact, a highly degenerate sample, in the sense that much of it must be excluded as
irrelevant and incorrect—thus the child learns rules of grammar
that identify much of what he has heard as ill-formed, inaccurate and inappropriate). The child's ultimate knowledge

of language obviously extends far beyond the data presented to
him. In other words, the theory he has in some way developed
has a predictive scope of which the data on which it is based
constitute a negligible part. The normal use of language characteristically involves new sentences, sentences that bear no
point-by-point resemblance or analogy to those in the child's
experience. Furthermore, the task of constructing this system
is carried out in a remarkably similar way by all normal language learners, despite wide differences in experience and ability.
The theory of human learning must face these facts.

I think that these facts suggest a theory of human intelligence that has a distinctly rationalist flavor. Using terms suggested by Peirce, in his lectures on "the logic of abduction," the
problem of the theory of learning is to state the condition that
"gives a rule to abduction and so puts a limit on admissible
hypotheses." If "man's mind has a natural adaptation to imagining correct theories of some kinds," then acquisition of knowledge of a sort that we are considering is possible. The problem
for the psychologist (or linguist) is to formulate the principles
that set a limit to admissible hypotheses. I have made detailed
suggestions in this regard elsewhere, and will not repeat them
here. Roughly, I think it reasonable to postulate that the principles of general linguistics regarding the nature of rules, their
organization, the principles by which they function, the kinds
of representations to which they apply and which they form,
all constitute part of the innate condition that "puts a limit on
admissible hypotheses." If this suggestion is correct, then there
is no more point asking how these principles are learned than
there is in asking how a child learns to breathe, or, for that
matter, to have two arms. Rather, the theory of learning should
try to characterize the particular strategies that a child uses to
determine that the language he is facing is one, rather than
another, of the "admissible languages." When the principles
just alluded to are made precise, they constitute an empirical
assumption about the innate basis for the acquisition of knowledge, an assumption that can be tested in a variety of ways. In
particular, we can ask whether it falls between the bounds
described earlier: that is, does it ascribe a rich enough innate-
structure to account for the acquisition of knowledge, but a
structure not so rich as to be falsified by the diversity of languages. We might also ask many other questions, for example,

how the schema that is proposed as a basis for acquisition of knowledge of language relates to the principles that "give a rule to abduction" in other domains of human (or animal) intelligence.

What I am suggesting is that if we wish to determine the relevance of linguistics to philosophy, we must investigate the conclusions that can be established concerning the nature of language, the ways in which language is used and understood, the basis for its acquisition. I think that these conclusions have interesting consequences for psychological theory, in particular, that they strongly support an account of mental processes that is, in part, familiar, from rationalist speculation about these matters. They support the conclusion that the role of intrinsic organization is very great in perception, and that a highly restrictive initial schema determines what counts as "linguistic experience" and what knowledge arises on the basis of this experience. I also think, and have argued elsewhere, that the empiricist doctrines that have been prevalent in linguistics, philosophy, and psychology in recent years, if formulated in a fairly precise way, can be refuted by careful study of language. If philosophy is what philosophers do, then these conclusions are relevant to philosophy, both in its classical and modern varieties.

At this point, I would like to turn to some of the critical analysis of this point of view that has appeared in the recent philosophical literature. . . .

It seems to me that Hilary Putnam's arguments are inconclusive, primarily, because of certain erroneous assumptions about the nature of the acquired grammars. Specifically, he enormously underestimates, and in part misdescribes, the richness of structure, the particular and detailed properties of grammatical form and organization that must be accounted for by a "language acquisition model," that are acquired by the normal speaker-hearer and that appear to be uniform among speakers and also across languages.

To begin with, Putnam assumes that at the level of sound structure, the only property that can be proposed in universal grammar is that a language has "a short list of phonemes." This uniformity among languages, he argues, requires no elaborate explanatory hypothesis. It can be explained simply in terms of

"such parameters as memory span and memory capacity," and
no "rank Behaviorists" would have denied that these are innate
properties. In fact, however, very strong empirical hypotheses
have been proposed regarding the choice of universal distinctive
features, the form of phonological rules, the ordering and organization of these rules, the relation of syntactic structure to
phonetic representation, none of which can conceivably be
accounted for on grounds of memory limitations. Putnam bases
his account largely on my "Explanatory Models in Linguistics,"
which examines in some detail the principle of cyclic application
of phonological rules, a principle that, if correct, raises some
rather serious problems. We must ask how the child acquires
knowledge of this principle, a feat that is particularly remarkable since, as already noted, much of the evidence that leads
the linguist to posit this principle is drawn from the study of
percepts and is thus not even available to the child. Similar
questions arise with respect to many other aspects of universal
phonology. In any event, if the proposals that have been
elaborated regarding sound structure are correct or near correct,
then the similarities among languages at this level, and the richness of the knowledge acquired by the child, are indeed remarkable facts, and demand an explanation.

Above the level of sound structure, Putnam assumes that
the only significant properties of language are that they have
proper names, that the grammar contains a phrase-structure
component, and that there are rules "abbreviating" sentences
generated by the phrase-structure component. He argues that
the specific character of the phrase-structure component is
determined by the existence of proper names; that the existence
of a phrase-structure component is explained by the fact that
"all the natural measures of complexity of an algorithm . . .
lead to the . . . result" that phrase-structure systems provide
the "algorithms which are 'simplest' for virtually any computing
system," hence also "for naturally evolved 'computing systems'";
that there is nothing surprising in the fact that languages contain
rules of abbreviations. Hence, he concludes, the only innate
conditions that must be postulated are those that apply to all
reasonable "computing systems," and no Behaviorist should feel
any surprise at this.

Each of the three conclusions, however, is vitiated by a

false assumption. First, it is obvious that there are many different phrase-structure grammars consistent with the assumption
that one of the categories is that of proper names. In fact,
there is much dispute at the moment about the general properties of the underlying base system for natural languages; the
dispute is not in the least resolved by the existence of proper
names as a primitive category in many languages.

As to the second point, it is simply untrue that all measures of complexity and speed of computation lead to phrase-
structure rules as the "simplest possible algorithm." The only
existing results that have even an indirect relevance to this
matter are those dealing with context-free phrase-structure
grammars and their automata-theoretic interpretation. Context-
free grammars are a reasonable model for the rules generating
deep structures, when we exclude the lexical items and the
distributional conditions they meet. But even apart from this
fundamental discrepancy, the only existing results relate context-
free grammars to a class of automata called "nondeterministic
pushdown storage automata," and these have no particularly
striking properties insofar as speed or complexity of computation are concerned, and are certainly not "natural" from this
point of view. In terms of time and space conditions on computation, the somewhat similar but not formally related concept
of real-time deterministic automaton would seem to be far
more natural. In short, there are no results demonstrating that
phrase-structure grammars are optimal in any computational
sense (nor, certainly, are there any results dealing with the much
more complex notion of base structure with a context-free
phrase-structure grammar and a lexicon, with much richer
properties, as components).

But there is no point in pursuing this matter, since what
is at stake, in any event, is not the "simplicity" of phrase-structure grammars but rather of transformational grammars that
contain a phrase-structure component, the latter playing a role
in the generation of deep structures. And there is absolutely no
mathematical concept of "ease of computation" or "simplicity
of algorithm" that even suggests that such systems have some
advantage over the various kinds of automata that have been
investigated from this point of view. In fact, these systems

have never really been considered in a strictly mathematical
context, though there are interesting initial attempts to study
some of their formal properties.[2] The source of the confusion
is a misconception on Putnam's part as to the nature of grammatical transformations. These are not, as he supposes, rules that
"abbreviate" sentences generated by phrase-structure rules.
Rather, they are operations that form surface structures from
underlying deep structures, which are generated, in part, by
phrase-structure rules. Although there has been considerable
evolution of theory since the notions of transformational generative grammar were first proposed, one assumption that has
remained constant is that the phrase-structure rules generate
only abstract structures, which are then mapped onto surface
structures by grammatical transformation—the latter being
structure-dependent operations of a peculiar sort that have never
been studied outside of linguistics, in particular, not in any
branch of mathematics with which I am familiar. To show that
transformational grammars are the "simplest possible" one
would have to demonstrate that an optimal computing system
would take a string of symbols as input and determine its
surface structure, the underlying deep structure, and the sequence
of transformational operations that relate these two labeled
bracketings. Nothing known about ease or simplicity of computation gives any reason to suppose that this is true; in fact,
the question has never been raised. One can think of certain
kinds of organization of memory that might be well adapted
to transformational grammars, but this is a different matter
entirely.[3] I would, naturally, assume that there is some more
general basis in human mental structure for the fact (if it is a
fact) that languages have transformational grammars; one of
the primary scientific reasons for studying language is that this
study may provide some insight into general properties of mind.
Given those specific properties, we may then be able to show
that transformational grammars are "natural." This would
constitute real progress, since it would now enable us to raise
the problem of innate conditions on acquisition of knowledge
and belief in a more general framework. But it must be emphasized that, contrary to what Putnam asserts, there is no basis
for assuming that "reasonable computing systems" will naturally

be organized in the specific manner suggested by transformational grammar.

I believe that this disposes of Putnam's main argument,
namely, that there is "nothing surprising," even to a Behaviorist, in the linguistic universals that are now being proposed and
investigated. Let me then turn to his second argument, that
even if there were surprising linguistic universals, they could be
accounted for on a simpler hypothesis than that of an innate
universal grammar, namely, the hypothesis of common origin
of languages. This proposal misrepresents the problem at issue.
As noted earlier, the empirical problem we face is to devise a
hypothesis about initial structure rich enough to account for the
fact that a specific grammar is acquired, under given conditions
of access to data. To this problem, the matter of common
origin of language is quite irrelevant. The grammar has to be discovered by the child on the basis of the data available to him,
through the use of the innate capacities with which he is endowed.
To be concrete, consider again the two examples discussed above:
the association of nominal phrases to base structures and the
cyclic application of phonological rules. The child masters
these principles (if we are correct in our conclusions about
grammar) on the basis of certain linguistic data; he knows nothing about the origin of language and could not make use of
such information if he had it. Questions of common origin
are relevant to the empirical problems we are discussing only in
that the existing languages might not be a "fair sample" of the
"possible languages," in which case we might be led mistakenly
to propose too narrow a schema for universal grammar. This
possibility must be kept in mind, of course, but it seems to me
a rather remote consideration, given the problem that is actually
at hand, namely, the problem of finding a schema rich enough
to account for the development of the grammars that seem
empirically justified. The discovery of such a schema may provide an explanation for the empirically determined universal
properties of language. The existence of these properties, however, does not explain how a specific grammar is acquired by
the child.

Putnam's discussion of the ease of language-learning seems
to me beside the point. The question whether there is a critical

period for language-learning is interesting,[4] but it has little relevance to the problem under discussion. Suppose that Putnam were correct in believing that "certainly . . . 600 hours [of direct method instruction] will enable any adult to speak and read a foreign language with ease." We would then face the problem of explaining how, on the basis of this restricted data, the learner has succeeded in acquiring the specific and detailed knowledge that enables him to use the language with ease, and to produce and understand a range of structures of which the data presented to him constitute a minute sample.

Finally, consider the alternative approach that Putnam suggests to the problem of language-acquisition. He argues that instead of postulating an innate schematism one should attempt to account for this achievement in terms of "general multi-purpose learning strategies." It is these that must be innate, not general conditions on the form of the knowledge that is acquired. Evidently, this is an empirical issue. It would be sheer dogmatism to assert of either of these proposals (or of some particular combination of them) that it *must* be correct. Putnam is convinced, on what grounds he does not say, that the innate basis for the acquisition of language must be identical with that for acquiring any other form of knowledge, that there is nothing "special" about the acquisition of language. A nondogmatic approach to this problem can be pursued, through the investigation of specific areas of human competence, such as language, followed by the attempt to devise a hypothesis that will account for the development of such competence. If we discover that the same "learning strategies" are involved in a variety of cases, and that these suffice to account for the acquired competence, then we will have good reason to believe that Putnam's empirical hypothesis is correct. If, on the other hand, we discover that different innate systems (whether involving schemata or heuristics) have to be postulated, then we will have good reason to believe that an adequate theory of mind will incorporate separate "faculties," each with unique or partially unique properties. I cannot see how one can resolutely insist on one or the other conclusion in the light of the evidence now available to us. But one thing is quite clear: Putnam has no justification for his final conclusion, that "invoking 'Innateness' only postpones the problem of learning; it does not solve it."[5] Invoking an innate representation of universal grammar does solve the problem of learning (at least partially), in this case, if in fact it is true that this is the basis (or part of the basis) for language-acquisition, as it well may be. If, on the other hand, there exist general learning strategies that account for the acquisition of grammatical knowledge, then postulation of an innate representation of universal grammar will not "postpone" the problem of learning, but will rather offer an incorrect solution to this problem. The issue is an empirical one of truth or falsity, not a methodological one of stages of investigation. At the moment, the only concrete proposal that is at all plausible, in my opinion, is the one sketched above. When some "general learning strategy" is suggested, we can look into the relative adequacy of these alternatives, on empirical grounds.

Harman's critique is . . . concerned with the matter of competence and performance. He begins by ascribing to me a view that I have never held, and have explicitly rejected on numerous occasions, namely, that "competence [is] the knowledge that the language is described by the rules of the grammar," and that a grammar describes this "competence." Obviously, it is absurd to suppose that the speaker of the language knows the rules in the sense of being able to state them. Having attributed to me this absurd view, Harman goes on to struggle with all sorts of purported confusions and difficulties of interpretation. But he cites nothing that could possibly be regarded as a basis for attributing to me this view, though he does quote remarks in which I explicitly reject it. Therefore, I will not discuss this part of his argument at all.

In Harman's framework, there are two kinds of knowledge: knowing that and knowing how. Obviously knowledge of a language is not a matter of "knowing that." Therefore, for him, it must be a matter of "knowing how." A typical speaker "knows how to understand other speakers"; his competence is his ability "to speak and understand the language described by [the] grammar" that describes the language. I do not know what Harman means by the locution "knows how to understand," but clearly he is using the term "competence" in a different way from what

I proposed in the work he is reviewing. In my sense of "competence," the ability to speak and understand the language involves not only "competence" (that is, mastery of the generative grammar of the language, tacit knowledge of the language), but also many other factors. In my usage, the grammar is a formal representation of what I have called "competence." I have no objection to Harman's using the term in a different way, but when he insists on supposing that his usage is mine, naturally, only confusion will result. Again, I see no point in tracing in detail the various difficulties into which this misinterpretation leads him.

According to Harman, the "competence to speak and understand the language" is a skill, analogous to the skill of a bicycle rider. Given his insistence that knowledge of language is a matter of "knowing how" (since it is obviously not "knowing that"), this is not an unexpected conclusion. But he suggests no respect in which ability to use a language (let alone the competence, in my sense, that constitutes an element of this ability) is like the ability to ride a bicycle, nor do I see any. The proper conclusion, then, would be that there is no reason to suppose that knowledge of language can be characterized in terms of "knowing how." I therefore see no point in the analogy that he suggests. Knowledge of language is not a skill, a set of habits, or anything of the sort. I see nothing surprising in the conclusion that knowledge of language cannot be discussed in any useful or informative way in this impoverished framework. In general, it does not seem to me true that the concepts "knowing how" and "knowing that" constitute exhaustive categories for the analysis of knowledge. Nor is it surprising that Harman finds it difficult to understand my remarks, or those of anyone else who is concerned with knowledge of language, given that he insists on restricting himself to this framework.

Harman tries to show that there is a fundamental incoherence in my proposal that in acquiring or using knowledge of a language (in developing "an internal representation of a generative system" or making use of it in speaking or understanding speech), the child makes use of an innate schematism that restricts the choice of grammars (in the case of acquisition) or an internalized grammar (in the case of language use). His argument seems to me unclear. As I understand it, it seems to proceed as follows. He argues that this internalized system must be presented in "another more basic language," which the child must come to understand before he can make use of this schematism to learn this language, or before he can make use of the grammar to understand speech. But this, he argues, leads to a vicious circle or an infinite regress. Thus if we were to say that the child knows the "more basic language" directly, without learning, then why not say also that he knows "directly the language he speaks," without learning; a vicious circle. Or, if we say that he must learn the more basic language, then this raises the question how the more basic language is learned, and leads to an infinite regress. This argument is totally invalid. Consider the case of acquisition of language. Even if we assume that the innate schematism must be represented in an "innate language," neither conclusion follows. The child must know this "innate language," in Harman's terms, but it does not follow that he must "speak and understand it" (whatever this might mean) or that he must learn it. All that we need assume is that he can make use of this schematism when he approaches the task of language-learning. So much for the infinite regress. As to the vicious circle, there is a very simple reason why we cannot assume that the child knows the language he speaks directly, without learning, namely, that the assumption is false. We cannot claim that every child is born with a perfect knowledge of English. On the other hand, there is no reason why we should not suppose that the child is born with a perfect knowledge of universal grammar, that is, with a fixed schematism that he uses, in the ways described earlier, in acquiring language. This assumption may be false, but it is quite intelligible. If one insists on describing this knowledge as "direct knowledge of a more basic language," I see no reason to object, so long as we are clear about what we mean, but would merely point out that there is no reason at all to doubt that the child has this direct knowledge. Hence there is no vicious circle, and no infinite regress. Similarly, if we consider the case of language use, there is neither incoherence nor implausibility. There is surely no infinite regress and no vicious circle in the assumption that in

language use (speaking or understanding) the user employs an
internally represented grammar. We can easily construct a model (say, a computer program) that functions in this way. I
therefore fail to see any basis for Harman's belief that there is
an infinite regress or vicious circle inherent in, or even suggested
by this formulation.

In the second part of his paper, Harman turns to my argument that current work in linguistics supports a view of language
and mind that has a distinctly rationalist flavor, and is in conflict with the empiricist views that have dominated the study
of language and mind in recent years. He asserts that to infer
a grammar from data, a model of language-learning must already have detailed information about the theory of performance.
This is an interesting proposal, and it deserves to be developed.
But I cannot go along with his rather dogmatic claim, hardly
argued in the paper, that this approach must necessarily be
correct, and that any other approach must fail to provide any
insight into the problem of acquisition of knowledge. I think
that the work of the past few years on universal grammar does,
in fact, suggest and in part support an interesting, rather classical approach to the problem of how knowledge is acquired. In
the absence of any argument as to why this approach must
fail to be illuminating, I see no reason not to continue with the
investigation of how principles of universal grammar might select a particular grammar on the basis of the data available.

Let us turn now to the issue of rationalist and empiricist
approaches to problems of language and mind. As Harman
points out, if we describe an innate schematism biased toward
(or restricted to) a specific form of grammar as part of the
"principles of induction used," and define "resourceful empiricism" as a doctrine that makes use of such "principles of induction" as this, then surely "resourceful empiricism" cannot be
refuted, "no matter what the facts about language [or anything
else] turned out to be." Of course, this new doctrine of "resourceful empiricism" would now incorporate "principles of
induction" that are, so it seems, quite specific to the task of
language-acquisition and of no general validity.

The concept "resourceful empiricism" so defined seems to
me of little interest. The issue that concerns me is whether

there are "ideas and principles of various kinds that determine
the form of the acquired knowledge in what may be a rather
restricted and highly organized way," or alternatively, whether
"the structure of the acquisition device is limited to certain elementary peripheral processing mechanisms . . . and certain analytical data-processing mechanisms or inductive principles."
(*Aspects*, pp. 47 f.) I have argued that "it is historically accurate as well as heuristically valuable to distinguish these two
very different approaches to the problem of acquisition of
knowledge," even though they of course "cannot always be
sharply distinguished" in the work of a particular person. (*Ibid.*,
p. 52.) In particular, I have tried to show that it is possible to
formulate these approaches so that the former incorporates the
leading ideas of classical rationalism as well as the modern variant
I have been describing, and that the latter includes classical empiricist doctrine as well as the theories of acquisition of knowledge
(or belief, or habit) developed in a wide range of modern work
(Quine's notions of quality space and formation of knowledge by
association and conditioning; Hull's approach in terms of primitive unconditioned reflexes, conditioning, and habit structures;
taxonomic linguistics, with its anyalytic procedures of segmentation and classification and its conception of language as a "habit
system," and so on). Needless to say, there is no necessity to
view the various attempts to study language-acquisition within
this framework; I can only say that I think it is both useful and
accurate. These alternatives can be made fairly precise and investigated in terms of their empirical consequences. Harman's
proposal to define "resourceful empiricism" in such a way as to
include both approaches, and to be, as he notes, immune to any
factual discovery, is merely a pointless terminological suggestion
and cannot obscure the difference between the approaches mentioned or the importance of pursuing and evaluating them.

To summarize, I doubt that linguistics can provide "a new
technique" for analytic philosophy that will be of much significance, at least in its present state of development. Nevertheless,
it seems to me that the study of language can clarify and in
part substantiate certain conclusions about human knowledge
that relate directly to classical issues in the philosophy of mind.
It is in this domain, I suspect, that one can look forward to a

really fruitful collaboration between linguistics and philosophy in coming years.

NOTES

1. Since the language has no objective existence apart from its mental representation, we need not distinguish between "system of beliefs" and "knowledge," in this case.

2. See, for example, S. Peters and R. Ritchie, "On the Generative Capacity of Transformational Grammars," *Information and Control*, forthcoming, and J. P. Kimball, "Predicates Definable over Transformational Derivations by Intersection with Regular Languages," *Information and Control*, II (1967), 177-195.

3. For some speculations on this matter, see G. A. Miller and N. Chomsky, "Finitary Models of Language Users," part II, in R. D. Luce, R. Bush, and E. Galanter, eds., *Handbook of Mathematical Psychology*, Vol. II (New York: John Wiley, 1963).

4. See E. H. Lenneberg, *Biological Foundations of Language* (New York: John Wiley, 1967), for evidence bearing on this issue.

5. Or for his assumption that the "weighting functions" proposed in universal grammar constitute the "sort of fact . . . [that] . . . learning theory tries to account for; *not* the explanation being sought." No one would say that the genetic basis for the development of arms rather than wings in a human embryo is "the kind of fact that learning theory tries to account for," rather than the basis for explanation of other facts about human behavior. The question whether the weighting function is learned, or whether it is the basis for learning, is an empirical one. There is not the slightest reason to assume, a priori, that it is to be accounted for by learning rather than genetic endowment, or some combination of the two.

There are other minor points in Putnam's discussion that call for some comment. For example, he asserts that since certain ambiguities "require coaching to detect," it follows that "the claim that grammar 'explains the ability to recognize ambiguities' . . . lacks the impressiveness that Chomsky believes it to have." But he misconstrues the claim, which relates to competence, not performance. What the grammar explains is why "the shooting of the hunters" (the example he cites) can be understood with hunters as subject or object but that in "the growth of corn" we can understand "corn" only as subject (the explanation, in this case, turns on the relation of nominalizations to deep structures, noted earlier). The matter of coaching is beside the point. What is at issue is the inherent sound-meaning correlation that is involved in performance, but only as one of many factors. Putnam also misstates the argument for assuming the active-passive relation to be transformational. It is not merely that the speaker knows them to be related. Obviously that would be absurd; the speaker also knows that "John will leave tomorrow" and "John will leave three days after the day before yesterday" are related, but this does not imply that there is a transformational relation between the two. Syntactic arguments are given in many places in the literature. See, for example, my *Syntactic Structures* (The Hague: Mouton, 1957); *Aspects of the Theory of Syntax.*

12

Linguistics and Philosophy

W. V. QUINE

Chomsky has expressed general doubts as to how much philosophy stands to gain from linguistics or linguistics from philosophy. But he did express the belief that linguistics contributes to philosophy in one quarter, by supporting rationalism as against empiricism.

With the following claim of Chomsky's, at least, we are all bound to agree:

We must try to characterize innate structure in such a way as to meet two kinds of empirical conditions. First we must attribute to the organism, as an innate property, a structure rich enough to account for the fact that the postulated grammar is acquired on the basis of the given conditions of access to data; second, we must not attribute to the organism a structure so rich as to be incompatible with the data.

All this I find indisputable. If this is rationalism, and incompatible with Locke's empiricism, then so much the better for rationalism and so much the worse for Locke. The connection between this indisputable point about language, on the one hand, and the disagreements of seventeenth-century philosophers on the other, is a scholarly matter on which I have no interesting opinion. But what does require to be made clear is that this indisputable point about language is in no conflict with latter-day attitudes that are associated with the name of empiricism, or behaviorism.

Reprinted with the kind permission of Professor Quine and the copyright holder from Sidney Hook, ed., *Language and Philosophy* (New York: New York University Press, 1969), pp. 95-98.

For, whatever we may make of Locke, the behaviorist is knowingly and cheerfully up to his neck in innate mechanisms of learning-readiness. The very reinforcement and extinction of responses, so central to behaviorism, depends on prior inequalities in the subject's qualitative spacing, so to speak, of stimulations. If the subject is rewarded for responding in a certain way to one stimulation, and punished for thus responding to another stimulation, then his responding in the same way to a third stimulation reflects an inequality in his qualitative spacing of the three stimulations; the third must resemble the first more than the second. Since each learned response presupposes some such prior inequalities, some such inequalities must be unlearned; hence innate. Innate biases and dispositions are the cornerstone of behaviorism, and have been studied by behaviorists. Chomsky mentioned some of that work himself, but still I feel I should stress the point.

This qualitative spacing of stimulations must therefore be recongnized as an innate structure needed in accounting for any learning, and hence, in particular, language-learning. Unquestionably much additional innate structure is needed, too, to account for language-learning. The qualitative spacing of stimulations is as readily verifiable in other animals, after all, as in man; so the language-readiness of the human infant must depend on further endowments. It will be interesting to find out more and more, if we can, about what this additional innate structure is like and how it works. Such discoveries would illuminate not only language but learning processes generally.

It may well turn out that processes are involved that are very unlike the classical process of reinforcement and extinction of responses. This would be no refutation of behaviorism, in a philosophically significant sense of the term; for I see no interest in restricting the term "behaviorism" to a specific psychological schematism of conditioned response.

Conditioned response does retain a key role in language-learning. It is the entering wedge to any particular lexicon, for it is how we learn observation terms (or, better, simple observation sentences) by ostension. Learning by ostension is learning by simple induction, and the mechanism of such learning is conditioning. But this method is notoriously incapable of carry-

ing us far in language. This is why, on the translational side,
we are soon driven to what I have called analytical hypotheses.
The as yet unknown innate structures, additional to mere quality space, that are needed in language-learning, are needed
specifically to get the child over this great hump that lies beyond ostension, or induction. If Chomsky's antiempiricism or
antibehaviorism says merely that conditioning is insufficient to
explain language-learning, then the doctrine is of a piece with
my doctrine of the indeterminacy of translation.

   When I dismiss a definition of behaviorism that limits it
to conditioned response, am I simply extending the term to
cover everyone? Well, I do think of it as covering all reasonable
men. What matters, as I see it, is just the insistence upon
couching all criteria in observation terms. By observation terms
I mean terms that are or can be taught by ostension, and whose
application in each particular case can therefore be checked
inter-subjectively. Not to cavil over the word "behaviorism,"
perhaps current usage would be best suited by referring to this
orientation to observation simply as empiricism; but it is empiricism in a distinctly modern sense, for it rejects the naive
mentalism that typified the old empiricism. It does still con-
done the recourse to introspection that Chomsky has spoken in
favor of, but it condones it as a means of arriving at conjectures or conclusions only insofar as these can eventually be made
sense of in terms of external observation.

   Empiricism of this modern sort, or behaviorism broadly so
called, comes of the old empiricism by a drastic externalization.
The old empiricist looked inward upon his ideas; the new empiricist looks outward upon the social institution of language.
Ideas dwindle to meanings, seen as adjuncts of words. The old
inner-directed empiricists—Hobbes, Gassendi, Locke, and their
followers—had perforce to formulate their empiricist standard
by reference to ideas; and they did so by exalting sense impressions and scouting innate ideas. When empiricism is externalized, on the other hand, the idea itself passes under a
cloud; talk of ideas comes to count as unsatisfactory except
insofar as it can be paraphrased into terms of dispositions to
observable behavior. Externalized empiricism or behaviorism
sees nothing uncongenial in the appeal to innate dispositions to

overt behavior, innate readiness for language-learning. What would be interesting and valuable to find out, rather, is just what these endowments are in fact like in detail.

13

Linguistic Innateness and Its Evidence

MARGARET ATHERTON and ROBERT SCHWARTZ

It has become increasingly popular of late to investigate the
abilities of animals to learn to use a language. Not only have
such phenomena as the dance of the bees, the songs of the
whales, and the squeaks of the dolphin received close attention,
but various attempts have been made to teach animals a natural
language. Most notable of these perhaps have been the efforts
to teach chimpanzees English. The Hayeses, for example, raised
a chimpanzee, Viki, in a home environment similar to that of a
pre-school child, but Viki never learned to utter more than a
few English words.[1] The Gardners have increased the performance capabilities of their chimpanzee, Washoe, by teaching her
sign language rather than spoken English, and Washoe is capable
of understanding and generating a limited set of new sentences.[2]
Premack has pushed the linguistic competence of his chimpanzee, Sarah, even further. By using arbitrary plastic pieces for
words, Premack claims to have taught Sarah certain rudiments
of English syntax and semantics. Sarah strings her plastic words
in grammatical order and seems able to answer questions, distinguish use and mention, deal with a range of sentences containing "some" and "all," and handle certain logical operations.[3] Just how far Sarah and Washoe can progress are taken
by these theorists to be open questions, limited as much by
experimental ingenuity as by the chimpanzees' capacities.

*We wish to thank David Rosenthal and Richard Herrnstein for helpful com-
ments.

Reprinted with the kind permission of the authors and the editor from *The
Journal of Philosophy* LXXI, 6 (March 28, 1974).

Now all these investigations of animal learning and communication are interesting in and of themselves, but each has been regarded as of wider theoretical significance. Every new instance of animal communication, especially those cases seeming to involve natural language, have been greeted as important evidence disproving the nativist thesis that there are special innate factors critically responsible for man's linguistic competence. This attitude is shared by friends of nativism as much as by its foes, for the nativist response typically has been to deny that what the animal communicates with is really a language, or that the limited symbol systems taught the chimpanzees have anything significant in common with English. But it is not clear why some animal's mastery of a natural language should contradict the theory of either the nativist or the non-nativist. If the anti-nativist rejected nativism because his learning theory required that any organism capable of learning could learn anything, then he might indeed insist on the existence of talking chimpanzees as important evidence in his favor.[4] But these grounds for rejecting nativism would seem also to imply the existence of talking foxes, goldfish, and amoebae, and this result is not one most non-nativists would be willing to subscribe to. Rejecting nativism ought to be compatible with a learning theory that can admit to differences in the learning capacities of humans and goldfish. Yet it is no more obvious why the existence of talking animals should present a challenge to the nativist's opposition to non-nativism. If organisms other than humans demonstrate an ability to talk, a reasonable nativist conclusion would seem to be that organisms other than humans possess the innate structures that underlie this ability. Surely the nativist has no reason for wanting to maintain that anything innate must of necessity be limited to one and only one species.

Of course, the link between nativism and species-specificity becomes apparent when the nativist, as he frequently does, allies his thesis with the more metaphysical claim that possession of natural language is *a* or *the* distinguishing feature of human mentality. For if man's uniqueness among beasts is to be characterized in terms of linguistic capacity, then it is obvious why someone maintaining this position should be bothered by talking animals. What is not so obvious is why a nativist theory of language entails or is entailed by species-specificity, and why the nativist, as opposed to any other theorist, should be the one to see natural language as definitive of or essential to human rationality. If the animal studies are to provide empirical grounds for settling the nativism controversy, these presuppositions or implications of nativist theory must be brought to the surface. And to do this, we must first have a clear statement of what sort of psychological theory a nativist account of language development could be.

Language competence could plausibly be linked with the *nature* of the species possessing the competence if, when the nativist claimed that such competence was innate, he meant it was present at birth; for, under the circumstances of so limited an amount of experience, there is little else available to explain the possession of such a competence except the constitution of the species in possession. This traditional expression of nativism opposes innate skills or behavior patterns to those acquired by experience; competences that are innate can be identified because no process of learning is needed. But, of course, this version of the nativist theory achieves its clarity at the expense of its veracity. The claim that language competence can be accounted for in terms of properties of the species because all humans talk from birth and no animals do is false, and so there is no need to look for remarkable animals to refute this claim. Nor is the veracity of the claim enhanced by revising it to say that humans come by their language without help from experience via some process like maturation. For, if it is false that humans come into the world equipped with a natural language, it is equally plainly false that they will develop one without a rich experience of a linguistic sort. The mental structure of each human cannot be so powerful as to tell the whole story with respect to man's linguistic skill.[5]

The nativist, however, still might want to distinguish what the animal does when taught a language from what the human does. He might argue that human language development is the result of a structure so detailed and highly specific that it is plausible to maintain that, although experience is required, the process involved in language acquisition is not one of learning after all. Rather, the process by which humans come to possess language might be thought to make use of experience in the way that the process of imprinting makes use of inputs from the environment.[6] In the case of imprinting, experience does play a role in shaping what is acquired, but only in the sense of triggering or filling in some pre-existing set. For example, some birds are said to be imprinted with the "concept" of a conspecific, rather than learning from experience what sort of species it belongs to. This is because, throughout its life, the bird will apply the behavior responses appropriate to a member of its species to whatever sort of moving thing it first spies after birth. Thus, although the content of the "concept," the actual object to be followed or mated with, is discovered by the bird in his environment, the form or pattern of the "concept" is part of the built-in structure or program of the bird. If language acquisition is to be described after this model, then it must be that we are to assume that humans come into the world equipped with the form of language (some would say the rules of universal grammar) whereas they discover the content, the particular nuances of their native language, in their own peculiar linguistic environment.

But can such a model derived from imprinting be shown to square in an illuminating way with the processes we observe to occur when a child acquires language? In the case of the imprinting bird, a relatively clear distinction between form and content can be made to seem applicable. The use of this distinction in the imprinting model is justified by pointing to the early occurrence of a behavior pattern that defines something as a conspecific, and to the inviolability of the behavior pattern once an object has been selected. No matter how inappropriate the object, the pattern of behavior is not corrected. But incorrigible rules of this sort do not appear to be a feature of language learning. Furthermore, this model, or other similar models postulating innate release mechanisms, would seem to require that humans be preset for language in such a way that mere exposure to a few instances of a particular language would be sufficient to trigger the acquisition device. No processes of trial and error, mistake and correction, supplementation and deletion, gradual change and improvement, etc., would be expected. But this view of how man acquires mastery of a language seems only a little more reasonable than postulating the competence full-blown at birth. The grammatical rules that characterize adult speech are not observed to crop up immediately in the linguistic behavior of the child. Instead, mastery of even the rudiments of adult semantics and syntax takes a period of several years. During this time, the child is continually bombarded with relevant experience he uses and incorporates with varying degrees of speed and success. He makes a number of false starts, improper substitutions, and misguided supplementations, and in the process of correcting mistakes shows himself to be sensitive to his continuing linguistic environment. There is, in fact, little reason to argue that human language acquisition is more like imprinting than it is like other cases of learning.

Here again, the animal learning experiments are not able to clarify matters. People have, for example, wanted to argue that the slowness with which chimpanzees acquire anything like a language suggests that they require something very different in the way of relevant linguistic experience from what human children use. But even if it could be shown that chimpanzees required a much richer teaching environment than human in order to learn, this would not in any way entail that humans do not *learn* language, that acquisition is merely a matter of triggering or filling in a present competence. So long as we take a balanced view of what goes on when language is acquired, it would be false to say that language is innate if this meant either that linguistic competence required no experience or nothing like learning for its acquisition. And this means that if nativism is to be an intelligible model of language development, it must be seen, not as an alternative to learning theory, but rather as part and parcel of some learning theory.[7]

But how is the nativist to incorporate the claim that language or the form of language is innate while still allowing for the importance of the linguistic environment? One approach has been to argue that the mental structure that provides the form of language makes its presence felt as a restriction on the types of languages that can, in fact, be learned. According to this view, the form of natural language (again, some would say this is specified by universal grammar) is innate in the sense that languages not of this form cannot be learned by humans (or

could be learned only with such difficulty and expense of time
as to be beyond human grasp for all practical purposes). Systems that violate the given form are unlearnable.

Here it should be tempting to ask the nativist what evidence he has for his claim. Has this limitation hypothesis ever
been directly tested? Is it even testable? Certainly there is no
evidence presently available that would show that a language
just like English but violating even one universal feature could
not be learned. Nor is there any established theory of cognition
that indicates that humans could not readily master some artificial language consisting of, say, a two-word vocabulary and
only one rule of syntax, even if that rule were not of the con-
strained sort. Indeed, the evidence we do have of man's ability
to break codes of serious or fanciful sort, uncover the regularities underlying varied series of numbers, pick up game rules
from watching the play, etc., suggests a more charitable view
of human cognitive capacities than this version of the innateness
claim allows. But perhaps even more to the point than consideration of man's general conceptual abilities, is that, even under
quite ordinary circumstances, most humans master a multiplicity of symbol systems seemingly not of "the form of natural
language." It is very easy to think of quite a lot of symbol
systems such as gestures, maps, diagrams, pictures, music nota-
tions, graphs, and imitations that are learnable but fail to answer
to the universals that can plausibly be provided for natural languages. Nor are there grounds to suppose that all these systems
could not be mastered without the use of a natural language.
Indeed, acquisition of some of these systems, like gestural, pic-
torial, and imitation schemes, usually precedes mastery of natural
language and most likely plays a role in its development.[8]

Perhaps the nativist might want to counter all this evidence
by replying that he never meant the structural restrictions on
learnability to apply to other sorts of symbol systems besides
natural language. Therefore, that humans can learn artificial
languages, make and break codes, and master various nonlinguistic symbol systems cannot refute his claim. But such a reply
would leave this version of the nativist claim most unclear. Can
it be that only systems of the specified form are to be considered natural languages? If so, then it is obvious that natural

languages not of this form would not be learnable, for there would be no such natural languages. Such a trivial claim would be weak grounds for what is supposed to be a new theory of language acquisition. Clearly, the experiences we have that lead to our having acquired a natural language, lead to our learning English, rather than some other language that would violate the supposed restrictions of universal grammar. This much is tautologous. But this does not in any way imply that, in other circumstances, with different experience, other symbol systems or languages not of the specified form could not or would not be learned. There seems to be no reason to believe that we will either learn languages of a particular form or nothing at all. That some of these other kinds of systems might be harder to master than natural language or that a language just like English but violating some "linguistic universal" would take longer to learn than English need not be denied. Not all symbol systems, like any other kinds of skill, need be attainable at the same rate. And the point of the limitation claim is further diminished once we admit that natural languages themselves take a considerable amount of time to learn, and it seems reasonable to allow that some other very simple "deviant" system could be learned more quickly than they can.

Even if some version of the limitation interpretation of nativism could be made plausible, moreover, it is unlikely the animal studies would be of much relevance. For to establish that some animal other than man can or cannot master English says nothing about what sorts of systems unlike English humans will be unable to master. Thus, construing the innateness hypothesis as telling us what cannot be learned seems unacceptable on empirical grounds. Such a theory, moreover, really give us no purchase on an account of how language is acquired. It would only give us a reason why some possible symbol system was not in use—it was one that could not be learned. But if there is thought to be some feature peculiar to the human mind, it is that, with appropriate experience, human beings *will* learn a language. It is this ability to learn the languages that they do learn, then, that, as nativists, we would want to appeal to mental structures to explain.

What the nativist must provide for us is not an account of

how mental structures prevent some languages from being learned, but rather an account of how such structures play a role in
determining the language that is learned. Now the current
cognitivist model of language use and acquisition is seen by some
nativists as providing just such a framework in which to develop
a distinguishing position for himself. On this account, learning
a language is seen as acquiring (mastering, implicitly knowing) a
set of hypotheses (the grammar) that generate and characterize
the language. Knowledge of these hypotheses is supposedly
what enables the learner to speak and understand the language.
And the task he has accomplished is said to be one of generating and choosing hypotheses on the basis of the evidence with
which he is presented. Indeed, the child learning his native
language is most often described as being in a situation analogous to that of a field linguist attempting to construct and
write a grammar for an unknown language.

This task of choosing the correct hypotheses, however, is
thought to be a very difficult task once we take into account
the pervasive effects of ordinary inductive indeterminacy. For,
as we know from studies of inductive logic, there will always
be countless alternative conflicting hypotheses compatible with
any nonexhaustive set of evidence. Therefore, to learn a language, the child must be in a position to choose from among
the set of hypotheses all compatible with his evidence and dif-
fering in their future projections. It is only reasonable, the
nativist argues, that we assume the existence of mental structures
determining the child's selection of one set of hypotheses rather than some other conflicting set. After all, what else is
left? If the child is not taught the rules explicitly, he must
make the inductive leap on his own. And if we consider that
all speakers of a language must end up with the same set of
hypotheses, even though the evidence (corpus of instances) each
has encountered is very different, the only reasonable way to
account for this uniformity is on the basis of innate structures
determining the selection.[9]

There are several formal points to be made concerning the
relationship between this model and a nativist theory. The first
is obviously that, if a nativist is willing to commit himself to
this model, then he has no reason for wanting to restrict its

application to human beings. The inductive problem that mental structures are introduced to solve will emerge whether or not animals are capable of fluent English. If the data underdetermine the hypotheses and if learning requires that the learner choose among hypotheses, this task will remain no matter how large or small the set of creatures capable of making such choices turns out to be. For the problem of learning raised by this cognitivist model is purely the formal problem of relating a finite set of data to an unbounded set of conflicting hypotheses. Further, since the underdeterminacy of hypotheses remains whenever the data are inexhaustive, talk about how slowly or fast language learning takes place is also beside the point. Whether it takes two years or ten to master a language, the instances experienced in any case cannot uniquely determine the hypotheses. Even at the end of ten years, logically there will still be an unbounded set of conflicting grammars from which to choose. It is hard, moreover, to see why the model has any special application to natural language. Clearly, the problem of learning almost any symbol system, when the teaching is by instances, can be described in its terms. Indeed, the scope of this model would seem to extend far beyond symbolic capabilities; in the acquisition of almost any sort of skill the hypothesis needed to generate and characterize the competence eventually possessed far outruns the data available to the learner.

But the scope of the model ultimately depends on the possibility of its realization in empirical terms. For it is important to recognize that, at least so far as language learning goes, the model is thoroughly metaphorical. Hypotheses, at least from the standpoint of inductive logic, can themselves occur only as part of some language or system of representation. An organism cannot actually entertain hypotheses in a stage of its development that necessarily precedes the symbolic. To make literal sense of an inductive-logic model dealing in evidence and hypotheses, there would have to be another prior symbol system in which to formulate the evidence and hypotheses. The hypotheses and their evidence cannot be formulated in the language being learned, for it is just this learning event that the hypothesis model is supposed to explain. And, of course, even if we assumed that the evidence and the hypotheses were available in some prior symbol system, the model as an account of how symbolic skills are learned must break down, since it leads to a regress. We will need a prior system for each symbol system in which the hypotheses for learning are encoded, in which to encode the hypotheses generated in the learning of that system.

The analogy between a language learner and a linguist provides a metaphor for language learning that becomes increasingly difficult to interpret as it becomes further extended. If we could find some sort of empirical interpretation of the notion of hypothesis that frees it from its linguistic connotations, it will presumably have little in common with the linguistic-based hypothesis that is a projection from a set of evidence. For if these "hypotheses" are to be literally based on *evidence,* the language learner must be held to be codifying the environmental inputs into evidence statements from which hypotheses are generated. The world does not constitute evidence; only statements, that is to say, conceptualizations of the world, can be evidence for a hypothesis. [10] Application of the inductive model would require seeing the child as classifying, or in some way codifying, the sentences presented him as *instances* of the hypotheses they will be taken to support. Thus, prior to mastering any grammar, the child must assign the structure to particular instances that the grammar as a whole will assign to sentences of this sort. But what interpretation of this model could possibly lend plausibility to the claim that a child, even before he can understand a language, codifies input into NP, VP, object of, etc., that "his" future grammar will assign to these sentences? [11]

In general, it is when we try to talk about how the language learner behaves in the process of learning a language that the evidence-and-hypothesis model lets us down most severely. There can be no literal sense made of the claim that the learner *has* evidence from which hypotheses are generated, nor can it be said that the learner *has* hypotheses. Certainly, he cannot be said to have these conflicting grammatical hypotheses in such a literal sense that he could be said to choose among them. Clearly, if there is no obvious way of dealing with the claim that the child has put himself in possession of even one hypothesis, or recognized evidence in its favor, the suggestion that *he* is choosing among many hypotheses in his possession is quite mystifying.

This is not to say, of course, that there is no similarity between the behavior of a linguist projecting hypotheses from evidence and the behavior of the learner. It certainly is true to say of the language learner that he ends up learning something, the English language, for example, and that this something he learns is both intimately related to the data he has available to him, an English-speaking environment, and is underdetermined by these data. It also seems reasonable to talk about the child's handling and producing new cases in the particular way that he does as generalizing on the basis of an inexhaustive, finite sampling of the language. And, since it is not a priori necessary that he "generalize" in one way rather than some other, that his competence or his behavior take the form that it does, something must determine the direction of the learning process. So, here, perhaps the nativist has, at last, come upon firm ground. Learning cannot occur against a true tabula rasa. In order to learn language, we must be predetermined by a particular mental structure so that we generalize or go on to handle future instances one way and not another. This predetermination can result only if our brain has a built-in bias, and it is this critical biasing factor that constitutes the innateness of natural language. To say that the form of natural language is innate means that innate mental structures determine that, when we are given a sufficient sampling of sentences, we project or generalize to grammars of one form rather than alternative conflicting forms equally compatible with the teaching corpus.

Though this interpretation of the innateness thesis may provide the nativist with a clear and empirically tenable position, its significance as an interesting account of language acquisition seems limited. For, once we strip from the notion of a critical biasing factor the surrounding aura of the inductive model, with its "evidence," "hypothesis," "selecting or choosing," "ordering of alternatives by a simplicity measure" or whatever, there is not much that remains of the innate mental structure whose existence we granted. We have already found that we cannot conceive of this innate factor as a *source* of language competence

that waits only for birth, maturation, or a few triggering experiences before manifesting itself. Nor is the particular "end
product," the particular symbolic competence we achieve, predetermined by the innate factor. For it is not as if we will end
up either with a system of the predetermined form or with
nothing at all, no matter what experiential input we have been
presented. Given some experiences, some sorts of environmental
input, a learner will acquire the English language, with different
input, French, with still different experiences, some non-
natural language or symbolic system, and, if the input is different enough, with the ability to play chess. All that is predetermined is that, given enough of the right kind of experience,
we will wind up with linguistic skill, and some features of the
brain must be responsible for enabling us to "go on" in the
appropriate way. But, now that we have cashed in the evidence-and-hypothesis model in terms of "what is learned" and
"input available," we cannot claim to have devised a model
that does much more than pose the problem of how learning
itself can occur. That we learn what we learn is undoubtedly
due in part to innate factors, but this does not go to show that
what we learn is innate.[12] And if in acquiring language we do
generalize to new instances on the basis of old, we should ask
what else anyone could have ever meant by *learning*, but that,
when exposed to a particular environment, an organism who
has learned some skill can "generalize," "project," or "is able
to carry on" in the right way. If we were the type of organism
that could not carry on appropriately, i.e., in a grammatically
acceptable manner, having been given a suitably rich linguistic
environment, we would not have, for example, a linguistic
capacity. For the ability to learn almost any skill is nothing
more than the ability to go on correctly. The gloss the nativist
adds is that there is no a priori connection between our experience and how we carry on or generalize. Logically, at
least, we could always have done otherwise, and that we do
things the way we do must depend upon the type of brain and
nervous system we have. But this is nothing we needed the
nativist to tell us.

All this is not to say there is nothing new that the nativist
believes he has to tell us, or that there is no position that the
nativist, with his talk of mental structures, is trying to take up

in opposition to the non-nativist. For, if everyone is willing to agree that learning a natural language depends on genetically given structures, there is less agreement about how task-specific are these inherited features which provide men with the capacity to learn a natural language. The nativist's stress on the importance of mental structures seems to result in his willingness to argue that the requisite structures are quite specific, and restricted to natural-language acquisition, whereas the non-nativist is more willing to commit himself to the view that inherited structures are more a matter of man's general cognitive capacities or "general multipurpose learning strategies," and even suggests that there is a faculty specific to the acquisition of natural language, distinguishable from, for example, a mathematical faculty.[13] Similarly, George Miller suggests that the problem of innateness be "redefined around the conjecture that there are innate language-specific mechanisms unique to human beings."[14] The commitment on the part of nativists to mental equipment that is task-specific, then, would seem to be an issue of disagreement for which the animal studies might be thought to provide relevant empirical data.

But even at this point it is necessary to be careful in interpreting the significance of the results of attempts to teach natural language to animals. Mere failure of some species to master English would not itself show that man's language ability is to be distinguished from his more general cognitive capacities. The nativist could gain support for his position from the failures of a particular species only if he were to assume that the animals are otherwise as cognitively gifted as humans and that failure to learn is not due to other features, such as lack of interest and motivation, or to the use of teaching methods poorly suited to the species.[15] In fact, it would appear that the separation of linguistic capacity from intelligence, by postulating, for example, a distinct faculty, might be argued for more strongly if some admittedly stupid animal, like a turkey, could master English. But in order to attribute mastery of a language to some animal, the animal would have to be able to apply the symbols of the language appropriately and act appropriately with respect to the statements of the language. And, of course, to the extent that an animal were to use a language appropriately, that is, in an *intelligent* manner, we would be inclined to raise our view of the animal's intelligence. So it is not very easy to dissociate an assessment of a capacity to learn a language from an assessment of intelligence as a whole.

The nativist's difficulties in maintaining task-specificity are further compounded in the case of man, for he must somehow separate man's general ability to deal with complex symbol systems of all sorts from the particular capacity to master natural language. Now one way the nativist might use animal language studies to push for this distinction would be for him to produce an animal unable to master English, but able to master some artificial language that he, the nativist, is willing to admit is of comparable complexity and expressive power. But the nativist, typically, has not come forward with evidence that animals without natural language capacity are able to handle languages as "rich" as natural language but not of the form of natural language. Nor does the nativist bring forth evidence that animals without natural language capacity are well equipped to master various nonlinguistic symbol systems such as maps, graphs, diagrams, mathematical systems, etc. Instead, the nativist is frequently the one who is at pains to point out how limited and how "stimulus-bound" are most systems of animal communication.[16]

Then what is it that inclines the nativist to ignore the area in which his interests apparently lie? The fact is that it is not at all clear at this juncture where the nativist's interests ought to be. For suppose he were right in claiming that, in order to account for man's capacity to learn natural languages, we must postulate other highly specific genetic endowments that can reasonably be seen as separate from or independent of man's general intellectual or symbolic capacities.[17] This would amount to maintaining that the additional, genetically inherited features have little to do with man's cognitive capacities to abstract, to see spatiotemporal dependencies, to recognize structural relationships, to organize, reorder, plan, and discriminate. So the more it could be argued that those features responsible for natural language *are different* from features that form man's general ability to symbolize and order his world, the less reasonable would be the claim that the species-specificity of natural language accounts for or provides insight into the nature of the human mind and its intensional life, or into man's rationality and, hence, his choices and responsibilities. A psychologist, of course, interested in language learning must postulate the existence of whatever capacities can be shown necessary for language mastery, whether or not any argument can be given for their independence. But to argue that the features responsible for natural language are so highly task-specific that they can be separated from cognitive life in general would be to strip the claim that natural language is innately *species*-specific of most of its metaphysical as well as its theoretical and philosophical interest.

NOTES

1. See K. J. Hayes and C. H. Nissen, "Higher Mental Functions of a Home-raised Chimpanzee," in A. Schrier and F. Stollnitz, eds., *Behavior of Nonhuman Primates* (New York: Academic Press, 1971), pp. 106-110.

2. See B. T. Gardner and R. A. Gardner, "Two-way Communication with an Infant Chimpanzee," *ibid.*, pp. 117-184.

3. See D. Premack, "On the Assessment of Language Competence in the Chimpanzee," *ibid.*, pp. 185-228.

4. Throughout we shall use the word "talking" to cover any cases of language mastery regardless of whether the medium be sound, movements, plastic signs, etc.

5. This fact about language acquisition clearly differentiates it from other skills or habits also claimed to be of innate origin, such as reflexes, certain perceptual constancies, or the pecking behavior of chickens, all of which might reasonably be held to be present from birth or to be a matter of maturation. Although often cited, the relevance of these cases to a discussion of language acquisition, where competence is clearly neither present at birth nor a matter of maturation, is quite minimal.

6. See K. Lorenz, *Evolution and Modification of Behavior* (Chicago: University of Chicago Press, 1965) or, for a concise statement of the issue, Lorenz's paper, "Imprinting," excerpted in R. Birney and R. Teevan, eds., *Instinct* (New York: Van Nostrand, 1961), pp. 52-64. That the imprinting model and other similar models that postulate preformed pattern sets or innate release mechanisms have influenced nativist theories of language can be seen in the frequent references these theorists make to the works of Lorenz and other ethologists.

7. In fact, it may well be the case that reflexes, instincts, and imprinting patterns are all shaped by experience, so that the behavior we typically observe is not untouched by processes of learning. Perhaps, then, there are no pure cases of structured or developed behavior patterns that are present at birth or merely require triggering to emerge. But if this is so, it still would not alter our point, for it would just show that not only language, but even simple instinctual behaviors cannot be described as independent of learning. For a discussion of this controversy see J. Hailman, "How Instincts Are Learned," *Scientific American* CCXXI, 6 (De-

cember 1969), 98-106; and various articles in Birney and Teevan, *op. cit.*

8. See, for example, J. Piaget, "Language and Thought from the Genetic Point of View," in *Six Psychological Studies* (New York: Random House, 1968), pp. 88-99; H. Sinclair-de-Zwart, "Developmental Psycholinguistics," in D. Elkind and J. Flavell, eds., *Studies in Cognitive Development* (New York: Oxford, 1969), pp. 315-336.

9. See, for example, J. Katz, *The Philosophy of Language* (New York: Harper & Row, 1966), pp. 261-266.

10. The point is that a given object, for example, a diamond, is not evidence for "All diamonds are hard." Evidence for this hypothesis are statements, propositions, beliefs, etc., of the form "diamond x is hard."

11. Sidney Morgenbesser has also pointed out that, in using the inductive model to account for the generation of "hypotheses," there is a tendency to confuse questions concerning the context of discovery with the problem of justification. Inductive logic attempts to evaluate hypotheses or tell whether they are supported by the evidence; it does not pretend to tell how we come by the evidence, or account for which hypotheses will be generated, given the evidence.

12. Thus to claim that a language or a particular set of languages or forms of language are innate, i.e., that the subject matter that we learn or come to know is innate, could only be misleading. If anything is innate in this context it is not the end product or what we know, but only those mental features which allow us to learn. And if this is correct, it would be confusing to call these learning capacities, innate knowledge or ideas; for this suggests that the ideas, the subject matter, is somehow predetermined or pre-existing. The ability to acquire knowledge or an idea is not itself knowledge or an idea. This may well be Locke's point, since he never intended to deny that the mind has unlearned biases, habits, and propensities.

13. See "Noam Chomsky and Stuart Hampshire Discuss the Study of Language," *The Listener* May 30, 1968), pp. 687–691; and Chomsky, *Language and Mind* (New York: Harcourt, Brace & World, 1968), chap. 3.

14. "Four Philosophical Problems of Psycholinguistics," *Philosophy of Science* XXXVII, 2 (June 1970), 183-199, p. 183.

15. The possibility that failure in many cases is a function of teaching methods is brought out in the works of Premack and the Gardners.

16. See Chomsky, *Language and Mind, op. cit.,* p. 61.

17. This, of course, is a large supposition, since even if these additional capacities evolved under the genetic pressures that developed language in man, it would be highly unlikely that these capacities would remain isolated and untapped for many other cognitive uses. We are not claiming, however, that cognitive capacities and skills are unisolable in any sense, a claim that, for example, data on aphasia and other brain damage suggests is false, but only pointing out some difficulties in the claim that these functions are specific to properties peculiar to natural languages.

Selected Bibliography

Armstrong, R. L. "Cambridge Platonists and Locke on Innate Ideas," *Journal of the History of Ideas* XXX (1969).

Atherton, M. "Tacit Knowledge and Innateness," *Philosophical Forum* 3 (1972).

Austin, J. L., D. M. Mackinnon, and W. G. Maclagan. "Symposium: Are There *A Priori* Concepts?" *Proceedings of the Aristotelian Society, Suppl. Vol.* XVIII (1939).

Bach, E., and R. Harms. *Universals in Linguistic Theory.* New York: Holt, Rinehart and Winston, 1968.

Barnes, J. "Mr. Locke's Darling Notion," *Philosophical Quarterly* 22 (1972).

Braken, Harry. "Innate Ideas—Then and Now," *Dialogue* VI (1967).

———. "Chomsky's Variations on a Theme by Descartes," *Journal of the History of Philosophy* 8 (1970).

———. "Minds and Learning: The Chomskian Revolution," *Metaphilosophy* 4 (1973).

Carmichael, L. "The Early Growth of Language Capacity in the Individual," E. H. Lenneberg, ed., *New Directions in the Study of Language.* Cambridge, Mass.: MIT Press, 1964.

Chomsky, Noam. "Explanatory Models in Linguistics." In E. Nagel et al., eds. *Logic, Methodology and the Philosophy of Science.* Stanford, Calif.: Stanford University Press, 1962.

———. *Aspects of the Theory of Syntax.* Cambridge, Mass.: MIT Press, 1965.

———. *Cartesian Linguistics.* New York: Harper and Row, 1966.

―――. "The Formal Nature of Language." In E. H. Lenneberg. *The Biological Foundation of Language.* New York: Wiley, 1967.

―――. *Language and Mind.* New York: Harcourt, Brace and World, 1968.

―――. "Knowledge of Language," *Times Literary Supplement* 68, 15 May 1969.

―――. "Comments on Harman's Reply." In Sidney Hook, ed. *Language and Philosophy.* New York: New York University Press, 1969.

Chomsky, Noam, and J. J. Katz. "What The Linguist Is Talking About," *Journal of Philosophy* 71 (1974).

Cohen, L. J. "Applications of Inductive Logic to Theory of Language," *American Philosophical Quarterly* 7 (1970).

Cooper, David. "Innateness: Old and New," *Philosophical Review* 81 (1972).

Danto, Arthur. "Semantical Vehicles, Understanding and Innate Ideas." In Sidney Hook, ed. *Language and Philosophy.* New York: New York University Press, 1969.

Edgley, R. "Innate Ideas," *Knowledge and Necessity.* Royal Institute of Philosophy Lectures. Vol. 3. London: Macmillan & Co., 1970.

Fodor, J. A. "The Appeal to Tacit Knowledge in Psychological Explanation," *Journal of Philosophy* LXV (1968).

―――. *Psychological Explanation* (New York: Random House, 1968).

Fodor, J. A., and J. J. Katz, eds. *The Structure of Language: Readings in the Philosophy of Language.* Englewood Cliffs, N.J.: Prentice-Hall, 1964.

Goodman, Nelson. "The Epistemological Argument," *Synthese* 17, (1967).

―――. "The Emperor's New Ideas." In Sidney Hook, ed. *Language and Philosophy.* New York: New York University Press, 1969.

Graves, C. et al. "Tacit Knowledge," *Journal of Philosophy* 70 (1973).

Greenberg, Joseph H. *Universals of Language.* Cambridge, Mass.: MIT Press, 1966.

―――. "Language Universals: A Research Frontier," *Science* CLVI (1969).

Greenlee, D. "Locke and the Controversy Over Innate Ideas," *Journal of the History of Ideas* 33 (1972).

Gunderson, K. "Descartes, La Mettrie, Language and Machines," *Philosophy* 39 (1964).

Harman, Gilbert H. "Linguistic Competence and Empiricism." In Sidney Hook, ed. *Language and Philosophy*. New York: New York University Press, 1969.

Katz, Jerrold J. "Mentalism in Linguistics," *Language* 40 (1964).

———. "The Relevance of Linguistics to Philosophy," *Journal of Philosophy* LXVII (1965).

———. *The Philosophy of Language*. New York: Harper and Row, 1965.

———. *The Underlying Reality of Language and Its Philosophical Import*. New York: Harper and Row, 1971.

———. *Semantic Theory*. New York: Harper and Row, 1972.

Kretzmann, N. "The Main Thesis of Locke's Semantic Theory," *Philosophical Review* LXXVIII (1968).

Lenneberg, E. H. "A Biological Perspective of Language." In E. H. Lenneberg, ed. *New Directions in the Study of Language*. Cambridge, Mass.: MIT Press, 1964.

———. *Biological Foundations of Language*. New York: Wiley, 1967.

———. "On Explaining Language," *Science* CLXIV (1969).

Loemaker, L. E. "Leibniz's Doctrine of Ideas," *Philosophical Review* LV (1946).

Lyons, John. *Introduction to Theoretical Linguistics*. Cambridge: Cambridge University Press, 1968.

Mackie, J. L. "The Possibility of Innate Knowledge." *Proceedings of the Aristotelian Society*. 1970.

McRae, Robert. "Ideas as a Philosophical Term in the Seventeenth Century," *Journal of the History of Ideas* XXVI (1965).

Miel, J. "Pascal, Port Royal and Cartesian Linguistics," *Journal of the History of Ideas* XXX (1969).

Miller, G. A. "Four Philosophical Problems of Psycholinguistics," *Philosophy of Science* 32 (1970).

Moravcsik, J. M. E. "Competence, Creativity and Innateness," *Philosophical Forum* 1 (1969).

Nagel, Thomas. "Linguistics and Epistemology." In Sidney Hook, ed. *Language and Philosophy*. New York: New York University Press, 1969.

Passmore, J. A. "Descartes, the British Empiricists, and Formal Logic," *Philosophical Review* LXII (1953).

Rescher, N. "A New Look at the Problem of Innate Ideas," *British Journal for the Philosophy of Science* 17 (1966/7).

Root, M. "How to Simulate an Innate Idea," *Philosophical Forum* 3 (1972).

Sampson, G. "Can Languages Be Explained Functionally?" *Synthese* 23 (1972).

Savile, A. "Leibniz's Contribution to the Theory of Innate Ideas," *Philosophy* 47 (1972).

Schwartz, Robert. "On Knowing a Grammar." In Sidney Hook, ed. *Language and Philosophy*. New York: New York University Press, 1969.

Sternfeld, R. "Reason and Necessity in Classical Rationalism," *Review of Metaphysics* XII (1958).

Stich, S. P. "What Every Speaker Knows," *Philosophical Review* 80 (1971).

———. "Grammar, Psychology and Indeterminacy," *Journal of Philosophy* 69 (1972).

———. "What Every Grammar Does," *Philosophia* 3 (1973).

———. "Competence and Indeterminacy." In *Testing Linguistic Hypotheses: Papers from the University of Wisconsin-Milwaukee Linguistics Group, Third Annual Symposium*. Milwaukee: Hemisphere Publishing, 1975.

Toulmin, S. "Brain and Mind," *Synthese* 22 (1971).

Wells, R. "Innate Knowledge." In Sidney Hook, ed. *Language and Philosophy*. New York: New York University Press, 1969.

Wilson, M. D. "Leibniz and Locke on First Truths," *Journal of the History of Ideas* XXVIII (1967).

Yolton, J. W. "Locke and the Seventeenth Century Logic of Ideas," *Journal of the History of Ideas* XVI (1955).

———. *John Locke and the Way of Ideas*. Oxford: Oxford University Press, 1956.